FROM CREATION TO DOOM

AMS Studies in the Middle Ages: No. 5

ISSN: 0270-6261

Other titles in this series:

FROM CREATION TO DOOM

The York Cycle of Mystery Plays

CLIFFORD DAVIDSON

AMS PRESS, INC.
New York

PR
644
.Y6
D38

Library of Congress Cataloging in Publication Data

Davidson, Clifford
  From Creation to Doom.

  (AMS studies in the Middle Ages; no. 5)
  Bibliography: p.
  Includes index.
  1. York plays. 2. Mysteries and miracle-plays,
English — History and criticism. 3. Bible plays —
History and criticism. I. Title. II. Series.
PR644.Y6D38 1984   822'.0516'09   83-45273
ISBN 0-404-61435-3

MANUFACTURED IN THE UNITED STATES
OF AMERICA

CONTENTS

ILLUSTRATIONS

Following Page 116

PREFACE

The present book, which was begun as long ago as 1971, owes much to those who encouraged and criticized my work during more than a decade while it was in progress. The book's inception can be dated from my first visit to York during the summer of that year, since prior to that time I had envisioned something more modest than the full-scale study which eventually developed. Further work in York was made possible by summer research fellowships and grants from the Faculty Research Fund of Western Michigan University. In 1978, aided by David E. O'Connor, now of the Department of Art History at the University of Manchester, who became a collaborator in the project, I completed a subject list of early York art that was published by Medieval Institute Publications. The preparation of the subject list, which I could hardly have finished without Mr. O'Connor's expert help, was necessary as a first step in systematizing the vast amount of art from the city of York in the late Middle Ages—art which needed to be accurately surveyed prior to the completion of the present book.

Many other scholars, of course, also aided and encouraged me in various ways, and I can only name a few of them here. Alexandra F. Johnston of the University of Toronto, who was instrumental in making me see the value of systematic study resulting first in the York subject list, encouraged me at a crucial time, and the work on the dramatic records produced by her in collaboration with Margaret Rogerson for Records of Early English Drama likewise facilitated my research. Elizabeth Giedeman of Western Michigan University aided me with Latin passages, and my wife, Audrey Ekdahl Davidson, gave me assistance with musical matters as these touch on the York plays. Nona Mason, a person with immense theatrical sense and wide knowledge, collaborated with me on the first published version, issued by

vii

Theatre Survey, of Chapter II, and though an attempt has been made to excise sections for which she was directly responsible from the current version of this chapter, her presence is still very much felt here and this section remains partly hers. I am particularly grateful to be able to use this chapter in this book.

During the summer of 1977 when I was doing work in York, I benefitted from the hospitality extended by Lynette Muir and her colleagues at the University of Leeds, whose intellectual vitality and kindnesses require mention here. C. B. L. Barr of the York Minster Library was also unusually kind and assisted me on a number of occasions when I might not have been able to solve certain problems unassisted. The photographic collection of the Centre for Medieval Studies of the University of York and especially the help of Margaret Brown need to be acknowledged, and in addition I am grateful for the opportunity to use the photographic archive of the National Monuments Record in London. Contact with other scholars at the International Congress on Medieval Studies held annually at my university as well as the medieval drama conferences at Alençon and Dublin also deeply influenced my work.

Other chapters of this book which have previously appeared in print and which are presented here with permission in revised form are Chapters III, VI, VII, and VIII, which were first published in *Mediaevalia, Annuale Mediaevale, Speculum,* and the *American Benedictine Review.* An earlier draft of Chapter IV appeared as a section in my *Drama and Art* (1977), designed as a handbook for research in early drama and the visual arts.

In addition to work in the York Minster Library, research for this book was carried out in the following libraries: the British Library; the Warburg Institute Library; the Bodleian Library, Oxford; the North Yorkshire County Library; the Borthwick Institute, York; the Library of the Centre for Medieval Studies, University of York; the University of Michigan libraries; the University of Chicago libraries; the University of Minnesota libraries; University Library, Cambridge; the Fitzwilliam Museum, Cambridge; the Cistercian Studies Library, Western Michigan University; and, last but not least, the Western Michigan University libraries, which also cheerfully supplied unusually large batches of inter-library loan materials with surprising efficiency.

Quotations from the York plays are from the edition recently edited by Richard Beadle, though in a couple of instances I have had to rely on the old nineteenth-century edition of Lucy Toulmin Smith to supply a reading imperfect in Dr. Beadle's edition. I also have not adopted Dr. Beadle's titles for the plays, but instead for more convenient reference I have used the titles as they appear in the Index of the Records of Early English Drama volumes edited by Professor Johnston and Dr. Rogerson since these reproduce more exactly the titles as they are extant in an early fifteenth-century list. Dr. Beadle's careful re-numbering of the plays, based upon recent bibliographic research, has, however, been used here. Thus the misplaced *Purification of the Virgin* play is moved into a location between the Magi play (XVI) and the *Flight into Egypt* (Play XVIII) where the dramatic records indicate it should be placed. Also, Beadle joins the Herod and Magi scenes presented by the Masons and Goldsmiths into a single play (XVI). An appendix gives the new numbering system along with the titles used for the plays in this book.

Permissions to use photographs of relevant examples from the visual arts as plates in the present book have been granted by the following: National Monuments Record; Mr. David O'Connor; the University of Glasgow Library; the Very Reverend Ronald Jasper, Dean of York Minster; Canon J. H. Armstrong, Rector of All Saints, Pavement; Canon B. C. Norris, priest in charge of St. Michael Spurriergate; and the Reverend J. R. Armfelt, priest in charge of All Saints, North Street.

Finally, I need to thank my department, which upon several occasions granted me a reduced teaching load to work on my York projects and otherwise encouraged my scholarship, and the Medieval Institute, which eventually provided space for an office that would hold my files, catalogues, and books. A small grant from the College of Arts and Sciences assisted with the cost of obtaining the photographs for the plates. I will not soon forget the encouragement in particular of Robert S. Davis, Chairman of the English Department from 1974 to 1978, and Otto Gründler, Director of the Medieval Institute.

March 14, 1983

I

THE VISUAL ARTS
AND
MEDIEVAL DRAMA
AT YORK

I

It has been long recognized that the visual arts in the late Middle Ages have much to teach us about the plays which were performed each summer, often at Corpus Christi time, in English cities such as York. Yet too much of the previous work in this area has been based on the doubtful supposition that the painters and carvers of the late Middle Ages frequently made representations of what they had seen on the medieval stage.[1] Thus M. D. Anderson has asserted:

> If, after seeing a majestic theme such as the Creation, the Flood or the Last Judgment, presented upon the small stage of a pageant cart, the carver of an alabaster panel or a roof boss was called upon to depict it within an even more restricted space, he would naturally have tended to reproduce the tableau which he remembered. By doing so he saved himself the labour of eliminating inessential details and achieved a design which his own experience had proved to be impressive. If we accept the probability that medieval craftsmen were thus inspired by the plays, it is certainly likely that what they show us in their work is some sort of a record of what they had seen on the stage.[2]

1

And W. L. Hildburgh, in his "English Alabaster Carvings as Records of Medieval Drama," writes:

> I am inclined to think that though the stage conceivably may sometimes have borrowed from static art incidents or specific grouping or gestures, the borrowing almost always was in the opposite direction—i.e., that the carver obtained, whether direct or through paintings, very much more inspiration from the stage than he bestowed upon it.[3]

While not denying that the stage might occasionally have influenced the visual arts, this study, however, rejects the notion that craftsmen and artists normally looked to the stage for inspiration. As scholars have recently begun to realize, such scenes as the Flagellation or Crucifixion in late medieval art are more often than not influenced simply by a literal reading of the biblical narrative.[4] In an age when fashions in art were moving in the direction of realism and perspective as a means of giving life to visual representations, the workmen responsible for painted glass, alabasters, woodcarvings, block books, and manuscript illuminations were, like the dramatists and players of the same period, intent upon asking how biblical and other sacred events must in fact have appeared. The craftsmen, artists, and players shared a common goal, which was to place the event before onlookers in such a manner that they would feel as if they had participated in that event. The appeal is quite frankly to the imaginations of those who look on, but in order to refrain from straining the audience's willingness to suspend disbelief, the visual arts and drama were content to share a common fund of details normally present in each scene. Hence in an edition of the *Biblia Pauperum* dating from perhaps the second quarter of the fifteenth century, the scene illustrating the Crucifixion includes the soldier with the spear that pierced Christ's side; this man is touching his eye with the fingers of his left hand, and is kneeling before the cross.[5] Those not already familiar with the legend will learn in part why he reacts in such a way if they will turn to the York play entitled *Mortificacio Christi*. The soldier is Longinus—or "Ser Longeus," as Pilate calls him as he puts the spear into his hand with orders to "Schoffe it þis tyde" into "Jesu side" (XXXVI. 296–97). Having

done what he is told to do, Longinus in the play is clearly meant
to drop to his knees in reverence as he speaks:

> O maker vnmade, full of myght,
>   O Jesu so jentill and jente
> Þat sodenly has sente me my sight,
>   Lorde, louyng to þe be it lente.
> On rode arte þou ragged and rente,
>   Mankynde for to mende of mys.
> Full spitously spilte is and spente
>   Thi bloode, lorde, to bringe vs to blis
>   Full free.
>   A, mercy my sucoure,
>   Mercy, my treasoure,
>   Mercy, my sauioure,
> Þi mercy be markid in me. (XXXVI. 300–12)

The full story of this blind soldier was known through a number of
sources, including Jacobus de Voragine's influential *Golden Legend*, which remarks that he was converted to Christianity "when
he saw the signs which followed upon the death of
Jesus. . . . But it is said that what led to his conversion chiefly
was that he was afflicted with a malady of the eyes; and by chance
he touched his eyes with a drop of the blood of Christ which ran
down the shaft of his lance, and immediately his eyes were
healed."[6] Both the York play and the scene in the *Biblia Pauperum*
attempt to make visible with some exactness the manner in which
the scene might have appeared to an observer upon the scene.

The example of Longinus demonstrates, I believe, the value of
studying the plays against the background of the visual arts. The
woodcut in the *Biblia Pauperum*, to which may be added other
examples from the visual arts (including the alabaster tables
described by Dr. Hildburgh[7]), defines appropriate gestures for
the actor playing Longinus. Furthermore, the composition of
the scene, the expressions on the characters' faces, and the properties in their hands all prove of value as evidence which throws
light on the ways in which the age visualized an event in biblical
history. The artists and dramatists were, after all, in the busi-
ness of visualizing the same sacred history.

II

Since it is a temporal art, of course, drama is able to be more immediately effective as a medium through which events in time may be communicated. Otto Pächt has shown how the visual arts of the twelfth century learned to include the temporal factor and to represent the progress of events in drawings and illuminations.[8] In spite of the impressive qualities of the medieval art such as that cited by Pächt, drama can do a better job with the task of presenting narrative, for it does not need to break temporal movement up into static tableaux. Yet for the later Middle Ages, the ways of perceiving sacred events in the visual arts were of immense significance. The discrete scenes that appear in pictorial narrative often form the basis for the scenes of religious drama. Obviously, the visual arts in Western Christendom have a kind of historical primacy, for during the period between the Emperor Constantine and King Henry VIII of England painting and sculpture preserved the continuity of tradition, while the ancient Roman drama was nearly to die under the weight of its decadence and a new mimetic form was to rise again within the Church. This latter development was assisted by the understanding that acting was a way in which the religious image could take on a new vividness.

Through the early dramatizations based on the *Quem queritis* trope — e.g., the ritualized scene described in the *Regularis Concordia* of St. Ethelwold — the Easter event of the empty tomb took visible shape as clerics, appointed to play the roles of the angels and Maries, created a *representation* of the original happening. Since dramatic illusion was not the aim of the dramatic presentation described in the *Regularis Concordia*, the man playing the angel did not need to wear wings, as would be expected in the later Middle Ages; he merely appeared wearing an alb and holding a palm before the place where the sepulchre was located. The three men representing the three Maries wore copes and carried censers as they approached the sepulchre. The tenth-century text explains:

> These things are done in imitation [*ad imitationem*] of the angel seated in the monument, and of the women coming with spices to anoint the body of Jesus.[9]

This is a scene often represented in the visual arts of that period, but the particular value of the dramatic exchange that follows in the *Regularis Concordia* is that the image is able to come to life through ritualized speech — i.e., through speech sung to the traditional plainchant melodies.[10] Like the art of the period, this drama is essentially associated with the hieratic principle that links the congregation with sacred events in history. Instead of attempting to create an illusion of reality which might teach people the hypothetical appearance of the event, it is here aware of itself as shadowing forth the eternal reality of the Resurrection. It creates an *image* of the original visit to the tomb, and hence in intention is as far removed from illusionistic drama as could be possible.

The *Quem queritis* exchange in the *Regularis Concordia* comes from an age when the image itself was regarded as participating in the essence of the thing or event imitated. As at a later time the king's crown would be indicative of the king's glory and his scepter of his God-given power,[11] so in the tenth century the religious image was associated in a very real sense with universal principles and with the structure of Christian reality. Neither romanesque art nor drama of the tenth century concerned itself primarily with perspective, realism, or illusionistic techniques — indeed, these techniques would have been regarded as involving a falsification of the truth which ought to shine through the religious image. Art and drama were fashioned as vehicles for something more important than the presentation of particulars intended to titillate the senses. Informed by the dominant philosophical realism associated historically with St. Augustine, the images of art and drama were designed to reveal glimpses of the eternal forms behind the temporal flux. They thus were intended to teach the way by which man might overcome sin and death just as Christ had overcome sin and death when he arose from the grave on the first Easter.

It is true that a high proportion of the iconography so profusely utilized in later medieval drama has its roots in the images of art of the earlier Middle Ages (e.g., Longinus makes his appearance in Anglo-Saxon crucifixion scenes). However, there are often changes, sometimes of a major sort, brought about by altered theology and by the introduction of radically different aesthetic values. The tendency to literalize (and hence to visualize) even biblical metaphors (such as the cup of sorrow mentioned during the Agony in the Garden) was part of the shift in emphasis toward a new interest in particulars and toward a new realism.[12] To be sure, the careful spatial arrangement of iconographic details was not rejected. But the emphasis has changed, and it is clear that both the visual arts and the drama receive their life from other sources than had been the case in the tenth century. Audiences and viewers of the fourteenth and fifteenth centuries are asked to place themselves imaginatively before the event and to see even metaphorical elements as literally present. Illusion has now become an acceptable technique in art and drama, for in re-creating the specific details the artists and dramatists reach out for a particularity that would have offended the purists of the earlier age with their interest in universals. These new artists could not, of course, return to the precise particulars that would have been present in the original event; they could only depict what the events *might* have been like in appearance.

In the art of York, the new style makes its appearance most vividly in the early fifteenth century in the glass painting of John Thornton of Coventry, who in 1405 was commissioned to glaze the Great East Window of the Minster. Most striking are the faces of the figures represented in the glass, for they are no longer the stylized representations of the fourteenth-century glass in the nave of the cathedral. Obviously in search of a master craftsman who could create a work of the highest quality, the cathedral authorities looked to Thornton, a man who represented the new fashion in design, to complete the immensely large East Window (approximately 1,680 square feet in size) which, according to the indenture, he must complete "within 3 years from the date hereof."[13] Clearly influenced by the movement toward perspective in art that we associate with the late fourteenth and fifteenth centuries in the North, Thornton's work is characterized by meticulous attention to details. His faces and figures are highly individualized, with careful handling of perspective and with a strong sense of design generally.[14]

Well in advance of the modernism in art which stressed realism and a literalistic handling of details and even metaphors, a number of important theological shifts had taken place. The most important of these deserves particular attention here — the change in emphasis in Christian theology from the Resurrection to the Crucifixion. It is no accident that the central incident chosen by early drama appears to have been the empty tomb of Christ, symbolizing his power over the powers of darkness, while the later vernacular cycle plays of England instead normally emphasize the Passion and Crucifixion whereby the Savior as the Second Adam triumphed over sin. In the liturgy, the altered emphasis may be traced by means of the new doctrine of the Eucharist which in part shifts the focus in the Mass toward the idea of the repetition of the event of Good Friday. In art and drama as well as liturgy, the new emphasis on the Crucifixion was accompanied by a demand for an emotional response and personal involvement when confronted with ritual or illusionistic repetition of the event.

The work of the York Realist, who sometime after c.1422 rewrote the majority of the plays dealing with the Passion in the York cycle, demonstrates how thoroughly the pageants in the York cycle had found their focus at once in the new theology and new aesthetic. It seems apparent that following c.1422 the city authorities decided to encourage the combining and refurbishing of certain of the most important pageants in the cycle, and in large measure the task was given to the anonymous writer we know only as the York Realist. It would not be frivolous to suggest comparison with the commission given to John Thornton to create the centrally located Great East Window in the Minster, for both Thornton and the York Realist represent new directions in the arts of the day. Hence special attention was directed toward those subjects which have a central location and emphasis in the cycle as a whole. Altogether, the length of the plays between the beginning of the Skinners' *Entry into Jerusalem* (XXV) and the end of the *Mortificacio Christi* (XXXVI) is more than 4600 lines — approximately one-third of the text of the entire cycle as it now appears in the Register (British Library MS. Add. 35,290). The realism of the York Realist, whose work appears in the Passion series throughout Plays XXVI, XXVIII–XXXIII, and XXXVI, has been well established[15] and, we might add, is in line with the "modernist" tendency in the visual arts in the early and middle part of the fifteenth century.[16]

In contrast to the *Quem queritis* dialogue in the *Regularis Concordia*, such a play as the (incomplete) *Agony and Betrayal* in the York cycle brings a vividness and a sense of precision to the biblical happenings that are dramatized. The costumes which the actors wore could no longer have been the liturgical garb of the early drama, but clearly must have reflected the more realistic garments worn by Christ and his apostles in representations of this scene in later manuscript illuminations and painted glass. Christ, no longer the divine warrior of Anglo-Saxon times, emphasizes the point that in order to save mankind, God had to become a man with all his frailty and in this form to overcome the devil. This was the theological position introduced by St. Anselm in his highly influential *Cur Deus Homo*. Anselm insists that since

> death had entered into the human race through *man's* disobedience, it was fitting that life should be restored through the obedience of *man*. When the sin which was the cause of our condemnation had its beginning from a woman, it was fitting for the author of our justice and salvation to be born of a woman. Since the devil, when he tempted *man*, conquered him by the tasting of a tree, it was fitting for him to be conquered by man's bearing of suffering on a tree.[17]

By likewise stressing Christ's humanity, the York Realist is led to dramatize those particulars which set forth his fear and suffering in the face of torture and death. Thus instead of speaking in formalized Latin verse as in the liturgical drama, the Christ of the York Realist utilizes a rich vocabulary which is at once lively and evocative. At the very beginning of the *Agony and Betrayal*, for example, Jesus emphasizes his very human fear as he tells us that his "flesshe dyderis and daris for doute of [his] dede" and that his "enemyes will newly be neghand full nere" with the purpose of threatening his "manhede" (XXVIII.2–4).

III

The close relationship between religious drama and sacred representations in the visual arts is due in part to similarity of purpose: both were designed as *devotional*. Devotion as a major purpose of drama had been, of course, recognized as early as 1220, if we are to believe an account of a Resurrection play at Beverley in that year when a crowd is said to have gathered around in the churchyard; they formed a ring and in their viewing were motivated "by delight or curiosity or devotion."[18] The York records demonstrate definitively that, following the establishment of the civic play cycle, the element of devotion becomes for the citizens a principal motive for presenting the plays. An entry dated 1422 in the *York Memorandum Book A/Y* specifically insists, for example, that the drama was instituted "for the important cause of devotion and for the extirpation of vice and reformation of customs."[19] The same impetus toward devotion clearly had as one of its effects the lavish decoration of churches with statues, painted cloths, glass, wall paintings, and other devotional objects and scenes.

We also learn from a Wycliffite tract, *A Tretise of Miraclis Pleyinge*, in British Library MS. Add. 24,202, that defenders of plays did indeed insist upon the spiritual efficacy of religious drama, through which men "leeven pride and taken to hem afterward the meke conversacioun of Crist and of hise seintis," and are "movyd to compassion and devocion, wepinge bitere teris." Furthermore, since some men will only "be convertid to God" through "gamen and pley," the use of "miraclis pleyinge and other maner mirthis" is approved by many. And finally, the important analogy with the painted image is listed:

> Also, sithen it is leveful to han the miraclis of God peintid, why is not as wel leveful to han the miraclis of God pleyed, sithen men mowen bettere reden the wille of God and his mervelous werkis in the pleyinge of hem than in the peintinge? And betere they ben holden in mennus minde and oftere rehersid by the pleyinge of hem than by the peintinge, for this is a deed bok, the tother a qu[i]ck.[20]

In spite of this clear statement in defense of the plays, the Wycliffite writer is, of course, hostile to drama. The thrust of his attack is based upon his understanding that the plays utilize *illusion*, which he sees as equated with falsehood, to promote the truths of religion.

The author of *A Tretise of Miraclis Pleyinge* is thus scandalized by the way religious drama makes a game of sacred events. He asserts that it is wrong to take "the most precious werkis of God in pley and bourde, and so [to take] his name in idil and so [to misuse] oure byleve."[21] Such playing, he insists, decreases religious respect and religious dread, which, like a nail holding two things together, is what holds man "Godward . . . and susteineth oure bileve to him."[22] In arguments that foreshadow the Puritan attack on the stage following the Reformation, he claims that plays are designed to please the world more than to please God, and hence are open to the charge of hypocrisy. It is, he charges, *deception* and/or hypocrisy to offer worship to "theire maumetrie." He draws a comparison with a lecherous person who insincerely acts out "verrey love"; hence the plays "ben not onely contrarious to the worschipe of God—that is, bothe in signe and in dede—but also they ben ginnys of the devuel to cacchen men to byleve of Anticrist, as wordis of love withoute verrey dede ben ginnys of the lecchour to cacchen felawchipe to fulfillinge of his leccherie." He continues:

> Bothe for these miraclis pleyinge been *verrey leesinge as they ben signis withoute dede* and for they been verrey idilnesse, as they taken the miraclis of God in idil aftur theire owne lust. And certis idilnesse and leesing been the most ginnys of the dyvul to drawen men to the byleve of Anticrist. . . .[23]

Here is a rejection of the whole modernist movement in art—a movement which, as we have seen, utilizes imagination and which often unashamedly sets out to inspire pious tears among those who look upon paintings and plays that represent emotionally charged scenes from sacred history.

The patrons of the drama in York in the fifteenth century obviously had very different ideas about the plays than those expressed in *A Tretise of Miraclis Pleyinge*, for they clearly understood them as a sincere way to honor God. To be sure, a secondary motive was to give honor as well to the city of York. But it is clear that the piety of the civic leaders was not antagonistic to the element of illusion in the drama or in the visual arts, for they contributed willingly not only to the yearly plays but also during this period to the beautification of city churches with, for example, elaborate and often splendid windows of painted glass. Parish churches in more affluent areas, such as North Street where many wealthy mercers lived, received exceptionally fine glass,[24] designed to draw the churchgoers' minds toward a meditative experience of the Christian story.

Miss Maud Sellers clearly gave a distorted picture of civic involvement in the plays when she insisted that they "were by no means the spontaneous expression of the sheer joy of life of men actuated partly by religious zeal, partly by social exuberance; the grudging craftsmen rather regarded them as an intolerable and vexatious burden, from which they were unable to free themselves."[25] The civic records do present evidence of guilds asking to have their financial responsibilities for the plays lightened, as when the armorers in 1444 complained about the high costs to individual members of the guild for their "pageant and play vpon corpus christi day." But the reason for their plight is important: "þe nowne powere and insufficience and ful fewe of Craft in nowmbre, þat we suffice not to mayntene nor vphalde þe charges and costes þat we bere yerely about þe bringyng furth of our pageant and play vpon corpus christi day with mony other costes. . . ."[26] Such complaints were to be expected as the high level of prosperity in the first part of the fifteenth century in York failed to be maintained, and many guilds found themselves less affluent than in previous years.[27] Thus, when the play originally performed by the masons was given to the minstrels, the reasons for the change in responsibility can be surmised, but there is no sign of reluctance in the ordinances of the minstrels:

> it is further ordeyned and by the consent of all the good men of the said Mystery or craft fully aggreed that the said ffelawship of Mynstrelles of their proper chardges shall yerely frome hensforth bryng forth and cause to be played the pageant of Corpus christi viz. the herold, his sone, twoo counselars and the Messynger inquyryng the three kynges of the childe Iesu sometyme accustomed to be brought forth at chardges of the late Masons of this Citie on Corpus Christi day in suche like semely wise and ordre as other occupacions of this Citie doo their pageantes.[28]

Obviously the Corpus Christi plays in York enjoyed a broad base of civic support, which finally was forced to give way in the face of ecclesiastical antagonism in Queen Elizabeth's reign.

The civic patrons of the plays apparently saw no harm and much benefit in dramatic performances which would bring to life the images known through biblical or liturgical texts, through sculpture, and through painting. Indeed, the records of the city of York show not only that the cycle was regarded as "instituted by ancient custom as a special cause of devotion and for the uprooting of vices and the reforming of morals,"[29] but imply that its characteristic features included affective images and *speeches*. Typical references to the expenses involved when the mayor, aldermen, and members of the city council *saw and heard* the Corpus Christi play from the house at the Common Hall Gates at the end of the fifteenth century[30] are proof that spectacle and spoken dialogue must generally have been regarded as distinguishing marks of the drama. The play, in other words, is a speaking picture.

IV

Since religious drama shares a close resemblance to scenes depicted in the visual arts in the late Middle Ages, one task of the critic ought to be to bring relevant information from the painting and sculpture to bear upon the plays in a manner that is critically sound and illuminating. Matters of dating and style may not without peril be handled in a naive way, and easy assumptions about "influences" must normally be avoided. It may at times be tempting to believe that the men assigned to play a certain scene in the Creation to Doom cycle might have studied a particular panel of painted glass in the cathedral. Such idle speculation will need to be set aside in favor of systematic use of the evidence in an attempt to solve more crucial questions about the manner of production and the meaning of the images.

Whenever possible, reference will be made to appropriate York art contemporary with the plays. Unfortunately, the centuries which divide us from the days of York's glory have not been kind to ecclesiastical art of the type germane to our purpose. Reformation, Puritanism, and neglect have destroyed much more than currently remains. The painted glass of the parish churches, for example, was once much more plentiful; if the lost glass and all the other lost art were extant, we would have more complete local records upon which to draw for our understanding of how various scenes and events were visualized in late medieval York. It was reported as late as 1730 that the East Window of Christ Church, formerly at King's Square, contained the Last Judgment, Pentecost, the Ascension, the raising of Lazarus, Christ before Pilate, the angels at the sepulchre, a *Hortulanus* scene, Christ carrying the cross, a Crucifixion, Christ in the sepulchre, and a Resurrection;[31] the Last Judgment alone could possibly have been of inestimable value in throwing light on the Mercers' play which concludes the York cycle.

Even in the instance of representations currently available in York glass, care must be taken not to be led astray. M. D. Anderson illustrates an interesting point about Noah's wife quite correctly by reference to a panel in Thornton's Great East Window in the Minster.[32] However, this panel must not be taken to demonstrate the design of an early fifteenth-century ark, for the bottom portion of the ark is a modern reconstruction made up of scraps of fourteenth-century canopy glass from elsewhere in the cathedral: the hull of the original ark has been lost totally.[33] Glass is extremely fragile, subject to damage from the vicissitudes of nature as well as man's malice and carelessness. In addition, it must be releaded approximately every 125 years—a task that has often been done, especially during the seventeenth through nineteenth centuries, with remarkable carelessness for the design. Unfortunately, the York glass has again in recent years received the benefit of restoration, often forcing misguided conceptions onto the glass, as in the case of an Assumption of the Virgin in the Chapter House restored as the Transfiguration and a Herod in St. Michael, Spurriergate, as Solomon (plate 7). Additionally, the reports on recent restorations are often incomplete so that the student cannot know the precise condition of each panel relevant to the study of drama.

It is, of course, very often necessary for various reasons to go directly to art from other locations in England and even to continental examples in order to illustrate certain critical points with regard to the plays. Everyone will recall that in the fifteenth century the art of the low countries was considered the most advanced and of the highest quality. The Flemish painters set the standards for the "modernist" movement of the day, and English art is sometimes, as we might expect, derivative. Any consideration of the visual arts in fifteenth-century England which entirely ignores all mention of the work of continental artists, especially of the Netherlands painters, would be hard to conceive. Nevertheless, the most rigorous attention ought of necessity be given to local or at least regional uses of iconography and of designs, since these normally and logically have the greatest bearing on the York plays. Additionally, in the use of the examples from the visual arts, it would seem to be critical to be acutely aware of matters of dating, and though earlier art might well throw light on later plays, the more nearly contemporary the example from the visual arts is, the more valuable that example becomes for our study.

V

Three final examples — Cain's weapon, the serpent in Eden, and the babe in the Nativity scene — will now be presented in order to illustrate the propriety and the difficulties of pursuing a comparative method such as the one described above.

1. Cain's use of an unbiblical jawbone to murder Abel will be remembered from a quip in Shakespeare's *Hamlet*: "That skull had a tongue in it, and could sing once. How the knave jowls it to the ground, as if 'twere Cain's jaw-bone, that did the first murder" (V.i.75-77).[34] The York *Sacrificium Cayme et Abell* is deficient at the point at which the murder should take place, since two leaves are missing and a later interpolation is introduced, but in all likelihood the murder weapon was a jawbone. In the Towneley *Mactacio Abel*, which may owe something in a general way to the original York play, Cain exclaims to Abel that

"With cheke-bon, or that I blyn, / Shal I the and thi life twyn" (ll. 324–25). In any case, the jawbone appears very prominently in a panel in Thornton's Great East Window (plate 1), and presumably it is the jawbone of an ass, as specified in the *Cursor Mundi*.[35] A similar iconographic detail may be observed in *Queen Mary's Psalter*, the *Holkham Bible Picture Book*, and numerous other English sources, while continental art, except within the range of English influence, more commonly shows Cain utilizing a club or one of various agricultural tools (e.g., in a window at Chartres, he uses a hoe, and in the mosaics at the Palace Chapel, Palermo, he uses an axe).[36] Hence in this instance attention to the visual arts makes possible the restoration of a vital detail missing in the incomplete text of one of the York plays.

2. In the case of the serpent who tempts Eve, Thornton's Great East Window (plate 2) provides useful though limited suggestions about the appearance of characters in the original productions of the York plays. "Why, what-kynne thyng art þou / Þat telles þis tale [of temptation] to me?" Eve asks. Satan answers: "A worme, þat wotith wele how / Þat yhe may wirshipped be" (V.52–55). The ambiguity, of course, has been entirely in the mind of Eve in original performances, for the audience would have seen perfectly well the nature of the archetypal betrayer. The devil, like the actor in a drama, is a pretender, in the York play promising to appear "In a worme liknes" (V.23). But for us today the shape of the fraudulent "worme" in the early productions can only be ascertained from late medieval examples, since these are the only records that exist. To these we must go if we want to discover what kind of a form Satan must have taken in this scene, and the most convenient representation to which we may turn is surely contained in Thornton's panel. The body of the serpent in Thornton's panel is wrapped around a tree, while the part of the left arm which is visible is clearly human. A serpent's garment with wings attached would seem to be what is represented in Thornton's glass, though it is impossible to learn more than the outline of the serpent's body from the panel in its present state since the glass of the body itself has been lost.[37] In the Chester plays, Satan puts on his "edders coate" on stage in preparation for the temptation of Eve,[38] while the Norwich

Grocers' play of *The Fall* utilized a "cote with hosen and tayle for the Serpente, steyned, with a [white] heare."[39] The serpent's head, in good condition in Thornton's glass, clearly represents that of a young woman, since this, following Peter Comestor, would have been quite conventional in England;[40] however, in dramatic productions there is no reason why the role would not have been taken by a boy actor. But in spite of the light which Thornton's work may seem to throw on the performance of the York *Fall of man*, it should not be taken as a direct record of dramatic activity in York or elsewhere. Thornton and the author of the York play were in fact only setting forth the same image in different media. In one case the extant record is an imperfect panel of painted glass which nevertheless reveals to us how a talented artist viewed the participants in the fall, while in the other case a dramatic text without illustrations presents a series of speeches which hypothetically could have taken place in Eden. The panel of painted glass and the dramatic text together provide an excellent example of the way in which the plays and the visual arts complement and help to explain each other.

3. The appearance of the Christ Child in the York *Nativity* play is more complex, and as far as I have been able to determine marks a departure from all the extant locally produced examples of the Nativity in scenes in the visual arts. Excellent fourteenth-century glass in York Minster shows Joseph on the right and the Virgin reclining in bed at approximately the same angle as in the *Benedictional* of St. Ethelwold (tenth century) but with the Child resting in a manger overhead. The York play, however, gives a radically different picture of the event. Joseph has left the ruined stable—a setting surely influenced by the Franciscan emphasis on the poverty of the place where Christ was born[41] which is specifically devoid of "cloth" and "bedde" (XIV.24). Left alone in the place where Jesus will be born, Mary prays for grace, experiences "grete joie" in her soul, and recognizes that she has given birth to a son who is at once God and man (XIV.45–56). It seems that these actions take place as she is kneeling, with the Child appearing on the ground before her following a painless birth. The child, whom Mary salutes as "my lord God" and "prince of pees," can have become visible in the play in only one way: as a

doll in the midst of a radiant mandorla. Dr. Hildburgh describes
the manner in which the infant in certain later alabaster tables

> is depicted as if lying upon a concave object, almond shaped
> in outline, which generally retains traces of painted or of
> carved rays and seems clearly meant to represent an aureole.
> In those tables the Child looks as if it were an unclothed
> doll laid upon a sort of long dish sufficiently concave to
> contain it, this impression being strengthened by the way
> the image appears on the scene, because it looks as if it
> rests only on the mandorla and is without other support.[42]

Such a scene, with the Virgin kneeling and adoring the Child,
appears in painted glass at Fairford, Gloucestershire, and in two
windows at the Great Malvern Priory Church, Worcestershire.[43]
   The source of this scene as thus represented in art and drama
has been traced to the *Revelations* of St. Bridget of Sweden,[44] who
at Jerusalem in 1370 had a vision in which she saw Christ's birth:

> And when all was thus prepared, the Virgin knelt down
> with great veneration in an attitude of prayer. . . . Thus,
> with her hands extended and her eyes fixed on the sky, she
> was rapt as in ecstasy, lost in contemplation, in a rapture
> of divine sweetness. And while she was engaged thus in
> prayer, I saw the child in her womb move, and suddenly in
> a moment she gave birth to her son, from whom radiated
> such an ineffable light and splendor that the sun was not
> comparable to it. . . . And so sudden and instantaneous
> was this way of bringing forth that I could neither discover
> nor discern how . . . she gave birth. Verily, though, all of
> a sudden I saw the glorious infant lying on the ground naked
> and shining. His body was pure from any kind of soil and
> impurity. Then I heard also the singing of the angels,
> which was of miraculous sweetness and great beauty. . . .
> When the virgin felt that she had already borne her child,
> she immediately worshipped him, her head bent down and
> her hands clasped, with great honor and reverence. And
> she said to him, "Be welcome, my God, my Lord, and my
> Son." Then as the child was whining and trembling from
> the cold and from the harshness of the floor where he was
> lying, he stretched out his arms, imploring her to raise him
> to the warmth and to her motherly love. The mother then

took him in her arms and pressed him to her breast, and
with her cheek and her breast she warmed him with great
joy and tender maternal compassion. She then sat down on
the floor and laid the child in her lap, and at once she
began to cover his small body. . . .[45]

Thus in the Fairford glass, the Child extends "His hands in expectation of being clasped to His mother's breast,"[46] and in the
York play the Virgin takes up the Child and begins to dress him
"in þis poure wede" (XIV.67). Thereupon the York play reintro-
duces Joseph, who, as in the Fairford window, returns on this
cold evening with a candle and is struck by the greater light radi-
ating from the child. Finally, the infant is placed in a manger,
where the two beasts so familiar from iconography miraculously
warm him with their breath. This final detail is borrowed from
the *Meditations on the Life of Christ*, which states:

and anone the oxe and the asse knelyng doune leyden doune
theire mouthes on the cratche, brethynge at her noses vpon the
child that they knewen by reason that in that cold tyme the
child so simply hiled had nede to be warmed in that maner.[47]

Thus is fulfilled, as Joseph explains in the York play, the prophecy which Habakkuk had "prechid" (XIV.136–38), for the child
has revealed himself "in the midst of the two beasts."[48] The
beasts are identified as an ox and an ass in the apocryphal *Pseudo-
Matthew*, which refers specifically to the text in *Habakkuk*.[49]

The treatment of the Nativity in the York cycle is not only evidence that this play could not on the iconographic evidence have
been written before c.1415–20, but also that the plays were deeply
influenced by the popular piety of the Franciscans who strongly
promoted the idea of the virgin birth and who stressed an emotional piety which would respond to the details recounted in St.
Bridget's vision.[50] This kind of piety will receive additional attention below in the discussion of civic attitudes toward
religious images and religious drama.

But the study of the York plays against the background of the
visual arts can also provide further insight into matters practical as well as matters theoretical. On the one hand, specific aspects of production such as costuming and stagecraft can receive

considerable illumination when painted glass and carvings are consulted. Then, on the other hand, a consideration of the phenomenology of the Fall and its consequences both in the Old Testament scenes and especially in the post-Resurrection scenes of the New Testament will bring drama and the visual arts together to provide a common understanding of the themes and images which the actors set out to elucidate in the plays.

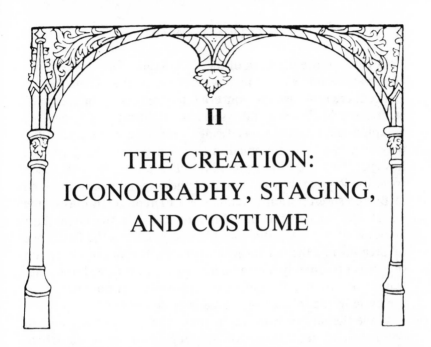

II

THE CREATION: ICONOGRAPHY, STAGING, AND COSTUME

Each performance of the extant English cycle plays, at York assigned in the late Middle Ages to various civic guilds, had as its starting point the introduction of the Creator immediately before the creation of the world. In the case of the York *Creation of Heaven and Earth* presented by the Barkers (i.e., Tanners), the extant play presents a particularly splendid opening for a cycle that was designed to display the events of salvation history from beginning to end in a manner which would reflect favorably on civic piety and would promote the glory of the city. The alliterative verse present in this play has been said to mark it as the work of the York Realist, the anonymous genius also responsible for making major revisions in the series of plays dealing with the Passion in this cycle.[1]

In the *Ordo paginarum ludi Corporis Christi* dated 1415 and included in the York records, the opening pageant is described as follows:

> Deus pater omnipotens creans et formans celos Angelos
> et archangelos luciferum et angelos qui cum eo ceciderunt
> in infernum.[2]

Since at other points this description, written by Roger Burton, the town clerk, seems to be referring to an earlier stage of the

York cycle before the work of the York Realist,[3] the above probably may be understood as not referring to the extant Play I.
Hence there is no need to concern ourselves about the "Angelos
et archangelos," which may seem to be inconsistent with the
Seraphin and Cherubin specifically mentioned in the text of the
play as it has been preserved in the Register. It would appear,
however, that the extant play did not in fact differ very much
from the iconography or design of the original pageant, which
in Burton's description is reminiscent of representations in the
visual arts such as the first Creation panel in the Great East
Window of York Minster that likewise combines the first stage
of Creation and the fall of the rebel angels. The author's intention
thus was presumably not to be innovative with regard to the action of the drama, but rather to improve the crucial opening of
the cycle in the interest of dramatic effectiveness.

While the author who was perhaps the York Realist may in
fact have been responsible for adopting a more up-to-date theological doctrine with regard to the reasons for Lucifer's fall,[4] his
treatment of the primordial event of Creation would seem in
most respects not to have made any radical departures from the
iconography which previously had pertained. The evidence is
that both costuming and pageantry at York were splendidly
elaborate, and hence when the author undertook to provide a new
text to illustrate the Creation event he most likely set out to retain
as much of the extant stage equipment as possible, perhaps for the
sake of economy. The extant play therefore probably represented
an advance primarily in the extended and affective use of
language in order that the drama might have a more direct impact on the emotions of the spectators than would previously
have been possible.

I

We are not merely speculating, however, when we insist that
this opening play of the cycle must indeed have been spectacular.
The modern productions of the York plays in York in Canon
Purvis' modernization and on an elevated platform stage before

the ruins of St. Mary's Abbey can hardly do more than hint at the extravagant fifteenth-century religiosity and deep respect for the ultimate mythic realities that are suggested by the text in the Register. The York *Creation of Heaven and Earth* introduces the awe-inspiring Creator of the whole universe enthroned on a raised area which represented heaven.[5] From this location, God appears as the One from whom all life flows and to which all life returns:

> *Ego sum Alpha et O[mega]: vita, via, veritas, primus et*
> *nouissimus.*

The five words which open these lines likewise appear on the open Book of Creation held by God at the very top of the Great East Window in York Minster. This tracery figure, created by John Thornton of Coventry in 1405–08, also holds up his right hand in blessing over the window which below depicts the beginning and end of history.[6] Of course, whether or not the God of the York play would have had held a similar Book of Creation (destined to be burned in the Last Judgment) when the early performances of this play were staged may again seem a matter for conjecture. But it is not impossible that during his first speech he might have held up a large book, either open with the words "Ego sum Alpha et O . . ." written in large letters, or closed.[7] God's first spoken words in English may then be understood as an explanation of the Latin text:

> I am gracyus and grete, God withoutyn begynnyng,
>   I am maker vnmade, all myghte es in me;
> I am lyfe and way vnto welth-wynnyng,
>   I am formaste and fyrste, als I byd sall it be. (I.1–4)

This God is the One from whom the world emanates and to which all things must ultimately return.

The first act of this God is to create the heavens and the nine orders of angels who are to give him everlasting praise, honor, and reverence (I.23–24). Surely the actors representing angels were somehow hidden at the beginning of the scene, and, when God declared his thought at lines 22–24, they rose up as if newly created and sang the *Te Deum*. If we may judge by the frequency with which late medieval representations of angels show them playing musical instruments—rebecs, organs, psalteries, etc.—in

painted glass and sculpture or carving (e.g., on the bosses on the
choir screen at York Minster, or on the hammer beams at All
Saints, North Street[8]), then we may conjecture that the music at
this point was not merely plainsong but rather something more impressive. Polyphonic music was, after all, regarded as the music of
heaven. Thus the first act of God's creation appropriately issues
forth into the exultant praises of the heavenly creatures. Here is
spectacle indeed! We must certainly believe that the actors who
impersonated the angels here and elsewhere in the cycle must
have been very skilful singers and instrumentalists. For example,
in the *Assumption*, twelve singing angels are required by the text
(XLV.105–17) and musical compositions are actually supplied.[9]
These compositions are not of the sort that could be handled by
fifteenth-century amateurs, but rather point to the fact that
angelic music must have been the responsibility of professional
musicians — men and boys — attached to the cathedral and town.

After the completion of the *Te Deum*, God, with a gesture
which indicates the playing area or *place* (*locus*) below, creates
earth and gives it to his angelic ministers on condition that they
remain "stabill in thoghte" (I.30). Those who fail this test are
promised that they will "Be put to my presone at pyne" (I.32).
Thereupon, he turns to Lucifer, "berar of lyghte," and commissions him as "master and merour of my mighte" (I.33–36).
Again, the scene issues into angelic song as heaven's creatures
sing "*Sanctus, sanctus, sanctus, dominus deus sabaoth,*" presumably here a portion of the *Te Deum* though the words also
appear in the standard item in the ordinary of the Mass. When
the music is completed, the actor playing God must retire, while
proud Lucifer, in revolt against his Maker and against the good
angels, insists upon his autonomy and his self-derived power
that "es passande my peres" (I.56). Discord is thus introduced
into a heaven previously associated with harmony. In contrast
to the Towneley *Creation* in which Lucifer actually sits in God's
seat ("how semys now me / To sit in seyte of trynyte") and thereafter attempts to fly upward in the heavens just as God does,[10]
the York play only calls for an argument among the angels with
regard to primacy and, when Lucifer boasts that he "sall be lyke
vnto hym þat es hyeste on heghte" (I.91), he and his followers

spectacularly tumble or fall downward from the platform which represents heaven. "Fra heuen are we heledande on all hande," one of Lucifer's cohorts cries (I.95). The event is illustrated in Thornton's Great East Window in the Minster, which shows Lucifer, already transformed into "a horrific red beast with the head of a monkey, the breast of a serpent and the legs of a bird," falling across a globe of wavy lines that represents the void.[11] Originally there was another falling angel, now almost entirely patch.[12] In the York play, the fall of Lucifer and his followers was possibly effected with the help of ropes, for we know that ropes were indeed used to assist actors to imitate flight in the Mercers' pageant of the Last Judgment. A Mercers' memorandum from 1464 lists 2d "for a rope to the angels,"[13] though in this instance the angels involved may have been the nine puppets mentioned in the 1433 indenture as designed "to renne aboute in þe heuen."[14] The indenture, however, does speak of a contrivance which God shall use "when he sall sty vppe to heuen With iiij rapes at iiij corners."[15] In the York Realist's *Creation of Heaven and Earth*, the fall of the rebel angels appears to have been triggered at the moment when God again emerged from behind the curtain or door or otherwise appeared on the platform which represented heaven.

The remainder of the play is divided between hell, where the evil angels terminate their fall, and heaven, the place where the stable angels and God comment on what has taken place and where the deity prepares to create new creatures to fill the empty earth. Hell was represented by the well-known hell mouth that commonly appears in medieval iconography. The 1433 Mercers' indenture specifically lists a "helle mouthe" as one of the properties for the Doomsday pageant,[16] while the 1526 inventory for the same pageant speaks of a "hell dure."[17] Surely in both these instances and in the York *Creation of Heaven and Earth* the conventional beast's mouth spouting smoke must be meant. The design is ubiquitous in medieval art, and many examples may be noted in the North of England. In illuminations, hell mouth commonly appears at the bottom of scenes which illustrate the Creation or fall of Lucifer (e.g., the *Holkham Bible Picture Book*, fol. 2^r, and *Queen Mary's Psalter*, fol. 1^v).

At Coventry, the records for 1557 show that 4d was paid "for kepyng of fyer at hell mothe."[18] The text of the York play seems to indicate a hell mouth which is similarly dirty and smoking.[19] Lucifer speaks of being beaten and burned upon his arrival at hell (I.102), while the second demon complains, "All oure fode es but filth . . . /We þat ware beelded in blys, in bale are we brent nowe" (I.106–07). And, as Lucifer, who is choking, indicates, they are being smothered "in smoke" (I.117).

The scene in which the angels fall is extremely lively and graphic in its assertion of particular details, and hence stands in direct contrast to the more dignified and ritualized scenes in heaven where God and the angels act according to the rule of what is proper. Such handling of material looks forward to the contrast in those plays in the Passion sequence which, written by the playwright whom we call the York Realist, set forth a strong contrast between a silent Jesus and a lively, undignified group of persecutors. In a sense, the setting up of such a contrast may be characteristic of the work of the Realist, whose retreat from earlier aesthetic principles perhaps made him insist upon the manipulation of vividly conceived scenes in order to involve his audience in the action of the drama.

II

"Stage costume," Glynne Wickham insists, "seems in general to have been kept in harmony with stage settings: that is to say, the unknown was interpreted in terms of the known."[20] While Wickham apparently would admit a certain degree of archaism in the garments worn by "representatives of both foreign and ancient founder races,"[21] he hardly appreciates the extent to which older fashions or variants of less rapidly changing liturgical garb must have been utilized in the plays. Study of costume in the visual arts shows that there is more stability in the manner in which certain figures are clothed than has sometimes been realized. It is through clothing that medieval artists working with purely visual media could express the element of time. Then, as in other semi-literate societies, "a long time ago" meant "in grandfather's time," and "ancient" and "old" were popularly indefinite terms that denoted "when grandfather was young or anytime before that time." Hence we ought not to be surprised to recognize a deliberate purpose in the artists' representation of God — i.e., of Being more ancient than any creature — as a man of grandfather's age and wearing either a garment no longer stylish or garb associated with religious ritual. Such must also have been the manner in which God the Creator appeared in the York *Creation of Heaven and Earth*.

The appearance of God in human shape according to the best anthropomorphic tradition and of grandfatherly age becomes somewhat more curious, however, when it is recognized that medieval theology often gave the credit for the Creation to the Son rather than the Father. The source of this belief may have been *Hebrews* 1.10: "And Thou, Lord, in the beginning hast laid the foundation of the earth; and the heavens are the works of thine hands" (AV). As late as Milton's *Paradise Lost*, it is the Son who sets forth out of heaven "On his great Expedition" to calm the "troubl'd waves" and to prepare "to circumscribe / This Universe, and all created things" (VII.193, 216, 226–27). Hence we might expect that the true identity of the Creator as the second person of the Trinity might have been represented in the York *Creation of Heaven and Earth* by means of the cross-nimbus.[22]

At the opening of the York *Creation of Heaven and Earth*, the actor playing God must have aimed at an appearance not so different from the deity who sits on the edge of the cosmos and creates the world in British Library MS. Egerton 1894, fol. 1^r, which M. R. James has dated[23] about 1360:

> . . . God, represented as a venerable bearded figure with long hair, and cross-nimbus, clad in a cope or mantle fastened by a morse on the breast, sits upon a bow or arch representing the immovable sphere. . . . God's *r*. hand is extended downwards in the attitude of blessing, and His *l*. hand rests on a closed book on His knee, over which His fingers are carefully portrayed.[24]

Some qualifications, of course, are in order, for it is unlikely that the "bow or arch" would have been included in the design of the staging which represented heaven in the performance of the York *Creation of Heaven and Earth*. As noted above, however, there is reason at least for conjecturing that the deity held a book at the beginning of the play.

At this point, the most reliable procedure in attempting to trace further the precise costuming and other props that might have been associated with God in the *Creation of Heaven and Earth* at York would seem once again to involve close examination of works of art such as painted glass, preferably from the same period as the play, from the city of York itself. Such information, as we have seen in Chapter I, can then be used to corroborate and refine information learned through a more general study of iconography. In York Minster today is a fifteenth-century window, known as the Te Deum window, a panel of which contains a representation of the Creator, with long hair and wearing a beard, in the act of circumscribing the creation. Although this window, which dates from c.1430 (the date when it apparently was installed in St. Martin-le-Grand, Coney Street, from which it was removed in 1722),[25] is in imperfect condition, the observer will see that it has much in common with the miniature described by M. R. James. Again we see the cross-nimbus and the archaic garment — a mantle which seems richly embroidered along the edges and is held together with some kind of clasp at his waist. While one hand holds an orb, the other holds a pair of compasses, symbolic of God's role as architect of the universe. Similar iconography may be observed in the illustration of God with compasses in the *Holkham Bible Picture Book* (fol. 2r), the Creation window at the Great Malvern Priory Church, and the important illumination by John Siferwas in the *Sherborne Missal* (c.1396–1407).[26] It also will appear in Milton's *Paradise Lost* as the circumscribing instrument that the creating deity uses:

> One foot he centred, and the other turn'd
> Round through the vast profundity obscure. . . . (VII.228–29)

It is unlikely that the God of the York *Creation of Heaven and Earth* held a set of compasses, even during the time he was creating earth in lines 25–32. Nevertheless, more important is the recognition that he unquestionably did extend his hand in blessing, perhaps in the manner of the illumination in the *Sherbourne*

Missal, upon the newly created angels below him and upon this terrestrial sphere. The costume worn by the actor playing God in this play would appear to have been a mantle or cope of an appropriately royal color. He very likely wore a wig and a mask such as appear in the Norwich Grocers' inventory of 1565: "A face and heare for the Father."[27] The evidence of the 1433 Mercers' identure and of the Te Deum panels now in York Minster would indicate that the wig and face with its beard—a mask—were all gold in color, as would be the cross-nimbus that he would be expected to wear. He also probably wore gloves.[28]

As the above indicates, uncertainties can never be removed from any attempt to discover with as much precision as possible how a particular character, such as the Creator in the York *Creation of Heaven and Earth*, would actually have appeared in productions at York in the fifteenth and early sixteenth centuries. So too in the depiction of the nine orders of angels, we can never regain with photographic accuracy the identical scene which greeted the eyes of the original spectators at York. The text in the Register has speaking roles for only two orders of angels—in addition, of course, to the evil angels. But surely, as in the Chester *Fall of Lucifer* which has speaking roles for all nine orders,[29] when the actor playing God spoke of the *nine* orders he had created ("I byde at be here/Nyen ordres of aungels full clere," ll. 22–23) more than two angels were made to appear. The Mercers' records show that several live actors (all of them almost certainly musicians) were utilized to play angels' roles, in addition to other sizes of angels represented by puppets in their pageant of Doomsday.[30] Presumably the different sizes of angels in the Mercers' pageant reflected the medieval understanding of the three hierarchies of angelic orders. While it may be argued that for the York *Creation of Heaven and Earth* a platform representing heaven might have provided space too limited for a large number of angels, logic in this instance would dictate a minimum of nine angels at the outset, though this number could well have included the evil angels as well. Assuming that after the fall two or three evil angels would have been removed from the heavenly choirs, six or seven would remain—a number not inconsistent with the number that seems to appear in the Mercers' records for the Judgment pageant.

The members of the audience at York must have known in advance what the orders of angels were supposed to look like in a general way, for they are a very common subject in the ecclesiastical art of this period. In addition to their appearance in the tracery of Thornton's Great East Window in the Minster, the nine orders are illustrated in three extant windows in York churches. Because of the difficulty with which Thornton's angels, high above the floor of the Minster, may be examined even today, the extant parish church glass will receive emphasis here on account of its accessibility. None of the examples in parish church glass follows exactly the description of the angelic orders in, for example, the influential *Golden Legend* of Jacobus de Voragine, but each offers something to our understanding of the iconography of angels as it informs the York *Creation of Heaven and Earth*. Even the fragmentary window from 1410-20 at All Saints, North Street — a church noted for its excellent painted glass — is of considerable value, especially since a seventeenth-century drawing of the glass in its original state has been discovered.[31] The All Saints glass was arranged in a manner consistent with the division of angels in the *Golden Legend*. The nine orders or "choirs" are divided into three rows, with seraphim, cherubim, and thrones — the orders that "are wholly turned to [God]"[32] across the top; with dominations, principalities, and powers — those who "are set to rule and command the whole universe of men"[33] — in the center; and with virtues, archangels, and angels — "the lower hierarchy"[34] along the bottom. Fragments of glass remaining in the window indicate that the angels had golden wings and feathered bodies. In many cases, the bodies were covered by rich robes or, in the case of the powers, by armor. The dominations and principalities wore crowns.[35]

In better condition today is the glass in the tracery of the St. Martin window in St. Martin-le-Grand, Coney Street. Here various orders of angels are clothed in different kinds of garments, including tunics, an alb, dalmatics with amices, a cope and almuce, and plate armor.[36] The armor is, of course, for the angel representing the order of powers. Unfortunately, the identification of individual orders in this window can be only tentative since, except in the case of powers and principalities, no tradition of costuming is being drawn upon. But it should be noted that here again some angels, probably the cherubim and seraphim, are made to appear without any outer garments over their feathery bodies.

The York Realist himself apparently understood the traditional roles of the various orders of angels, for to his Seraphin and Cherubin he gives lines that are indicative of their conventional associations with love and knowledge, respectively. If these roles were likewise understood by the actors (and we have reason to believe that they were), any robes or garments worn by these angels would certainly have been red for the Seraphin and probably purple for the Cherubin, who would perhaps have been holding the Book of Knowledge, as in the All Saints, North Street window.[37] But most certainly the actors impersonating angels did appear wearing feathered costumes to represent the feathery bodies of the angelic creatures. Such bodies are most splendidly illustrated in York in the window in St. Michael, Spurriergate, in the well-preserved panel representing the cherubim.

While it would be very nice if the York dramatic records would somewhere corroborate the description of the angels' costumes in the York glass, they unfortunately fail to provide a description more complete than the mere lists in the Mercers' accounts and the 1433 indenture from the same guild. It is clear, for example, that the angels wore wings, though we cannot be so certain about their design. And what color were the angels' wings? Were they gold as they were commonly represented in iconography and as they probably were at Coventry?[38] While specific answers to such questions are not likely to be forthcoming, the evidence, derived from the visual arts as well as from the Coventry records and the Norwich Grocers' accounts, points toward the theory that the basic garments for an angel were a set of leather stockings and a leather coat;[39] upon these, feathers apparently could be fastened and wings attached. M. D. Anderson suggests that stage angels in general may have had much in common with the appearance of the carvings of angels at Beauchamp Chapel, Warwick, where these heavenly creatures are grandly set forth with "Pointed rays [of light] . . . hang[ing] from their collars" and with "feathered tights with richly jeweled belts and

collars."⁴⁰ For York, however, the extant illustrations of the
nine orders in painted glass seem to provide the soundest guide
to the angels which God has created in the *Creation of Heaven
and Earth*. White feathered coats and stockings seem to be called
for, along with some standard symbols (e.g., the book associated
with the cherubim, and a set of balances with the thrones, as in
the glass at St. Michael, Spurriergate). The use of certain
liturgical garb and/or robes of archaic style, along with some
armor for powers, would certainly have been appropriate, at
least for the lower orders.⁴¹ At Coventry, the Cappers' accounts
listed albs and "surplisses" for angels, while the Drapers' records
for 1556 list "iiij dyadymes."⁴² The presentation of the angelic
orders in the York cycle would hardly have shared the simplicity
of the appearance of the angels in the dramatic exchange described
in the *Regularis Concordia* of the tenth century.

The fall of Lucifer presents, of course, some special problems.
At first Lucifer would not have been distinguished from the
other angels except that he would have been represented as brighter
and more beautiful. At the point at which he attempted to place
himself in a position of usurped authority in heaven, he may
have received a crown from another angel, as in the *Holkham
Bible Picture Book* (fol. 2ʳ), or he may, perhaps more appropriately, have appeared as self-crowned.

After the fall, Lucifer and the other evil angels must undergo
a transformation. In drama, it is not possible that the transformation from angels to ugly demons could have taken place in
mid-air, as in the panel in the Great East Window of York
Minster. But some idea of how the transformation took place in
the staging of the York *Creation of Heaven and Earth* is to be
derived from the fifteenth-century glass in one of the lights of
the East Window, South Aisle, in St. Michael, Spurriergate,⁴³
which illustrates Lucifer fallen but as yet in his feathery angelic
costume among fully transformed and hairy demons. The chief
of demons here seems to answer the description in the Chester
banns: "the deuell in his ffeathers. all Rugged and rente."⁴⁴ The
glass contains the text: "de celo cecidisti lucifer corrusti qui
militabas"⁴⁵ (cf. *Isaiah* 14.12: "How art thou fallen from heaven O
Lucifer, son of the morning! how art thou cut down to the ground,

which did weaken the nations," *A V*). Obviously, upon arrival at hell mouth, the actors portraying the evil angels would begin changing their angelic garb for the grotesque masks and hairy coats of devils. Perhaps there was actually room within the entrance of the smoking hell mouth to accommodate the transformation, which would need to be somewhat more complete than the "Claw-gloves and a mask hurriedly snatched up" suggested by M. D. Anderson.[46] White and red and gold need to be exchanged for black and blue, the colors mentioned by Lucifer at line 101: "My bryghtnes es blakkeste and blo nowe."

Evidence for coats and masks for demons comes from the records of the York Mercers. The 1433 indenture calls for "iij garmentes for iij deuels vj deuelles faces in iij Vesernes,"[47] while the 1526 inventory mentions "ij dewell cottes" and "ij dewell heddes."[48] The earlier document proves that the demons in the Doomsday pageant wore masks with two faces; such masks are, of course, common in the visual arts in representations of devils. Similar garments apparently prevailed at Coventry, where in 1477 "the demons Garment" needed mending and in 1498 "the demones hed" required "peynttyng."[49] We also learn from the Coventry records that, like the angels' coats, the devils' coats were at least in part made of leather.[50] That hair was not merely painted on is also shown by the Coventry Drapers' accounts, which specify "heare for the demons cotts and hose."[51] Thus at York the fully transformed demons accompanying the fallen Lucifer in the glass of St. Michael, Spurriergate, have bodies covered with hair, as does the demon standing before St. Martin in one of the panels of the St. Martin window in St. Martin-le-Grand, Coney Street. One of the demons in the glass of St. Michael, Spurriergate, has two faces, both of them bestial.

From lines 101–02 of the York *Creation of Heaven and Earth* comes evidence that the demons also may have carried clubs or staffs, which they used to beat each other. Both staff and club appear in the Coventry accounts; the demon in the Smiths' pageant apparently used a staff, while the Cappers' devil carried a club made of canvas and painted.[52] The latter, of course, would underline the foolishness or absurdity of the devil's actions—the same emphasis that may be detected in the illustration of the

fool holding a limp club, apparently made of cloth, in an illuminated initial accompanying Psalm 14 in Bodleian MS. Don. d.
85.[53] Instead of inheriting eternal bliss, the fate of the fallen
angels is to be beaten and burned.

III

The York *Creation of Heaven and Earth* does not, of course,
complete the story of the Creation as it is told in *Genesis*. In the
York cycle, it is followed by three short plays, which their nineteenth-century editor, Lucy Toulmin Smith, entitled *The Creation, to the Fifth Day, God Creates Adam and Eve*, and *God
Puts Adam and Eve in the Garden of Eden*. It is tempting to try
to date these plays earlier than the first play in the cycle, but it
would nevertheless be hazardous to assign a date on the basis of
either style or iconography. Each of these plays illustrates one
or two images only, and provides speeches clearly designed to
vivify the tableau set forth on the pageant wagon.

The Plasterers' play, which treats the Creation up to the fifth
day, indeed requires only one actor, Deus, who reviews the state
of things and comments that "Syne þat þis world es ordand
euyn,/Furth well I publysch my power" by bidding a "firmament" to appear (II.29–32). Thereupon God proceeds to command the existence of the creation up to the forming of man.
These events find their parallel in representations of the Creation in the visual arts. Four panels immediately following the fall
of the rebel angels in the Great East Window by John Thornton
in York Minster thus illustrate the creation of the firmament, of
plants, of the sun and moon, and of fishes and birds, while a fifth,
which was reported to be a "jumble" before the recent restoration,[54] shares the subject of the creation of the animals with the
creation of Adam. In the Plasterers' play as in the panels by
Thornton, the newly created plants, birds, and animals would
need to be made visible in some symbolic way. When God creates
fishes and birds, for example, he minimally would be required to
do no more than to make the sign of blessing directed at perhaps
two or three representations, made of wood, cloth, or alabaster,

which would make their appearance at the appropriate moment. At the Great Malvern Priory Church, God stands in the midst of a landscape and looks toward the right. His hands are extended, "from the left of which two birds (now mere outlines) fly away, while the right holds a fish."[55] Such effects in drama were certainly technologically possible at York, and indeed the flight of the newly created birds seems to be called for by the text. At the end of the playlet, Deus declares:

My blyssyng haue ȝe all;
The fift day endyd es. (II.85–86)

The moving of the creation of the beasts up to the fifth day leaves the creation of Adam and Eve as the lone event to be accomplished on the sixth day.

As drama, the Cardmakers' *Creation of Adam and Eve* is hardly a great improvement over the previous play, for its presentation of the image of Adam's creation and of the making of Eve from Adam's "lyft rybe" (III.38)[56] lacks the inspired language of the York *Creation of Heaven and Earth*. Nor is the handling of the action very skilful, since, as in the Plasterers' play, the drama opens with a clumsy recapitulation of what has just happened. Unlike the York Realist's work in the series of plays on the Passion in which one play moves into the next almost as if no break were intended between them, Plays II and III show the marks of their origin as parts of a processionally staged drama played at various stations throughout the city.

Play IV, the Fullers' *Prohibition of the Tree of Knowledge*, continues, however, precisely where the previous play has left off. But in the Register it is written in a sixteenth-century hand and is one of the items entered in 1559 by John Clerke.[57] The innocent Adam and Eve in this play as in the Cardmakers' play apparently wore garments of white leather similar in design to the white leather body stocking which seems to have been worn by Christ during the Flagellation and other Passion scenes in the York plays. At Norwich, an inventory of the properties for the Grocers' play of *The Fall* in 1565 included not only a "Rybbe colleryd Red," obviously for use in the creation of Eve, but also "2 cotes and a payre [of] hosen for Eve, stayned" and "A cote

and hosen for Adam, steyned."⁵⁸ In his discussion of the staging
of the creation of Adam and Eve in the Towneley cycle, Martial
Rose cites an important stage direction from the Cornish plays:
"Meanwhile are got ready Adam and Eva aparlet in whytt lether
in a place apoynted by the conveyour and not to be sene till they
be called and thei kneel and ryse."⁵⁹ A magnificent panel of
painted glass at Great Malvern Priory Church shows God indi-
cating the forbidden fruit to the kneeling Adam and Eve, who
are nude with very white skin.⁶⁰ The Malvern glass represents the
moment when God in the Fullers' play threateningly points out
"The tree of good and yll" from which if they eat they will bring
disaster upon themselves and all their descendants (IV.56–59). It
is a warning that Deus repeats twice again (IV.66–69, 83–95)
before giving the couple his blessing and leaving the scene, presumably making way for the arrival of Satan in the next pageant,
which will be the Coopers' play of the *Fall of Man*.

IV

In spite of all that we are able to learn about the conditions of
performance in the case of the York *Creation of Heaven and
Earth* and the three short Creation plays which immediately
follow it in the Register, answers are not available to all our
questions. There is a great deal, for example, that we would like
especially to know about the style and technique of acting used
in the fifteenth and sixteenth-century productions of these plays.
The middle of the fifteenth century apparently marks the rise of
the professional player in England: the first use of the term *player*
(meaning stage player, one who acts in plays or interludes) recorded
in the *Oxford English Dictionary* is dated 1463/4. The York
records show evidence of professionalism not only with regard to
the hiring of musicians but also with regard to the employing of
actors.⁶¹ As drama designed specifically to appeal to the taste of
the citizens of York, the opening play of the cycle in particular
need not have been a creaky amateur production only worthy of
Shakespeare's Bottom the Weaver. The Barkers, to whom the
York *Creation of Heaven and Earth* is given in the Register,

surely must have shared the desire to present their portion of the cycle as a way of honoring their Lord God and bringing glory to their city. And in spite of the inferiority of their texts, the plays staged by the Plasterers, Cardmakers, and Fullers must have involved their best efforts as well.

III

AFTER THE FALL

A comparative method involving study of the York plays and analogous representations of subjects in the visual arts may suggest some new ways of approaching the vexed question of the selection of episodes in the portion of the cycle based on the Old Testament. Agreement seems fairly general that all theories which purport to explain the choice of episodes as determined by liturgical readings, by typology, or by the medieval understanding of the seven ages of man[1] can never provide adequate explanations of the principles of selection. Let us for the time being put aside any attempt to identify the mechanism or principle which allowed certain plays to "evolve" within a certain pattern. Instead, if we are willing to consider the phenomenology of the plays in the Old Testament series, they suddenly make very good sense.

No argument defending a tightly-knit "organic unity" of the plays in the York cycle between the Fall and the Annunciation is either possible or desirable, but throughout these plays there is observable a more or less consistent treatment of the issue which rightly ought to be most prominent in any representation of the early history of the race according to the Christian myths. This issue involves the marked alteration in the human condition following the fall from the idyllic state experienced in the Garden

of Eden. Choice obviously has entered into human life, but it is
not so simple a matter as the Dominican Thomas Aquinas apparently believed when he expressed confidence that the intellect
through the imparting of rational knowledge would produce a
desire in the will to perform virtue and eschew vice.[2] Through
the Fall, demonic forces have made their way into the very spiritual and psychological make-up of man. Men can become wil-
fully blind: they can sever their relationships with their kinsmen
and their Creator. Or they can, through openness and sensitivity
to the divine realities, overcome the effects of the Fall. The tendency of the one kind is toward vice, the other is toward virtue.

The presentation of scenes from the early history of the race
is, of course, the province of much medieval English and continental art, and here too the examination of meaning and structure must lead to the conclusion that no merely interesting images
are being presented for their own sake. The visual arts illustrated
the important events of the sacred story not scientifically and
dispassionately, but with a view to understanding their true significance. The approach of the painter or sculptor was hence
very much like the dramatist or actor who attempted to present
in livelier fashion the same images and the same events.

I

For the history of mankind as interpreted by the York plays,
the crucial moment is the fall of man. As portrayed in the
Coopers' *Fall of Man*, the age of innocence in the Garden is very
brief for Adam and Eve, who are created in the morning and are
fallen already at noon. After the Fall, in the Armorers' *Expulsion from the Garden*, Adam laments:

> Allas, in blisse kouthe we noȝt bee,
> For putte we were to grete plenté
>   At prime of þe day;
> Be tyme of none alle lost had wee,
>   Sa welawaye. (VI.88–92)

Irreparable loss is the result of allowing themselves to be deceived
by the "tales vntrewe" of the hypocrite Satan (V.123). Thus in

this play the audience is taken back to the time when the race was founded — a time marked by a touch of bliss against which all later sorrow may be judged.

In contrast to any strictly typological interpretation of Play V, our understanding of the dramatic handling of the Fall ought to conclude that, like representations in the pictorial arts of the late Middle Ages in England, this work focuses most upon the moral and physical disaster brought upon mankind. The "gamys" and "glee" enjoyed by our innocent parents in the morning of sacred history are gone (VI.86–87), and they are overcome by shame at their naked state. Adam expresses his severe anxiety about his nudity — "Oure shappe for doole me defes" (V.129) — and Eve suggests that they take up "fygge-leves" (V.131). Their discomfort is proof that they have something to hide. "Full wondyr fayne I wolde hyde me,/Fro my lordis sight," Adam exclaims (V.135–36). As in the series of panels painted by John Thornton in the Great East Window of York Minster, the transgression is immediately followed by divine intervention. In Play V, God orders Adam and Eve out into the "erthe" where they will "swete and swynke,/And trauayle for [their] foode" (V.161–62) (see plate 3), and calls upon his "Cherubyn" to "dryve these twoo" out of the Garden (V.166–67). The angel is not present as the agent of expulsion in the scriptural account in *Genesis*, which only notes that after "the Lord God . . . drove out the man," he stationed "at the east of the garden of Eden cherubims, and a flaming sword which turned every way, to keep the way of the tree of life" (3.23–24). But in Thornton's Great East Window and in the York plays, the angel acts to expel man's first parents, who are still nude. Thornton's painted glass shows the angel placing one hand on Adam's shoulder — a very common gesture[3] (see also plate 3) that probably was repeated in the Armorers' play, where the divine messenger also tells Eve that she shall as punishment bring forth her children in pain and woe (VI.69–72).

It is extremely unlikely that the medieval audience of Plays V and VI in the York cycle would naturally have been led to think about the typological significance of the Fall, which in the *Biblia Pauperum* and elsewhere points to the Temptation of Christ by Satan. This is not to say that medieval men failed to think of Christ as the second Adam and of the Blessed Virgin Mary as the second Eve who miraculously brought forth her Son without travail; however, the focus of the plays, even while preparing the way dramatically for the life of Christ which will follow later, is upon the human condition as encountered in a post-lapsarian world.

Primarily we note an Adam and Eve totally discomfited and desiring to hide from the reality represented by God. Having fallen from obedience, they expect punishment — and they receive stern treatment indeed. After they are expelled from Eden, they argue and fall into despair. "On grounde mon I never gladde gange, / Withowten glee," Adam complains (VI.161-62). Normally in the visual arts the next scene would be the scene in which "Adam delved and Eve span," as in the *Speculum Humanae Salvationis*,[4] the fifteenth-century painted glass at Great Malvern[5] or the fourteenth-century illumination in the *Bohun Psalter* now in the Bodleian Library,[6] but this is not represented in the York cycle or in Thornton's Great East Window. Yet in the plays the idea that Adam will be condemned to joyless labor is directly conveyed in a manner that must have made a deep impression on fifteenth- and sixteenth-century audiences.

The pattern established by the fall of man hence is essentially different from the fall of the rebel angels. When Lucifer and his cohorts fell, they first impressed audiences with their arrogance and pride — factors which separated them from the spectators and made them the objects of hatred at the same time that their absurd hopes made them the butt of laughter. In falling into a sado-masochistic hell, they appeared to receive what they deserve. Thereafter, they become simultaneously sinister and comic — angels of darkness who are at once foolish and malicious. On the other hand, Eve and Adam are deceived by Satan who, to be sure, appeals to their pride. But they eat almost reluctantly, and when then they voice their regret it is with a terrible sense of despair that is in no way funny. The relationship established with the deity has been broken, and in their alienation man's first parents lose all the joy which they formerly possessed. They are repentant — a sign that their despair actively is working for good within their souls. Hence when Christ, the second Adam, comes after the Crucifixion to rescue Adam and Eve during the

Harrowing of Hell, he will be able to offer them salvation (XXXVII.385–88).[7] But in the meantime the primordial couple has established a pattern which will resound through history.

This pattern as set forth in the story of Adam and Eve involves an essential conflict between *hope* (nourished by obedience and overcoming despair to re-establish communication with God) and a *despair* which brings together all the negative aspects of the sin of Adam and Eve as observed in Plays V and VI in the York cycle. The immediate effects of the Fall are to bring unhappiness, sin, and death into human life, as in the sixteenth-century Rouen glass panels recently inserted in one of the windows of York Minster. In this expulsion scene, the nude Adam and Eve with their hands bound have in attendance the allegorical figures of Poverty, Toil, Sorrow, and Credulity as well as the Seven Deadly Sins.[8] Once the machinery of the allegory is stripped away, the image in the Rouen glass, like the York plays, presents us with the condition of natural man as a precarious and fragile state in which he must struggle to extend his existence in an environment that has become hostile. The natural condition for man in such an existence seems to be joyless despair, yet the memory of paradise lost breeds a desire to return to felicity and a hope that through renewed obedience communication with the deity might bring about this happy end.

II

Hope and despair hence become the essential elements in the dialectic of the play which follows the Armorers' *Expulsion from the Garden*. This play is the Glovers' *Sacrificium Cayme et Abell*, which, as we have seen, is not extant in complete form in the Register and which also contains an interpolation in a sixteenth-century hand. However, in spite of the fragmentary nature of the text, enough is present to document the manner in which the images communicated by the scenes are designed to illustrate the binary pattern of hope and despair. Thus Abel in his first speech announces his sincerè obedience and devotion: "I worshippe þe with worthynes" (VII.36). He is a good steward, recognizing that it is only proper for God to have his share in sacrifice "sen [he] it sent" (VII.42).[9] As the first shepherd and a worthy keeper of sheep, he likewise looks forward typologically to the divine Shepherd (i.e., Christ).[10] While hence Abel on several levels represents hope, Cain from the very first epitomizes its opposite, which is despair. He makes fun of Abel's piety, and responds to his brother's plea that he too is required to fulfil "Goddis biddyng blithe" (VII.49–50) with the following inappropriate words:

> Ya, daunce in þe devil way, dresse þe downe,
> For I wille wyrke euen as I will. (VII.52–53)

He substitutes his own *will* for the divine will, and hence becomes an emblem of disobedience to divine authority.

Cain's despair is a logical extension of his wilful isolation and alienation. He is unable to "set [his] hope high, to the good of all goods."[11] So he serves himself, placing narrow self-interest above service to the Maker of all things. As the first son of Eve born after the Fall, Cain clearly represents the lapsarian principle in mankind. Medieval theology popularly regarded him as a child of sin.[12] He offends against kinship, and in him all human ties are dissolved.[13] In the Towneley cycle, Cain's acts are regarded as foreshadowing all later deeds of ingratitude and malice, as when Judas betrays Christ. The Towneley Pilate, speaking to the Jews who maliciously attempt to destroy Jesus, calls them "kamys kyn" (*Conspiracy*, l. 639). And in the fragmentary Towneley *Suspencio Iude*, Judas calls himself a member of "that Cursyd Clott of Camys kyn" (l. 17).[14] For the medieval Church, Judas is, of course, the prime exemplar of despair, for his hopelessness in the end leads to his utterly horrifying suicide—an act early represented in art as opposed precisely to the death of Christ in the Crucifixion, which ultimately is the source of hope for all Christians. Hence as early as the fifth century the artist responsible for an ivory now in the British Museum placed the betrayer Judas, hanging by his neck and utterly alone, on the left, while on the right Jesus on the cross is attended by the Virgin and St. John at the moment when Longinus (with a spear now lost) opens the side of the Savior.[15] Judas' attitude toward self-interest and profit and his act of malice in betraying his Master to death are both already present in Cain, whose name, according to St. Ambrose, means "getting"[16] in keeping with his refusal to tithe or sacrifice sincerely — and who, as everyone knows, killed his own brother. Cain is also linked with Christ's betrayer in the frieze on the West front of Lincoln Cathedral, where he curiously holds a bag or purse — an emblem which he shares with Judas.[17] Indeed, Cain's followers — those who are destroyed at the Flood, tyrants such as Pharaoh and Herod, Judas, the Jews who oppose Christ and his religion — are set in permanent opposition to obedient Abel, Noah, Abraham, and the Apostles and other Christians who are Christ's followers before and after the Resurrection. Through these two sets of characters, the York plays establish a dialectic of despair and hope.

The York *Sacrificium Cayme et Abell* hence builds on the understanding of Cain set forth long ago in St. Ambrose's *Cain and Abel*.[18] Ambrose wrote:

> I am inclined to hold that . . . we have reference to two classes of peoples. In disposing for the Church's use the faith of His devoted flock, God has made ineffective the perfidy of the people who fell away from Him. The very words of God seem to establish this meaning: 'Two nations are in your womb; two peoples stem from your body.' These two brothers, Cain and Abel, have furnished us with the prototype of the Synagogue and the Church. In Cain we perceive the parricidal people of the Jews, who were stained with blood of their Lord, their Creator, and, as a result of the Child-bearing of the Virgin Mary, their Brother, also. By Abel we understand the Christian who cleaves to God, as David says: 'It is good for me to adhere to my God,' that is, to attach oneself to heavenly things and to shun the earthly.[19]

The idea of "two nations" is familiar from St. Augustine, who named them Babylon and Jerusalem. However, in the visual arts the usual equivalents of Ambrose's "two classes" are the Synagogue and the Church. A window in the east wall of the vestibule of the Chapter House at York contains late thirteenth-century painted glass showing Synagogue and Church,[20] which also find representation at Lincoln[21] and elsewhere. In Bodleian

Library MS. Auct. D. 3. 5 (fol. 1),[22] an illuminated initial typically depicts the Synagogue as a maiden blindfolded, holding a broken banner with her right hand, and dropping the tables of the law from the other hand. In the York glass, she has a crown which is falling, while the Church, above, is crowned and is holding a cross and a small model of a church.[23] The Church triumphs ultimately, just as ultimately the descendants of Abel will inherit bliss. Cain's kin, on the other hand, lack such hope and, failing to grasp the vision shared by those who are obedient and pious, can only despair.

It should be noted, of course, that the analogy of Cain and the Synagogue and of Abel and the Church may not be pressed too far in any discussion of the *Sacrificium Cayme et Abell*. This colorful imagery is not directly present in the York play, though its presence as background can hardly be denied. When the play takes up the biblical narrative, however, it focuses instead on pictorial details more closely related to the events being dramatized.[24] The tendency of biblical interpretation, especially under the influence of the friars, was now more toward literalism and away from the more intellectualized figural schema preferred by earlier exegetes.[25] Yet, from the standpoint of the entire cycle, the role of Cain and Abel remains immensely significant, for it confirms the pattern of the Fall which will resonate through the entire series of plays until finally the "two classes" of people will be separated on the Last Day of history. Cain in particular demonstrates how the negative aspects of the Fall attach themselves to men of the blind "nation" which devotes itself to self-interest and which hence is unable to recollect the bliss lost by the race when their parents ate of the forbidden fruit. In sharp contrast are those who, like Abel, devote themselves to obedience to a higher Good.[26]

Cain's refusal to sacrifice is thus crucial.[27] This act actually provides the first scene of the York play, though the Register breaks off at line 70, where two leaves are missing, before his refusal can culminate in his impious and hence unsatisfactory rendering of sheaves to his Creator. This scene is implied in the panel in the Great East Window of the Minster, which shows grain and sheep, the offerings tendered by Cain and Abel. More complete is the Cain and Abel story in the *Holkham Bible Picture Book,* which illustrates in graphic detail the rebellious Cain and obedient Abel. Here (fol. 5), as in the Towneley *Mactacio Abel,* the two sacrifices are shown: in contrast to the clean-burning sacrifice of Abel, Cain's offering smokes vilely and stinks "like the dwill in hell" (l. 283) — and the smoke mingles with the smoke of hell-mouth immediately below the altar.[28] Between the two brothers stands God, approving the one on his right and condemning the faulty sacrifice on his left. Thus too at the Last Day will the Judge give his approval to those arrayed on his right and his curses to those on his left.

The next miniature in the *Holkham Bible Picture Book* (fol. 5^V) illustrates the murder with the jawbone of an ass, as discussed above in Chapter I, and also Cain's reaction after the murder. At the bottom left of the illumination, Cain, with a sour and unrepentant look on his face, appears to be saying to the dead Abel, as in the Towneley play, "lig down ther and take thi rest; / Thus shall shrewes be chastysed best" (ll. 326–27). On the right he impudently looks up at God, who personally speaks to him as in the biblical account. Appropriately in the Towneley play his arrogant disdain alternates with fear. Like Adam immediately after the Fall, he expresses a desire to hide himself: "Into som hole fayn wold I crepe" (l. 337). God, however, very soon calls to the quaking Cain, whose saucy rebelliousness quickly returns. In the York play, God is replaced by an angel, whose role is parallel to the angel of the Expulsion, for he sends the sinner into the field to till the soil.

There is, however, a terribly important difference between Adam sent forth to labor in the soil in Play VI and Cain's treatment in the *Sacrificium Cayme et Abell.* The angel does not tell Cain that he will earn his bread with the sweat of his brow, but that his labor henceforth will be fruitless:

> Þou shall be curssed vppon þe grounde,
>   God has geffyn þe his malisonne;
> Yff þou wolde tyll þe erthe so rounde
>   No frute to þe þer shalle be fonne.
> (VII.106–10)

In the *Holkham Bible Picture Book* (fol. 6), as in the Towneley *Mactacio Abel,* Cain is actually seen plowing. The illumination pictures him with a medieval plow pulled by a team which includes an ass and two oxen — an impressive technological advance, certainly, over the spade which weary Adam typically uses to turn over ground. The plow appears to be traditionally linked to Cain, the tiller of the ground, and as a symbolic attribute it underlines the hopelessness of his occupation. Cain in the Chester plays laments that he will "never thryve" (II.702).

Cain thus is cursed to till the fruitless ground, which will not bring forth any produce as a result of his labor. What is presented here is a traditional picture of despair. Medieval theologians, following Augustine and Gregory, described despair in terms of sterility and lack of growth.[29] God's grace, made available through hope and faith, is like water necessary to make the soil fruitful, according to Gregory.[30] Cain has successfully severed himself from the sources of life. Until Lamech will end his life with a misdirected arrow — a scene commonly represented in the visual arts[31] but dramatized in the English cycles only in the N-town Plays where it forms an episode in the play of Noah (ll. 142–97) — Cain will suffer the pangs of those who are "dampned without grace" (*Chester* II.666). Early in the *Sacrificium Cayme et Abell*, Cain seems driven by anger — a sign of the irascible passions which, according to Aquinas, are associated with despair.[32]

At the end, Cain is overcome with fear, the emotion more typically identified with despair. Completely out of touch with any remembrance of bliss past, he moans that his "synne it passis al mercie" (VII.119). Like Judas later, he feels he has committed a sin so unforgivable that repentance is impossible. All he now can do is to live out his cursed life without any hope whatever.

III

At the opening of the *Building of Noah's Ark*, Deus comments that men have already become so wicked that "they make me to repente / My werke I wroght so wele and trewe" (VIII.17–18). These men also, like Cain, have inherited all the negative qualities inherent in the Fall, and, for their inability to live lives based on hope, God will work their destruction. The world will be made

"Al newe" through the Flood, which will "[de] stroye medilerthe" (VIII.25–28). God's instrument of renewal will be one single obedient man, Noah, who is addressed by the deity as "my seruand" — the terminology reminiscent of the precise service wrought by Abel, the exemplar of good stewardship.

God's speech to Noah also opens a series of panels on the Flood in painted glass at the Great Malvern Priory Church. God is seen at the upper left "out of white clouds and a glory of gold rays."[33] Below on the right, an aged Noah responds to the divine presence by kneeling and raising up his hands. The text below refers to the Vulgate (*Genesis* 6.13) and indicates that this is the moment when God appeared to Noah and spoke to him.[34] Noah's response underlines his faith and obedience, both of which sustain him steadfastly during the long period when he secretly is building the vessel of salvation. His only worries in the play concern his age ("I am full olde and oute of qwarte," VIII.50) and his lack of skill ("of shippe-craft can I right noght," VIII.67), but God helps him to overcome all obstacles. He gives the builder strength and specific advice as he works on the ark.

It is no accident that this play at York was given to the Shipwrights, who must have produced a pre-fabricated ark that could be assembled in minutes, though surely it must have taken longer than the time apparently allowed by one modern critic, who would have the entire play performed in nine minutes.[35] And perhaps this ship, once it had been assembled, may have been used as well for the following play of *Noah's Ark during the Flood*. In contrast to some symbolic arks in the visual arts,[36] the Shipwrights' vessel must have resembled an actual ship such as would normally sail out of the port of York by way of the Ouse River. As in a miniature in Bodleian MS. Barlow 53, dated 1420–30,[37] Noah, working alone, takes up his carpenter's tools and hews a board, whereupon he joins and sets the pieces together. He drives "nayles" and inserts "a revette," then takes his "rewe" (rule). The hull of the ark now appears already to be assembled. The result would appear to be a substantial vessel at least able to hold eight actors, though it surely was less elaborate than the ark utilized in the Plough Day pageant at Hull.[38]

Completion of the ark in the York Shipwrights' play apparently did not involve rigging, which prominently figures in the original glass in the panel representing the Flood in Thornton's Great East Window in York Minster. Similar attention to rigging had been present in the accounts relating to the Plough Ship at Hull.[39] However, once the hull of the ark is finished, Noah in the York play is merely commanded to set up "dyuerse stawllys and stagis" to accommodate the animals and birds he is to take aboard (VIII.124–31). These are obviously set up very quickly, and may be simply some rooms atop the hull as in a thirteenth-century illumination in Bodleian MS. Lat. th. b. 1.[40] Nothing so complex as the usual three-tiered ark (e.g., on a nave boss in Norwich Cathedral[41]) could be so rapidly assembled. Yet it is likely that this superstructure would involve *three* "stawllys" or compartments, since the ark was held to have a potent symbolic meaning as a representation of the Church—and in medieval number symbolism, the number for the Church is three. The Church is, of course, the institution that should provide the means of hope against the realities of individual death and the destruction by fire that eventually will overtake the world. Gregory the Great hence explained that the ark had three levels arranged in the shape of a pyramid, with reptiles and beasts below and birds and man above: thus is the ark like the Church, which contains a greater number of carnal men, along with a smaller number of spiritual men and with one man, Christ, who is without sin, at the highest level.[42] The arrangement suggested above for the York ark would thus provide a practical solution to the demand that the ark have a tripartite structure, since the reptiles, animals, and birds could easily be shifted to the two enclosures on each end, while the central area could be reserved for Noah and his family.

At the beginning of the play of *Noah's Ark during the Flood*, produced by the Fishers and Mariners, Noah's promise to fill "With beestys and fewlys my shippe" (VIII.149) must already be realized, for, unlike a panel in the Noah series in the painted glass at Great Malvern[43] and the Chester play of *The Deluge*, there appears to be at York no procession of animals and birds entering the ark.[44] After a long monologue in which Noah

laments the disaster coming to the world and recollects that it is
a disaster predicted by his father Lamech, his children arrive at
the ark and announce: "Fader we are all redy heere, / Youre biddyng baynly to fulfille" (IX.47–48).

At this point is inserted the lively episode of Noah's shrewish
wife, who refuses to do as she is bid — i.e., she will not obediently
follow orders from her lawful husband. This story has its source
in Eastern legend, and has been observed in English art as early
as the illustration in Caedmonian MS. Junius XI (p. 66), which
has been described by Sir Israel Gollancz as follows: "On the
right hand, one of the women, whom we may assume to be
Noah's wife, seems to be unwilling to mount the ladder, and is
expostulating with one of the three sons."[45] Similar reluctance
has been observed in painted glass at the Great Malvern Priory
Church,[46] and in *Queen Mary's Psalter* the episode appears
along with further remnants of the ancient tale, which posits the
devil's plan to use Noah's wife as an instrument whereby the
floating of the ark might be prevented.[47] In this manner she is
made to appear as a second Eve with all her negative qualities —
an interpretation of her character that would have seemed quite
logical to the medieval mind, which would have remembered
that Noah's wife, like Eve, is also a mother of the entire race.
The York play, however, has stripped away everything associated
with the legend except Uxor's recalcitrance and unwillingness to
enter the ark. (Instead of coming into the ark, she wants to go
"to towne," IX.81, and then she wishes to return home for her
goods and, later, for her "commodrys" and "cosynes," IX.143.)

As a person with no respect for God's will as revealed to her
husband Noah, Uxor is perhaps allegorically representative of
"the recalcitrant sinner . . . who refuses to repent and enter the
church" symbolized here by the ark.[48] Her blindness at first
toward the great spiritual and existential realities is as marked as
Cain's, but the difference is also underlined in the play: her mood
mends after she has entered the symbolic ark.[49] Between line 55,
when the son first announces himself to his mother as Noah's messenger, and lines 151–52, when she laments that her friends "Are
ouere flowen with floode," the drama presents a very lively and
much admired farce. It is farce characterized by all the precision of

detail that is associated with the meticulous artistry and attention to detail of the glass painter John Thornton.[50] But the farce
is calculated to set off the absurdity which marks the behavior
of those who, self-deceived, fail to understand the desperation
inherent in the fallen condition of man. Such wilful blindness
obviously needs to be taken in hand—i.e., the negative and self-
destructive side of the post-lapsarian personality requires coer-
cion when it interferes with the divine command. As a warning,
the farce takes on a more serious meaning too in the light of the
typological explanation of the Flood at the end of the play: the
world has been ravaged now by water and, in spite of God's promise through the image of the rainbow that it will not happen again,
this event looks forward to the time when "it sall ones be waste
with fyre, / And never worþe to worlde agayne" (IX.301-02).

The survival of Noah through obedience, faith, and hope
may be regarded as a remedy for despair. Even if in dramatic
production the specific allegory of the Ark = Church is lost, the
phenomenological lesson is clear: he who keeps the lines of
communication open with the deity and obeys the divine commands will be given hope of salvation on the Last Day when the
deluge shall be fire instead of water.

IV

In the Parchmentmakers' and Bookbinders' *Abraham and
Isaac*, the lesson of obedience is continued in a drama which is
more overtly based on typology than any of the other Old Testa-
ment plays in the York cycle. Figurally, Abraham represents the
Father willing to sacrifice his only Son, and Isaac is a type of
Christ.[51] Isaac, as a sermon in Mirk's widely-known *Festial* ex-
plains, "was fygur of Crystys passyon long or he wer borne. . . ."[52]
The liturgy of the Feast of Corpus Christi, through the sequence
Lauda Sion written by Thomas Aquinas, contains an explicit
reference to the sacrifice of Isaac as a figure foreshadowing Christ.
A similar reference is found in the Canon of the Mass, which com-
pares the ritual act to "the sacrifice of our forefather Abraham"[53]
The entire matter is described by the Chester Expositor:

> By Abraham I may understand
> the Father of heaven that cann fonde
> with his Sonnes blood to breake that bonde
> that the dyvell had brought us to.
> By Isaack understande I maye
> Jesus that was obedyent aye,
> his Fathers will to worke alwaye
> and death for to confounde. (*Chester* IV.468-75)

Hence in the York play the Father-Son relationship is arranged to stress parallels between the Old Testament event and the Passion and Crucifixion.

It is, of course, in the character of Isaac that the typology presented in the York play is concerned. Following Peter Comestor, Isaac is not the child normally expected, but is a man approximately as old as Christ at his Crucifixion.[54] His father notes that his son "is of eelde to reken right / Thyrty ʒere and more sumdele" (X.81-82). An Isaac of similar age appears on a misericord at Worcester Cathedral[55] and formerly in the wall paintings, now lost, in the choir at Peterborough[56] — in both instances carrying the faggots of wood for the sacrifice in two bundles shaped like the cross over his shoulders. In other representations of Isaac in the visual arts which show him younger than in the York play, he nevertheless carries the wood for his sacrifice.[57] The York version of the story sees the journey which will lead to the sacrifice on the mount start, as required by the biblical account, with an ass led by servants and carrying the wood (X.109-10). When they approach the mount, Abraham and his son leave the ass and servants in order to go up together. The father now orders Isaac to carry the wood: "þis wode behoues þe bere / Till þou come high vppon yone hill" (X.151-52).

When Isaac in the York play is told that he will be the sacrifice, he accepts his role at once since it is God's will. On one level, however, he cannot restrain his dread: his natural fear and anxiety threaten to overcome him. At one point he expresses his fear, as Rosemary Woolf has noted, in terms of a paraphrase of the Office for the Dead: "dere fadir, lyff is full swete, / The drede of dede dose all my dere" (X.279-80).[58] Such a reaction, however, does not disqualify him as a type of Christ. Indeed, the

Franciscan *Meditations on the Life of Christ*, which so deeply influence the plays on New Testament topics, strongly stress Christ's
fear and apprehension when looking forward to the anguish
which he should suffer. This fear is especially important, for it
underlines the point so significant for the *Meditations* (and for
the York plays): Jesus must die as a human being, and his perfect humanity must atone for the imperfect humanity shared by
all other men since Adam's disobedience in the Garden.[59] Isaac's
fear, like Christ's, is not a sign of sin.

As everyone knows, Isaac will not in fact be sacrificed: the deity
will send an angel to stay the hand of execution and will provide a
sheep for the offering. The sheep is also, of course, a type of the
Lamb of God who will actually be slain for men's sin.[60] It rein-
forces the appropriateness of Abel's offering and looks forward to
the Lamb which is a standard attribute in the visual arts of John
the Baptist,[61] whose role is to announce: "Behold the Lamb of
God, which taketh away the sin of the world" (*John* 1.22, *AV*).

But all of the typology evident in the York *Abraham and Isaac*
only enriches and gives additional meaning to the basic pattern established by the Fall: through obedience and a will attuned to the
divine commands, an individual may banish despair. Abraham's
obedience hence is at the center of the York play as it is also the
central lesson of the biblical story. In the visual arts, Abraham,
pictured alone, was early associated with obedience, as in the
Bamberg Apocalypse (c. 1000).[62] This interpretation is especially
made clear in the twelfth-century *York Psalter*, in which in
separate illuminations the sword held by the angel of the Expulsion and the sword raised by Abraham (plates 3–4) are not only
identical in appearance but are held at the same angle in approximately the same space within the outline of the miniature. In
the Expulsion, the sword threatens Adam and Eve for their disobedience; in the sacrifice of Isaac, an angel stays the sword
with his hand as a response to Abraham's obedience.[63] The York
play opens with a monologue in which Abraham proclaims that
the lines of communication between himself and his Maker (who
"alle þis world has wrought," X.1) are open. Because he has been
able to establish "frenshippe" with God (X.12), Abraham, an
old man, "þus fro barenhede has [been] broghte" (X.5). His son

Isaac is a reward for obedience and is a sign of divine favor and hope. As despair is traditionally associated with sterility, so Abraham is given a hope which historically will be expressed through his fertile progeny. God has told him that his "seede shulde be multyplyed / Lyke to þe gravell of þe see, / And als þe sternes wer strewed wyde" (X.15–17).

The divine testing which Abraham endures when the angel commands the sacrifice of Isaac hence demonstrates that the patriarch does not merely do lip service to a loving God because he has been well treated. Abraham will not allow communication with the deity to break down, but will remain perfectly obedient in his heart in spite of the horrible task that is laid upon him. But unlike God the Father, he will not actually need to surrender his only son in sacrifice, and God will see that Abraham is rewarded for his steadfastness, which is precisely opposed to the attitude expressed by Cain in the *Sacrificium Cayme et Abell*. Because he puts his possessions and himself above things of higher value, Cain is led toward the quintessence of despair. On the other hand, because Abraham puts obedience and trust in God above everything else, he is given his son a second time when he is told to substitute the lamb as an offering. The typology contained in the plays looks forward to a more permanent solution to the problem presented by the fallen condition of man, while the presentation of Abraham as an exemplar of obedience points toward the immediate cementing of divine-human relations in a manner that delineates the structure of hope.

Abraham and Isaac are founders of a chosen people, just as at a later time Christ will establish a new people whose lives are characterized by hope. These people of hope are precisely set off against the people of despair (Cain, Pharaoh, Herod, Judas, the Jews unchanged by the message of Jesus) and against those whose blindness, permanent or temporary, prevents them from seeing the absurdity of their acts.

V

The final play, *Pharaoh with Moses*, of the Old Testament series in the York cycle tells the Exodus story (Miss Smith's title is *The departure of the Israelites from Egypt, the ten plagues, and the passage of the Red Sea*), for which the Hosiers were responsible. Here we see Cain's kin set in opposition to the chosen people, the descendants of Abraham who are now the followers of Moses, an apostle of hope, in a unique drama which is poetically and theatrically superior. Pharaoh brags:

> All Egippe is myne awne
>   To lede aftir my lawe,
> I will my myght be knawen
>   And honnoured as it awe. (XI.9–12)

The tyrant's will is placed above respect for divine and human relationships that are essential in the post-lapsarian world. Like Cain, he stresses *possession* — in Pharaoh's case, not merely of some sheaves of grain but of an entire kingdom. Such selfish rule is fated to break down the fabric of the society and eventually to lead to a national and personal disaster for the sovereign. Paradoxically, the very "pees" (peace) that he proclaims at lines 13–14 becomes the occasion for dissension, because the condition upon which he insists is obedience that will dissolve the Jews' ties to their Creator. Since they will not sever their ties with God voluntarily, Pharaoh brags that he will thrust them down into bondage.

The author of this play deliberately provided a sharp contrast between the bragging, abusive Pharaoh and Moses, who is introduced alone at line 85. Moses (who surely was presented as the horned man of tradition, as in the figure sculpture from St. Mary's Abbey, York, now in the Yorkshire Museum)[64] immediately speaks of the "Grete God" whose power is passing all creatures and who "governes euere in gud degree" (XI.85–86). Here is a man who, as leader of the chosen people, does not share any blind illusion about human power arising within any individual human being. Hence as God's instrument he will oppose Pharaoh. This is the man to whom God himself will appear in the burning bush near Mount "Synay" (XI.92ff). It is a scene originally represented in the glass at Great Malvern where apparently, as in the *Biblia Pauperum*, Moses was seated and taking off his boots in the presence of God.[65]

Deus, directly communicating with Moses through speech, reminds him of his previous special relationship with Abraham, Isaac, and Jacob (whose story is missing from the cycle but who is a popular figure in the visual arts); these men had been promised that they should be blessed with a great progeny—a fact that has already been commented upon by Pharaoh, who has marvelled that the Jewish population in Egypt has increased from only 70 to 300,000 "Withowten wiffe and childe,/And herdes" in only four hundred years (XI.51-58). God will send the obedient and trusting Moses to Pharaoh, representative of "folke of wykkyd will" (XI.142). The Egyptian leader will be warned that he must let the Israelites go—even though in his malice he wishes to see them stay in his country in slavery.

Rosemary Woolf has pointed out that the confrontation between Moses and Pharaoh contains foreshadowing of the Harrowing of Hell, when Satan, using even a similar vocabulary and the same "jeering tone," refuses at first to believe the claims of Christ, who has at last come to rescue his people and to give them salvation.[66] The York author would appear to be building on the typology set forth in the *Speculum Humanae Salvationis*, which insists upon the escape from Egypt by the Israelites as a figural foreshadowing of the release of the Patriarchs from hell at the Harrowing.[67] But what the York *Pharaoh with Moses* really presents is a dramatic version of a confrontation between the forces of evil, of selfishness and the power of the creative principle which controls the cosmos. Hence Pharaoh's exercise of false sovereignty and wilful disobedience provokes the expected response. After Moses lifts up his miraculous rod or "wande"[68] without changing Pharaoh's attitude toward the Israelites, he prays that "God sende sum vengeaunce sone" (XI.251). God does precisely this: messengers come in quickly to report the well-known plagues of Egypt, which are presented in a rather lively telescoped fashion.

Pharaoh, like Cain, has acted out of envy as well as pride against one who represents a standard of obedience that allows him to have a religious and spiritual hope. In particular, Pharaoh is angered when he hears that the Israelites have left and are commencing their wandering in the wilderness—a wandering

58 CREATION TO DOOM

that, like the journey undertaken by the individual Christian, will terminate in the promised land. He wrathfully announces that he will follow them:

> Horse harneys tyte, þat þei be tane,
> Þis ryott radly sall þam rewe.
> We sall not sese or they be slone,
> For to þe se we sall þam sew.
> Do charge oure charyottis swithe
> And frekly folowes me. (XI.389–94)

Like the infidel that he is, Pharaoh impiously advises the Egyptians to "Hefe vppe youre hartis ay to Mahownde," who, he believes, "will be nere vs in oure nede" (XI.401–02). (In spite of the anachronism, Mahound or Mohammed is the appropriate god for him to call upon, since from the time of the crusades the prophet of Islam had appeared universally as a symbol of infidelity.) How the pursuit is effected and how the Red Sea is represented are unclear: not enough is known to reconstruct the staging with absolute certainty. Moses and the other Israelites, who by now have already crossed the sea, have had the advantage of the sea, controlled by Moses' "wande," standing "On aythir syde . . . / Tille [they] be wente, right as a wall" (XI.377–80). Lacking the realism which would be afforded by a ditch such as may have been used in stationary production,[69] the Hosiers probably merely arranged for some red cloth — a stage property which the guild itself ought to have been qualified to produce — which could be held up to illustrate the sea wall and then dropped upon the Egyptian army to simulate drowning. It seems highly unlikely that anything other than pursuing foot soldiers would have been represented, in spite of Pharaoh's call for a horse and chariot. Yet the visual arts provide some spectacular illustrations of the drowning in which a cart in the midst of the sea is a central detail, as on a striking boss in the nave of Norwich Cathedral.[70]

At the conclusion of the play, the wicked Pharaoh and his followers have died for their deeds — i.e., they have received the death promised as a reward for disobedience in the Fullers' play (IV.66–69). The negative aspects of post-lapsarian nature are swallowed up in the waters of the Red Sea. Not surprisingly, this event was also regarded as typologically foreshadowing the baptism of Christ and hence the sacrament of baptism generally.[71] Salvation from despair and danger is thus celebrated by the Israelite boy who cries out at the end of the York Play:

> Nowe ar we wonne fra waa
>   And saued oute of þe see,
> *Cantemus domino*,
>   To God a sange synge wee. (XI.405–08)

Singing here, like the singing of Noah's family in the ark upon the receding of the Flood (IX.260 and late marginal note at 266: "*Tunc cantent Noe et filii sui, etc.*"), affirms the kinship of obedient human beings with their Creator, who has rescued them from deluge and death. Through their song, they are able to attune themselves to the heavenly harmony or standard of angelic singing which has been observed in the *Creation of Heaven and Earth* and which again will be displayed in the *Offering of the Shepherds* at the time of the Nativity.

The Israelites who have been rescued from the sea have no reason to hide from the wrath of an angry God since they are among the people who in St. Ambrose's classification are associated with salvation through their obedience and their determination to act upon the commands of God. For them the lines of communication are kept open, and the deity protects them from an act of destruction that looks forward to the great catastrophe at the end of time. But even that catastrophe, frightening though it may seem to all who have tender consciences, will not finally affect the blessed, who will then be invited to enter the gates of bliss. For them, on the Last Day the negative aspects of the postlapsarian condition will be forever cancelled. However, for the second class of people, including Pharaoh and all other wilful or blind followers of Cain, the Last Day will bring the ultimate vengeance upon those who have been responsible for breaking the ties of kinship which ought to link them in hope to their Maker.

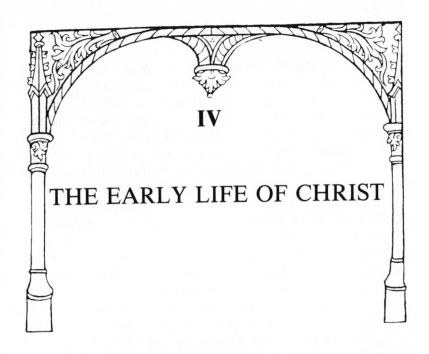

IV

THE EARLY LIFE OF CHRIST

I

The hope of the human race springs from the new beginning that is established through the coming into time of Christ as at once human and divine. Hence the plays which dramatize the Old Testament stories are only prelude to the crucial drama of the Incarnation and, later, the Passion and Crucifixion — the two themes most commonly illustrated in the visual arts of the late Middle Ages. It is, of course, in the Infancy series that the York cycle moves into the presentation of essential devotional tableaux, which are balanced against contrasting scenes such as the terrible *Slaughter of the Innocents*. Plays XII–XX, including the *Purification of the Virgin* which was misplaced in the Register, are indeed designed in the manner of devotional images in the visual arts, to which were added action and speaking parts. Hence each play is tightly controlled by the image at its center — a visual image which is attached to traditional dialogue taken from such sources as the liturgy, sermons, the *Meditations on the Life of Christ*, the *Golden Legend* of Jacobus de Voragine, the *Revelations* of St. Bridget of Sweden, and other writings.

The presentation of the critical events of the Christian story on pageant stages at York along a specified route[1] was carefully

controlled by the city Corporation, which was anxious to see
that the plays should be of high quality and a positive reflection
on the honor of the civic establishment. In 1476, the Council
gave authority for four of "þe most Connyng discrete and able
playeres within þis Citie" to be called before the mayor and
given authority to examine "al þe plaiers and plaies," with the
intent to exclude from playing of "insufficiant personnes either
in Connyng voice or personne."[2] Quality control was also en-
forced through having the city clerk present with the Register at
the first station, at the gates of Holy Trinity Priory.[3] Great care
was also taken to see that the city was ready for this festival, its
procession, and its plays at Corpus Christi time. In 1544, it was
decreed that "every howseholdr that dwellith in the hye way ther
as the sayd procession procedith, shall hang before ther doores
and forefrontes beddes and Coverynges of beddes of the best
that thay can gytt and Strewe before ther doores resshes and
other suche fflowers and Strewing as they thynke honeste and
clenly for the honour of God and worship of this Citie. . . ."[4]

The images at the core of each play in the Register are more
often than not closely connected with the details noted in the
Ordo entered in the *York Memorandum Book* in 1415.[5] Recent
study of this document, as well as a second list also entered by
Burton, has given attention to erasures and later changes or
those written in a different hand,[6] and we now can trace somewhat more confidently the history of some of the individual
plays in spite of broad areas where we can surely never expect all
the information we would like to have. In some cases, we are
now allowed some calculated guesses, as in the case of the
Founders' pageant for which the description has been altered in
the 1415 *Ordo*. Did changes in the *Ordo* correspond with changes
in the play itself? The second list explains this play's subject
matter as follows: "Ioseph volens dimittere eam occulte."[7] Surely
we have something here which suggests a stable central image
like the scene as depicted in the visual arts. Nevertheless, in the
dramatic working out of the play, its form in the Register actually presents a series of tableaux linked together — a series which
would seem to be indicative of some possible internal expansion

during the fifteenth and sixteenth centuries.

In *Joseph's Troubles about Mary* as it appears in the Register, Mary is on one side praying, while Joseph expresses his unhappiness about being "begiled" by a woman mysteriously pregnant (XIII.64). His doubts, of course, will not be set to rest until, as Mary had promised, God sends him a sign. The angel comes to him just as it had in a sixth-century ivory relief now in the Museo Arcivescoville, Ravenna,[8] where likewise the message of the angel is clearly that Mary's son is truly sent from heaven and that he should take his wife to "Bedlem" where "sall a childe borne be" (XIII.280–81). The bottom portion of the sixth-century ivory shows Joseph lovingly assisting Mary, who is very pregnant and riding on an ass, while the angel is helping to lead the animal. At the end of the York play, however, Joseph and Mary merely set out for Bethlehem, thus eliminating the need for a beast of burden in a play that would have been more conveniently played without such a creature.

While it would be dangerous to assert that the direction of revision in any play in the York cycle must inevitably be from simple to complex, that is indeed the direction that is suggested by the comparison of the play with the *Ordo* of 1415 and with Burton's later list. As in the case of the visual arts and of architecture during the fifteenth century, elaboration was commonly part of the plan to increase the effectiveness of a work. In the instance of *Joseph's Troubles about Mary*, we may guess that additional weight might have been given to Joseph's monologue—a speech that clearly gives us the impression of insight into a character at once basically fair-minded but nevertheless somewhat irascible. His mood is immediately contrasted with Mary's, and hence provides a kind of background against which her perfection might be displayed. But we are on more solid ground when we base a theory of elaboration in this play on the addition in the Register of two characters not mentioned in Burton's lists: two girls who mediate between Joseph and Mary. They are Mary's companions and serve to speak up more bluntly in her favor than would be permitted in the Virgin's own speeches. When one of them insists that Mary has seen "no man" except "an aungell" who feeds her once each day (XIII.123–29), Joseph explodes with the ironic accusation that the "aungell has made hir with childe" (XIII.135). If this is an addition, it makes good dramatic sense, and also suffices to underline in an important way the ultimate absurdity of unbelief in the face of the divine realities represented by the Incarnation. Richness of detail, as in York art of the fifteenth century, is not without its purpose as an aid to producing a devotional setting.

In the plays as in the visual arts, therefore, rewriting and elaboration may have been in part a response to new styles and new fashions in both design and iconography. Thus, as we have seen in Chapter I, a new way of visualizing the Nativity could attain wide popularity after about 1420 and hence could be a dominant influence in the visualizing of scenes in painted glass, alabasters, etc. The new iconographic pattern is the one established by the popular *Revelations* of St. Bridget of Sweden, and it is used in the York *Nativity* (Play XIV) as well as in illustrations in the visual arts, including woodcuts in early service books produced on the continent for use in York and the surrounding region.[9] In 1415 Burton had listed "obstetrix" in addition to Joseph, Mary, the new-born Child in the manger between the ox and the ass, and the angels who will announce the birth of the infant to the shepherds in the following pageant.[10] Midwives made their appearance in the older form of the Nativity play, as in the liturgical *Officium Pastorum*[11] and in the Chester cycle where they certify Mary's virginity and attest to Jesus' divinity (*Chester* VI.525–63). In the new form of the Nativity, however, the midwives are actually unnecessary, though it might not be obligatory to exclude them since the N-town cycle still includes them. We are reminded that iconography was not static but constantly developing and changing, though as we have seen older forms did not necessarily die out when newer iconography was adopted.

II

The Infancy series in the York cycle actually begins with the Spicers' *Annunciation to Mary* (Play XII), which is introduced by a prologue spoken by a "Doctour" that indeed would have provided quite an adequate introduction to a production of the plays stripped of its Old Testament material, for it presents a recapitulation of the entire background for the events hereafter dramatized. Finally, at the end of his speech, the "Doctour" tells of action that must be pantomimed on stage: God commissions Gabriel to go to the Virgin Mary at Nazareth. These events, as M. D. Anderson has noted, are represented in the fifteenth-century transept bosses of Norwich Cathedral, where (1) God summons Gabriel, who holds "a curiously shaped staff"; (2) Gabriel walks out through the gate of heaven and (3) arrives at the door of Mary's house; and (4) the angel enters the house in order to (5) deliver the message of the Annunciation.[12] In the York play, the visual images dissolve into drama enlivened by speech when Gabriel begins *singing* ("*Tunc cantat angelus*") and delivering his well-known message to Mary:

> Hayle Marie, full of grace and blysse,
>   Oure lord God is with þe
> And has chosen þe for his,
>   Of all women blist mot þou be. (XII.145-48)

These are the words which often appear in abbreviated form on a scroll in the visual arts, as in the full page illumination in the *Bolton Hours* (fol. 35ᵛ) and also in some examples of painted glass at York.[13] The angelic song shortly continues, then Gabriel brings the divine "bodword" or message to the Virgin, who will chastely bring forth a Son who "sall be God and called God sonne" (XII.153-62).

Presumably, while Gabriel is intoning or saying these words, he kneels before the Virgin — a posture that establishes the central image within this play and communicates its attitude of devotion to the audience. This is the posture that the angel assumes in the *Bolton Hours*, in several important representations of the Annunciation in York Minster,[14] and in the *Biblia Pauperum*.[15] It is, however, with less certainty that we approach the position of Mary at the opening of this play. While in the visual arts associated with York Mary is often standing (at the right) before the angel (who is on the left), the play might well have presented her at first in prayer. Painted glass in St. Olave's

Church in York has been described as follows: "[She] is rising from a chair with her l[eft] hand still holding the page in the book from which she was reading before the coming [of] St. Gabriel. The book rests on a richly covered lectern which at first sight looks like a part of her dress."[16] Mary at prayer is widely illustrated, as in the manuscript illumination, which has a slight connection with York, removed from the Rennes Psalter and now in the *Beaufort Hours*.[17] In *Joseph's Troubles about Mary*, she is described as sitting "at hir boke faste prayand" (XIII.81), a posture that would have been regarded as traditional. When she is shown with her book in late medieval art, it is sometimes open at *Isaiah* 7.14,[18] a passage that has been quoted by the "Doctour" who speaks the prologue to play XII at line 61: "*Ecce uirgo concipiett, et pariet filium, etc.*" At Great Malvern, the open book appears on a prayer desk before which Mary kneels with raised hands.[19] She similarly kneeled on the tomb of Thomas Dalby (d.1525) in the choir of York Minster.[20] Whether standing, sitting, or kneeling, however, at least one of her hands normally is raised in surprise and expectation, or her hands are placed across her breast.

In the visual arts, Mary's response to the angel's words was sometimes represented, as in the glass at Great Malvern and in the *Biblia Pauperum*, through her words "Ecce ancilla domini fiat michi secundum verbum tuum" on a scroll. The words are translated in the York play as follows:

> Goddis handmayden, lo me here
>   To his wille all redy grayd;
> Be done to me of all manere
>   Thurgh thy word als þou hast saide. (XII.189–92)

This is her acceptance of her mission. As the fifteenth-century Middle English lyric "I Syng of a myden" has said it, Mary *chose* to be God's mother: "kyng of alle kynges to here sone che ches."[21] It is therefore during or immediately following this speech that the miraculous conception takes place. The angel has already promised that the "haly gast in þe sall lighte" (XII.177), and now, apparently kneeling as in the *Meditations on the Life of Christ*,[22] she comments on her love for God, speaks the words quoted above, and is impregnated by the Holy Spirit. "Þus," says John Mirk in a sermon in his influential *Festial*, "scho conceyued our Lord Ihesu Crist in euerlastyng joy to all þe world."[23]

There are no stage directions in the York play to indicate what visual effects are involved. Most likely a dove representing the Holy Spirit descends to her ear or breast, as in various examples of York art and also most late medieval Annunciations.[24] We have evidence also that the dove was in fact utilized in drama on the continent during the fourteenth and fifteenth centuries.[25] The technology for the descent of the dove would be similar to that utilized for the birds sent out from the ark in Play IX, where carved or ceramic birds are apparently made to move along a string between one location and another. In the *Annunciation*, the string or strings would be gilded to represent light. One alternative (or addition) to the dove might be a miniature doll, representing the soul of Christ, descending in a like manner from heaven, as in certain works of art influenced by Franciscan theology.[26] Thus in glass in St. Peter Mancroft, Norwich, and in the Mérode Altarpiece by the Master of Flémalle, a tiny figure representing Christ's soul carries a miniature cross (to show the connection between the Incarnation and the Crucifixion, also illustrated, as in plate 5, in the Crucifix on the lily of the Annunciation, and descends toward the Virgin.[27] Evidence for the influence of this iconography may be claimed in York art. In the illustration in the *Bolton Hours* from York (c.1420), the soul of Christ is shown along with the dove — a not untypical arrangement — and in the Gdansk Joys of the Virgin triptych, formerly believed to have been carved at York, the Child in his descent from the mouth of the Father holds a cross over his shoulder.[28] Finally, it may also even be possible that all of the above suggestions were set aside at York, with the descent of the Holy Spirit merely represented by beams of light, which could have been shown rather spectacularly by burning tow. One thing, however, is certain: some kind of visual effect is definitely needed to preserve the integrity of the image which is at the heart of this scene in the York play.

In medieval thought, the conception of Christ is the most important moment within history, for it is the moment when the Incarnation takes place. Medieval audiences would have expected this supreme devotional image not to be excluded from the play. Representation of it in drama must have been a solemn reminder to pious Christians at York that their Savior became man as an expression of divine love. Indeed, it is hard to see how less pious spectators could fail to be impressed by this sight. Certainly in the visual arts the Annunciation received the greatest attention from artists. Margaret Rickert describes the beauty of the example from an illuminated book presumably associated with York:

> The colours in this miniature are so unbelievably lovely that no description, much less a reproduction, can give any idea of their quality. Typical are the deep ultramarine of the Virgin's cloak contrasting with the softest salmon pink of the angel's mantle and also those of the donors. The background is pale red with a pattern in gold and tiny touches of red and blue to give it life. God and some angels (in the upper left corner) are ultramarine (to balance the Virgin's blue) and the ceiling is vermillion, contrasting with the green of the canopy and the cloth covering the *prie-dieu* and the book. The inscriptions and all the decorative ornament are in gold except the lettering on the book and scroll, which is black.[29]

Immediately after the Annunciation, Play XII in the York cycle shifts to another scene which is again ordered around a precisely defined devotional image. The topic is the Visitation, in which Mary goes to her cousin Elizabeth. This is normally the scene which follows the Annunciation in the visual arts. In an early fourteenth-century painting by Pacino di Bonaguida, both episodes are illustrated within a circle painted on a Tree of Life: the Annunciation is on the left, with the Child and the rays of light breaking the circle, and the Visitation is on the right.[30] The latter event was particularly emphasized by the Franciscans, among whom it came to be celebrated on a feast day which in 1389 entered the calendar of the whole church.[31] But the scene had long been popular in art, and had appeared in England as early as the seventh century when it was carved on Ruthwell cross.[32] In York art which is extant, no example of this scene remains from later than the thirteenth century.[33] The image as presented in the York play is designed to elicit devotion to the Virgin, who appears here as the Mother of God. Tender emotion is joined with gesture — a touching of hands or an embrace — and a ritual act of blessing in which Elizabeth speaks the famous words "Blissed be þou anely / Of all women in feere, / And the frute of thy body / Be blissid ferre and nere" (XII.205–08). At the end of the play, a sixteenth-century stage direction indicates that the *Magnificat* be sung ("*Tunc cantat*"), presumably in Latin and by Mary.

III

Music also provides a very natural addition to visually perceived devotional image in the presentation of the play of the Chandlers' *Offering of the Shepherds*. The angels have been made ready for their song during the previous play, according to Burton's 1415 list. The song is not recorded in the Register, but its text is clearly the standard biblical item. The words of announcement to the shepherds are actually sung by a single angel, who perhaps even comes down to the three shepherds and stands before them as in a panel of late thirteenth-century painted glass in the Northeast window of the Chapter House at York. But the shepherds too are musicians, and attempt not only to imitate the angelic song at lines 63–64 but also to "make myrthe and melody" as they seek the Child with "sange" (XV.84–85). In the earlier *Shrewsbury Fragments* upon which the York play appears to be based, the third shepherd comments: "For solace schal we syng / To seke oure Saueour."[34] In iconographic tradition, the shepherds to whom the announcement is made had been musicians as early as the sixth century.[35] They play bagpipes in the *Holkham Bible Picture Book*, fol. 13, and in an embroidered fourteenth-century band in the Victoria and Albert Museum.[36] The same instrument is held by one of the shepherds in *Queen Mary's Psalter*.[37] The glass of the Great Malvern Priory Church shows an angel, who appears above, while below are shepherds, one of whom holds a pipe.[38] In the Coventry *Pageant of the Shearmen and Taylors* (309-11), the first shepherd makes a gift of his pipe to the Christ Child:

> I haue nothyng to present with thi chylde
> But my pype; hold, hold, take yt in thy hond;
> Where-in moche pleysure that I haue fond.[39]

The first shepherd in the York play also must be an instrumentalist for he too offers to give the Child his "horne" (XV.77)—a promise that he does not carry out, for his gift will be a brooch with "a belle of tynne" (XV.103).

In the York play, a star has apparently appeared in the sky (XV.15), where it will remain until the Magi also have found their way to the Child. In the Coventry *Pageant of the Shearmen and Taylors* (l. 588), a child appeared in the star. The *Shrewsbury Fragments* speak of "ȝone brightnes" which "wil vs bring/Vnto þat blisful boure" (A.29-30). The star, according to the *Golden Legend*, was extremely bright and "was not fixed in the firmament, but hung in the air near the earth."[40] It is, of course, by following the star that the shepherds find their way to the Nativity scene where they will adore the Infant. As separate scene, the *Adoration of the Shepherds* is fairly late in medieval art. Nevertheless, the only major examples at York are thirteenth-century—a panel of painted glass in the Chapter House and a miniature in a York Psalter (British Library MS. Add. 54,179, fol. 92ᵛ)—though there is a fine woodcut in the printed York *Hours*[41] and also a Flemish woodcarving now at the Bar Convent.[42] This scene received impetus from the Franciscan emphasis on poverty and the friars' observation that Christ's birth was first announced to the poor.[43] While the shepherds' gifts of a bob of cherries, a bird, and a ball in the Towneley *Secunda Pastorum* specifically reflect Christ's Passion, Resurrection, and ultimate sovereignty,[44] the gifts in the York *Offering of the Shepherds* seem only to underline the humility of the participants in the scene of adoration. As in the *Shrewsbury Fragments* (A.43), the third shepherd in the York play gives a horn spoon (XV.124), while the second gives "Two cobill notis vppon a bande" (XV.112), and, as noted above, the first gives a brooch (XV.103). The audience at this point is encouraged to *imagine* that it is present at the events being depicted.

After the shepherds depart "mak[ing] mirthe as we gange" (XV.131), the story of Christ's birth and attendant events continue rapidly through the following pageants, which likewise follow the established pattern of organization about central images which are shared with the visual arts. There is, to be sure, some confusion in the Register about the texts of the Masons' (later, Minstrels') Herod and Goldsmiths' Magi scenes, which are printed together as Play XVI by their most recent editor. But the scenes which are set forth are nevertheless again structured about elements familiar to art historians. Herod as tyrant, who at the opening of the Mason's scene makes false claims to sovereignty, here enters the cycle as the dangerous antagonist of the Child. The king is the irascible man whose anger is expressed vividly in the well known roof bosses in Norwich Cathedral.[45] His unreasonable expectations underline the false grandeur of his court, enriched in the play by the presence of musicians, we can be sure, after the Minstrels took over participation in the *Herod Questioning the Three Kings* scene in 1561. First Herod appears in his court, perhaps wearing a dark mask[46] and through his appearance belying his claim to beauty when he brags about his freshness and fairness "of face" (XVI.17). The soldiers, setting the tone for the Slaughter of the Innocents which is the logical outcome of the tyrant's malice, insist that they will "with countenance full cruel" put down any rebellious subjects (XVI.43). Then the three kings appear at court in a scene illustrated in a panel of painted glass in the Northeast window of the Chapter House at York and in a miniature in *Queen Mary's Psalter*.[47] The latter representation is particularly interesting because it shows Herod's crown slightly askew on his head. It is also possible that Herod may have been given a demon crown in this play, as in the previously noted fifteenth-century glass (unfortunately restored incorrectly as Solomon) in St. Michael, Spurriergate, York[48] (plate 7).

In the Goldsmiths' scene, the meeting of the three kings, who are independently travelling to Jerusalem, is represented. All of them are following the star, of course. Unlike the meeting of the three Magi in the *Très-Riches Heures* of the Duke of Berry, the kings in the York play are not on horseback (Magi journeying on foot are also present in the Chapter House glass[49]), and they do not have large retinues of followers. This scene is thus set off against the episode of the meeting of Herod and the three kings. The news they bring, as we might expect, causes Herod to explode with anger. "Nay," he insists, "I am kyng and non but I" (XVI.180). Play XVI in the text recently established by Richard Beadle then continues with the arrival of the three kings at Bethlehem, where they "seke a barne þat all shall bylde" (XVI.289). Here is one of the most famous of all the episodes from the Christian story as told in the visual arts, for the Magi will now kneel one at a time before the infant and present their gifts. This, along with the Annunciation and the Nativity, is one of the three subjects chosen from the life of Christ prior to his death for the roof bosses formerly in York Minster.[50] In the *Biblia Pauperum* and in the glass at Great Malvern, the eldest king, his crown placed on the ground beside him, is kneeling in adoration before the Mother and Child while the two others stand by awaiting their turn.[51] A similar but earlier example is contained in one of the lights of the East Window of the North Aisle in All Saints, North Street, York, where the kneeling king holds his crown as he presents the gift of a gold cup.[52] In contrast to the impious Herod, whose sovereignty seems to him to be deeply threatened by the news of the arrival of the Christ Child, the pagan kings (whose names, according to the *Golden Legend*, are Gaspar, Balthasar, and Melchior)[53] are not afraid to put aside the symbols of their sovereignty in the face of a greater power. Like the wise shepherds who in Play XV appear to know the significance of the Incarnation in advance (XV.1–32), the kings understand remarkably well the means of salvation which is being offered to mankind. The audience likewise through the devotional image is encouraged to understand the events in the same manner.

When the Magi have offered their gifts to the Child, they set forth again apparently on foot to return to the envious Herod, who, they have been deceived into thinking, will "come hymselffe and make offeryng/Vnto þis same" (XVI.363–64). However, at this point the third king, Balthasar, suggests that they "reste a thrawe" (XVII.366). This bit of unmotivated action is necessary to set the scene for the next devotional image to be presented: the angel coming to the sleeping kings to warn them that Herod "has malise ment" and that they should go home by "othir waies" to their countries (XVI.373–77). If representations such as the miniature in *Queen Mary's Psalter* are to be taken as a guide, the three kings, all wearing their crowns, would need to get side by side into a bed where once they are asleep, the angel would appear to them.[54]

Following the Adoration of the Magi is, according to Burton's lists,[55] the rather long (460 lines) play of the *Purification of the Virgin*, which was finally entered in the Register following an order in 1567 but not in its proper place.[56] Instead, the scribe placed it where there was space between the *Travellers to Emmaus* and *Doubting Thomas*. The action takes place forty days after Jesus's birth, when, according to "Moyses lawes," the mother must undergo the rites of Purification (XVII.191–95). So Mary and her husband are required to take up "ij dove-byrdes" and "a lambe" for their offering (XVII.237) and go to the Temple. The Christ Child himself is "the lame of God," they recall (XVII.263), and hence they are able to eliminate the need for the second and more expensive offering which they otherwise could not afford. Thus they will arrive at the Temple with only the two doves, which they carry in a "panyer" or basket (XVII.252), and their infant. When they have entered the Temple, they kneel and "offre . . . vp to God meekly/Our dewe offrand" (XVII.279–80). After the presbyter has prayed to God that their offering might be accepted, the prophetess Anna appears—and an angel tells Symeon to go forth to the Temple. When he arrives, he too praises the Virgin and her Son in a long speech which culminates in his famous "In peace lorde nowe leyf thy servand/For myne eys haith seyn that is ordand. . ." (XVII.415–16). The scene is designed to bring together all the elements normally present in representations in the visual arts, as an example from York Minster glass (c.1350) will show:[57] Mary is holding out the Child to Symeon, who stands behind the altar. Joseph stands behind the Virgin, as does another feminine figure, who holds a candle and, originally, also a basket with doves. An interesting window at Fairford—a window of later date—presents some similar features;

here Mary has a servant who with one hand holds a bird cage of wicket which contains two doves, while with the other hand she holds a candle.[58]

The iconography described above is not unique, but it has been described as characteristic of Northern art.[59] One of the women in a representation of the Purification in a window at Great Malvern also holds a candle, as does a figure which surely is Anna in the *Biblia Pauperum*.[60] Mary herself along with other feminine figures holds candles in an alabaster discussed by Dr. Hildburgh and in the illustration in the *Speculum Humanae Salvationis*.[61] The candles definitely appear in the Chester play in which Joseph speaks: "A signe I offer here alsoe/of virgine waxe, as other moo,/in tokeninge shee hase lived oo/in full devotion" (*Chester* XI.143–46). Presumably, candles would also be appropriate in the York play, for Symeon has spoken of God's "light" which has "shynyd this day" (XVII.421). Indeed, the Purification was specifically remembered in the York calendar on February 2,[62] the feast day popularly known as Candlemas. As Mirk notes, "holy chyrch maketh mynde þys day of candels offryng. ȝe seen, good men, þat hyt ys comyn vse to all crysten men forto come to þe chyrche þys day, and bere a candyll yn processyon, as þagh þay ȝedyn bodyly wyth oure lady to chyrch, and aftyr offyr wyth hyr yn worschip and high reuerens of hur."[63]

IV

Following the ceremonious occasion celebrated in the *Purification*, the York cycle turns in quick succession to two other scenes extremely well known through representations in the visual arts. The Marshals' *Flight into Egypt* (Play XVIII) and the Girdlers and Nailers' *Slaughter of the Innocents* (Play XIX) are again organized about specific devotional images normally shown in the visual arts. The *Flight into Egypt* hence opens with introductory matter which prepares the way for Joseph's dream[64] in which the angel Gabriel appears again to warn him of the danger:

> For Horowde þe kyng gars doo to dede
> All knave-childer in ilke a stede,
> Þat he may ta
> With ʒeris twa
> Þat are of olde. (XVIII.55-59)

And he advises:

> Tille he be dede, away
> In Egipte shall ʒe beelde. . . . (XVIII.60-61)

Thereafter, Joseph prepares Mary for the trip, which will shortly begin after a little domestic argument such as the Middle Ages loved to depict in drama, narrative, and the visual arts. The beginning of the journey may have differed from illustrations in painted glass and in other representations, since, in spite of the reference to riding at lines 205-06, it is not altogether certain that the usual ass was present in the acting area.

The *Slaughter of the Innocents* is one of liveliest and most moving plays in the entire cycle. While it does not perhaps achieve the consummate art of the earlier Fleury play on this subject, it nevertheless is extremely spectacular and moving in its own right. Herod here will open the pageant with a rambling and presumably comic speech in which he stresses again his sovereignty and his devotion to "Mahounde."[65] It soon is realized that he has been "noyed of newe" (XIX.41) ever since the three kings passed through on their way to see the Christ Child. The conditions are thus prepared for his explosion into anger when he hears that the kings have returned to their own countries without advising him with regard to the Child. His anger is indeed so extreme that he will calm down only when his counsellors advise killing *all* male children of Jesus' age in the area of Bethlehem.

The events which follow are clearly recorded in painted glass, manuscript illuminations, etc. The soldiers, who are dressed like contemporary knights, move quickly into the platea, where they proceed to kill young children. The children are normally nude as a symbol of their innocence, and some of them are accompanied by mothers who react understandably with anger and hysteria. As in so many representations of the event in the visual arts, the soldiers' actions are set off against the king on one side where he is watching and taking a kind of angry and vicarious pleasure in what is going on. In some examples such as a panel in the East Window of St. Peter Mancroft, Norwich, however, Herod from his throne actually participates in the butchery by brutally hacking an infant to pieces. At Fairford, he appears alone and is prominently stabbing a child. The excellent glass in a light in one of the windows in the South Choir Clerestory at York Minster (plate 6) shows the tyrant likewise encouraging the dreadful strokes of the soldiers. Here a soldier in plate armor holds up a sword with a tiny child impaled upon it, while a mother in grief leans over a richly decorated cradle—perhaps a cradle holding Herod's own son who, according to the *Golden Legend*, was killed along with the others.[66] More is made of the conflict between the mothers and the soldiers in the glass in St. Peter Mancroft, where at the top a woman is violently attempting to restrain a soldier who has impaled her infant on his sword. The woman is reminiscent of the mothers in the York play who will die if necessary to save their dear sons (XIX.199–201, 204–06). In the play, the hapless infants are surely represented by cloth dolls or dummies which are vigorously slashed by the mean-spirited soldiers.[67] When the atrocities are completed in the York play, the soldiers leave the platea and return to Herod, to whom they report their deeds. That he has in fact been looking on from his throne all through the massacre does not remove the need for the soldiers' report, which functions as a final speaking tableau that will show Herod's failure to be satisfied concerning Jesus' death. His failure to be satisfied will set off, of course, a final towering rage. He fears (correctly) that "þat boy be fledde," and insists that he will not be able to sleep till he is destroyed (XIX.270–73).

The series of devotional images which are at the core of the scenes telling the story of the early life of Christ terminates in the illustrations that accompany the episode of the twelve-year-old Christ among the learned men in the Temple. This episode is given dramatic representation in the York Spurriers and Lorimers' play of *Christ and the Doctors* (Play XX), which presents (1) the discovery by Mary and Joseph on the road from Jerusalem that the Son is missing, (2) Christ's participation in a disputation in the Temple, and (3) his recovery by his mother and Joseph. Of these, only the first is not found in the visual arts, though the second and third are normally brought together within a single illustration. Hence most common is the depiction of the moment when Mary and Joseph (now a very old man who often, as in *Queen Mary's Psalter*, uses a cane)[68] arrive on the scene. In the Magnificat Window at Great Malvern, the Child, who is sitting on a throne, is encircled by the doctors, who are dressed in academic garb, including gowns with hoods and black caps.[69] Similar academic garb is shown in the painted glass panel (c.1375) in the choir of York Minster.

Examination of the York play will show that the scholastic argumentation, which begins with the first Magister's *question*,[70] is not to be taken too seriously. It is the image which is at the core of the scene which is being presented here. In a sense, the audience is intended to receive something of the flavor of a medieval argument in a university without much of the substance. Before Christ has proven himself to be wise through any statements, the Child is invited to sit in a master's chair! (XX.95). The devotional image at the core of the play involves a Child who has not received education and yet who causes the most learned holders of masters' and doctors' degrees to respect him. Not surprisingly, Joseph the carpenter is very class-conscious as he sees the Child among the theologians in the Temple, while Mary totally fails to understand the argumentation. But their simple piety nevertheless makes them highly sympathetic, and at the end of the play the young lad must return with them to remain until his Ministry is to begin.

V

THE MINISTRY PLAYS

In contrast to the Infancy and Passion plays in the York cycle, the presentation of sacred scenes from the Ministry series may at first seem abbreviated and perhaps disappointing. In spite of apparently very great dramatic possibilities, the subjects dramatized are quite limited, giving attention only to the events of the Baptism, Temptation, Transfiguration, the woman taken in adultery, and the resurrection of Lazarus (Plays XXI–XXIV) prior to the culmination in the Entry into Jerusalem and the Last Supper (Plays XXV, XXVII). It should be recognized that this list of plays in the Register is not complete, however. For example, in the early fifteenth century there had been a dramatization of the Marriage at Cana by the Vintners,[1] whose play was never transcribed into the Register; as late as 1566, the omission of the transcript of this play is noted in the dramatic records of the city.[2]

The lack of interest in more fully dramatizing the scenes of the Ministry seems to have been shared by the other civic cycles in England, with a similar pattern to be noted in the Cornish *Passio Domini nostri Jhesu Christi*[3] and in the visual arts of the later Middle Ages. As Émile Mâle notes, "The miracles which fill so large a place in the art of the catacombs—the healing of the paralytic, of the woman with the issue of blood and the man

born blind, the raising of the widow's son and of the daughter
of the centurion, rarely or never appear in the thirteenth-century art."[4] This pattern holds also for the fourteenth and fifteenth centuries, as Mâle explains. The Ministry scenes that are
regularly displayed in art are only the Baptism, the Marriage at
Cana, the Temptation, and the Transfiguration, to which may be
added the scene of the raising of Lazarus.[5] These scenes are also
the ones that English art contemporary with the drama tended
to emphasize, though when measured against the large number
of extant or lost Infancy and Passion scenes the frequency of
occurrence of the Ministry scenes is not great. In York art, some
subjects appear but little or not at all.

Nevertheless, if the Ministry plays in the York cycle are understood as preparation for the Passion and as establishing the potential power over sin and death that will be available through the
divine-human hero who is Christ, their function in the full context
of the cycle drama play becomes recognized as very important indeed. It is not merely a matter of filling the gap between the Infancy
and Passion, but of *preparation*. Just as between the conclusion of
the Christmas season and the events remembered during Passion
week are the Epiphany season and Lent, so too the plays dramatized the revelation of Christ's nature to the world and the mood
of expectation that looked forward to the great matter of Holy
Week. The Ministry events begin, of course, with the baptism of
Christ by John the Baptist—precisely, according to tradition,
thirty years after the Magi adored the Child.[6] The Temptation,
however, is to be regarded as closely associated with Lent, the
season of fasting for the whole Church; indeed, the Gospel for the
first Sunday in Lent presents the story of this event in Christ's life.
Therefore as Lent is anticipatory of Holy Week and Easter, so in
the York cycle are the Ministry plays anticipatory of the plays
which will dramatize the suffering, death, and Resurrection.

I

Seen as preparation for the great Holy Week drama, therefore,
even the seemingly rather dull *Baptism of Christ* (Play XXI),

presented by the Barbers but superseded in the sixteenth century by a new and now lost play text, must have provided important devotional tableaux which would lay the ground for under-standing the soteriological work of overcoming the great dragon Satan and his cohorts. Though perhaps the extant text of this play does not generate much excitement from a purely aesthetic standpoint, it nevertheless evokes on the level of the imagination what would have been seen had the spectators been present cen-turies earlier at the baptism by John, whose act would seem to fix for the remainder of historical time the form of the Christian sacrament of baptism through which men achieve rebirth in order to make them eligible for entry into heavenly bliss. As Christ explains in the play, the historical event is to be regarded as mirroring forth a pattern for all to follow; indeed, he is the pattern to be followed without exception, and through his will the water of baptism contains the power of the Holy Spirit to cleanse men and women from the sin inherited from Adam and Eve (XXI.92–105). Yet we must not assume that the play is merely presenting doctrine here, for once again the principal purpose appears to be to set forth the scene in a joyful and de-votional way.

Symbolically, the *Baptism of Christ* foreshadows the victory over sin and death that will culminate in the Harrowing and Resurrection. Jesus explicitly states:

> The dragons poure ilk a dele
> Thurgh my baptyme distroyed haue I; (XXI.157–58)

and thus he reflects here the words of the psalmist that were regarded as prophetic: "Thou didst divide the sea by thy strength: thou brakest the heads of the dragons in the water" (*Ps.* 74.13, *AV*). In a sense, the later events of Christ's life were always present from the very beginning, from the time of his conception. Hence an Annunciation in York Minster glass (c.1420) presents the usual lily (*candidum lilium*) that is a con-stant iconographic feature and gives this feature an unusual twist, for upon the lily is a crucifix — a reminder also, perhaps, that the death on the cross occurred on the same day, March 25, as the Annunciation.[7] Thus the Baptism of Christ also links together the baptismal sign with the later signs of victory and triumph. For the congregation of the faithful, the result of the events to come in Christ's life will be health and life for those who are baptized and who trust in him. At the end of the scene in the York play, John the Baptist speaks both in play and in earnest when he asks the blessing of "þat barne þat Marie bare" upon the entire crowd of spectators (XXI.174–75).

An examination of York art will show that the role of John the Baptist in the institution of the sacrament of baptism was not regarded as unimportant. It will be seen that in addition to the scenes showing the historical event, even representations which simply show John as a standing figure are indeed symbolic reminders of his role with regard to baptism. In the late thirteenth-century glass in the Chapter House vestibule, he is displaying the Agnus Dei, toward which he is pointing. The meaning here is clear: as a prophet, John plays a crucial role in revealing the Lamb of God who has died for the sins of men to save them from death if they will submit to baptism and to catholic belief. There were several relics of John the Baptist in the Minster,[8] and one record of an image of him at the Altar of the Holy Trinity in the church of St. Michael, Spurriergate, is also particularly revealing. In 1458, John Dautre requested burial in front of this image because of the special veneration he had always felt for it.[9] We know that an alabaster image of the saint was given to anchoress Lady Alice Derby at St. Clement's Nunnery in 1474, while several extant scenes in art also show the martyrdom of this figure—an incident that was additionally reflected in the St. John's heads usually carved in alabaster for use in private meditation. Such, for example, was the "Sanct John Baptist heid of Amyas liyng in a platur of tree, gyltid and gratid w^t stonys" presented to St. Mary's Abbey by John Fell in 1506.[10]

In art, John the Baptist is usually easily recognized because he wears a coat of camel skin, very often with the head of the animal hanging down. In a panel in the East Window of Holy Trinity, Goodramgate, he wears a cloak over this rough garb, and he holds a book on which is the Agnus Dei with a pennant representing the Resurrection. This window was the gift of John Walker, rector of the parish, in 1470. It is significant that the donor himself, wearing a white surplice, appears in the glass, with special devotional intent directed at the Corpus Christi panel at the top of the central light. The Corpus Christi subject, which shows the wounded body of Christ along with the other persons of the Trinity, has been connected with the powerful Corpus Christi Guild, of which the donor was a member.[11] But John the Baptist must have been very important for him also, since the figure appears immediately to the left of the Corpus Christi panel. Presumably as one of Walker's patron saints, the Baptist provided a model for life; hence his image was surely indicative for the fifteenth-century clergyman of an opening into a life attuned to the divine realitites.

Examples of local art suggest not only rather precisely the appearance of the Baptist, but also the tableau at the center of the York *Baptism of Christ*. This is very fortunate, since no rubrics are included in the play at the actual point of the baptism. We have a description of what will happen when the angel foretells the event to John (XXI.65–71), but in the Register even this breaks off without completion. The scribe apparently has skipped over several lines without copying them—an oversight noted in a marginal note in the sixteenth-century hand of John Clerke but never corrected. From the angel's extant words we know that the heavens will open and the "holy gost schalle doune be sente," and that the voice of the Father will "Be herde full riʒt" (XXI.66–70). But the words to be spoken by the latter are not herein given, nor are they indicated in the text of the play below at the point where the baptism is performed. We would expect a speech by the Father here—a speech proclaiming, as in the N-town play, "This is my welbelovyd chyld . . ." (ll. 92ff). It is unlikely that abridgment of the text of the play at lines 71ff would have been deliberate, for the heavenly response to the baptism is not the voice of the Father but the celestial music we would expect to follow—two angels singing *Veni Creator spiritus*,[12] presumably while the dove of the Holy Spirit descends. In three important fourteenth-century panels of York glass, Christ is standing in the Jordan, represented by water which rises up as if in a mound over his legs, in the presence of John the Baptist and an angel. However, in none of the examples is God the Father present;

the emphasis is not on the opening of the doors of heaven to reveal the Father but upon the descent of the Spirit upon the figure being baptized, who also stands in the presence of a heavenly angel. The dove has been present in iconography since catacomb art and the Baptistry at Ravenna, while the earlier tendency had been for the indication of the presence of the Father by his extended hand from above in blessing. In the late Middle Ages, however, the hand was normally translated into the figure of the Father, as in a painted panel from Lüneburg (c.1410–20) where his hand holds a scroll with "Hic est filius meus dilectus in quo mihi complacui."[13]

In transforming the scene from the static tableau of the visual arts to the speaking tableau of the York play, the dramatist, the Barbers who were the sponsors of the play, and the actors could thus be content to present a simple pageant that, in spite of its spectacular descent of the dove (from an opening on an upper level of the pageant) and the music, really was not technically complex. If the finances of the Barbers were limited, however, they nevertheless were able to afford to hire two singing men to play the roles of angels. Quite possibly they would also have expended some ingenuity upon the water which was to cover Jesus at least in part — a detail that iconography would appear to have demanded. Would they have used a painted panel to represent the rising water which perhaps covered him to his thighs? Would the pageant wagon have been fitted with a slightly lower level to represent Christ's stepping into the river?

A final and rather interesting question concerns the possible stage properties utilized in the York Baptism play. The text of the play is silent here, but there is evidence for the use of some kind of container rather than the hand for pouring water over the figure of Christ. Often this would be a saucer-shaped dish or a shell. In a painted glass panel of c.1320 in York Minster, John pours from a bottle, but this is a late insertion. Nevertheless, at Great Malvern, fifteenth-century glass showing the Baptism has a bottle-shaped vessel[14] — a vessel of a kind the Barbers would surely have been able to supply without difficulty. Whatever the manner of pouring the water, the effect of the sacrament as cleansing and health-giving would have been felt to be appropriate for the Barbers, a guild whose vocation included involvement in the healing arts.

Following the Baptism, according to the 1415 *Ordo*, was the previously noted *Marriage in Cana*,[15] a seemingly unusual intrusion between the previous play and the Temptation which we would normally expect to see next in the cycle. As noted above, the Baptism is associated with the octave of Epiphany, followed by the Marriage at Cana on the second Sunday after Epiphany and with the Temptation falling within the Lenten season. This order has been shown to have influenced the scenes illustrated in glass at Great Malvern Priory,[16] and also provides the explanation we need for the sequence of plays in the York cycle. Thus, though the wedding at Cana would appear to have been intended for the Register *following* the Temptation,[17] attention to liturgical practice would suggest the correctness of the order noted in the *Ordo* of 1415.

In the Smiths' *Temptation in the Wilderness*, there is a continued emphasis on overcoming the power of that great dragon Satan and on Christ's role in providing a model of human behavior. He will be a mirror by which men may test their lives. Yet in the visual arts the Temptation is not as common as we might suppose, and at York no medieval examples are recorded later than the thirteenth century. A panel of painted glass from c.1285 in the Chapter House merely shows Christ holding up his hand against two devils, while an even earlier illumination in a York psalter (British Library MS. Add. 54,179) illustrates Satan's fall from the roof of the temple into hell — a scene which follows the depiction of the third temptation in the *St. Albans Psalter*. The York play, like the illuminations in the *St. Albans Psalter* which show the three temptations, is nevertheless designed to illustrate the manner in which the fraud of the devil is overcome[18] in order that the stage might be set for the triumph to be achieved through the Passion. However, the showing of Satan in an actual disguise (e.g., as a hermit or friar) did not begin until the sixteenth century.[19]

As Rosemary Woolf points out, the three temptations that are offered to Christ in the Temptation seem to be precisely parallel to those which caused man to fall in Eden.[20] In the *Temptation in the Wilderness*, the devil, who opens the play with comic bragging and bluster, fails to lead Christ into the sins of gluttony, vain-glory, and covetousness, with the result that the events of the Fall are reversed. Christ is, after all, the *second Adam* whose moral perfection regains once more the upright posture which the first Adam had lost in primordial time. In the end, therefore, the devil must, as in the illustration in the York psalter in the British Library, return to the place where he will suffer great pain (XXII.175-80), while, following the comfort given to Jesus by the angels, the Son raises his hand in blessing to the audience. "I knawe," he concludes, "my tyme is faste comand, / Now will I wende" (XXII.209-10).

Christ's divine power—power joined to humility—finds particular expression in the next play in the York cycle. The Curriers' *Transfiguration* presents, however, a subject for which no examples whatever are recorded in early York art, though there is, as noted above, a fake produced in the post-war restoration in the Chapter House where an Assumption in painted glass has been mistakenly "restored" as this scene.[21] We may note also that the current feast of the Transfiguration was not regularly celebrated until c.1475, and that earlier the practice had been to include the account as the Gospel in Lent as a lesson of hope in a time of penitence and fasting.[22] This is consistent with the design of the York Transfiguration play, for here Christ who has overcome the dragon in the Baptism will appear with "Hely" from Paradise and also Moses, briefly released from "þat dongeoun" from which the Savior will later draw the souls of the deserving at the Harrowing. There is additionally here a spectacular showing of Christ's divinity, apparently effected by stripping off his outer robe to show shining white garments (probably no means of illumination was used) and by adding in place a gold mask of the kind that we know was used for the deity, as in the Te Deum window formerly in St. Martin-le-Grand at York and now in the Minster. The effects were not surprisingly very "dazzling."[23] But perhaps even more spectacular in the York play is the appearance of God the Father, who descends in a cloud, according to the stage direction. Obviously, a quite elaborate pageant would have been necessary for such an action—a pageant with a strong framework and an upper level, as in the case of the Mercers' wagon. The mountain or mound on which Christ, Elijah, and Moses appear may be a standard piece of theatrical scenery perhaps, but the descent of the Father, while not involving machinery regarded as particularly unique, nevertheless completes the "sight" with a remarkable glimpse beyond the surface of mundane events. The audience is also invited to look beyond the physical characteristics of the persons involved, and to see the reality that is as yet hidden even from the disciples Peter, James, and John. In another sense, the Father's words in this play are the promised certification of the role of the Son in the appointed soteriological scheme—a scheme that requires the death of Christ on the cross and his subsequent Resurrection.

II

In the *Ordo* of 1415, three separate plays dramatized the dinner at Simon's house, the woman taken in adultery, and the bringing of Lazarus back from the dead.[24] Assigned to the Cappers, Play XXIV in the Register, however, only brings together first the woman taken in adultery[25] and thereafter the story of Lazarus's death and resurrection. The manuscript is, unfortunately, defective even within this play, with two leaves missing, the second being particularly serious since it contained the section in which Jesus, having arrived at the house of Mary and Martha, prepares to raise their brother from the dead. Nevertheless, the play, in contrast to the previous three plays, functions in an important way to set forth the power of the Savior from the standpoint of those who are in need of God's grace—i.e., from the standpoint of the entire human race. The first part of Play XXIV details Christ's power over *sin*, and the second illustrates his power over *death*.

With regard to its iconography, this play has considerable interest, especially in the matter of its resurrection scene. Following the break in the text at line 171 caused by a missing leaf in the manuscript, Christ orders that "This stone" be removed "and sette on syde." Surely he is referring to the top of a coffer-type

tomb such as was used in medieval England. The twelfth-century
York Psalter at the University of Glasgow thus shows Lazarus
in his grave clothes rising up from this kind of tomb, the cover
of which has been removed though it is not visible in the miniature.[26] The cover of Lazarus's tomb is actually "sette on syde" in
an illumination in the *De Bohun Psalter* (Bodleian MS. Auct.
D. 4. 4, fol. 243ᵛ), which is dated c.1370–80.[27] While it is useless
to speculate about the design of the lost panel from the East
Window of Christ Church, King Square, which was recorded in
the eighteenth century,[28] the evidence from extant art nevertheless seems to establish many details of the scene as it might have
appeared in the play. For example, at the line *"Lazar, veni
foras"* (XXIV.184) we may assume that the actor playing Jesus
may have reached down to take the hand of the man as in the
Glasgow psalter. In a printed York Missal (1533), Lazarus is
shown in a small woodcut kneeling as he comes out of the tomb
with grave clothes falling away; his hands are joined in prayer,
while Jesus holds up his right hand in blessing (sig. fiᵛ). The
play then presents the first words of Lazarus upon his resurrection as praise to the one who raised him from the dead on the
fourth day. He continues:

> By certayne singnes here may men see
>   How þat þou art Goddis sone verray.
> All þo þat trulye trastis in þe
>   Schall neuere dye, þis dar I saye. (XXIV.190–93)

But the lesson of Lazarus' victory over death is not a simple
one, nor could it be understood in terms of the self-contained
unit of the Capmakers' play in the Register even if we had the
missing leaves to complete the text. For the play looks ahead to
other events wherein the power and the glory of the Christ-hero
will be asserted; as a man who like all of us is *homo viator* in this
world, Jesus will set forth on a journey at the end of this play
toward Jerusalem, the earthly city where he will establish the
right of his brothers and sisters — i.e., all members of the race — to
hope for a heavenly city which is beyond death.

As Rosemary Woolf points out, the York *Entry into Jerusalem*
and the *Last Supper* tend to be more closely associated with the

Ministry group than with the Passion.[29] These plays are the
final preparation for the Passion, however, as they show Jesus'
coming to Jerusalem, where he will institute the Eucharist and,
later, suffer on the cross. The first of these plays, presented by
the Skinners, may well have involved staging quite different
from any other play in the cycle, for it is hard to see how a usual
pageant stage setting would have played any part in this production. The text of the play calls for a castle (Bethphage, identified
as a *castellum* in the Vulgate), a sycamore tree (often, as in the
Holkham Bible Picture Book, visualized as a willow[30]) for the
publican Zache,[31] and the gates of Jerusalem. The castle, where
the disciples are sent to find the ass with its foal,[32] surely needed
only to be merely suggested, perhaps by a painted panel, but the
two other locations are crucial. A tree which would support a
man need not be very elaborate, however, though the gates of
Jerusalem ought to be more than the simplest kind of cut-out
form and ought to be strong enough to sustain figures of wel-
coming citizens. Again, reference to the *Holkham Bible Picture
Book* is instructive for its visualizing of detail. In fourteenth-
century glass in York Minster, Christ is riding the ass without
bridle (it has only a rope halter[33]) as he raises his hand in blessing toward those upon and before the city walls and gates,
which are open to receive him. One of the figures at the top is
throwing down a branch which is not a palm but a sprig from
some other tree, probably a willow,[34] while the man standing
beside the gate may be the porter. The central tableau here as in
the play is the procession, which the text of the drama describes
as "With braunches, floures and vnysoune" and "With
myghtfull songes" sung by children (XXV.262–63).

The procession, which must move across the playing area, is
clearly modelled on the Palm Sunday procession, as painted
glass from Fairford makes very clear. O. G. Farmer describes
the scene:

> In the foreground, the Saviour riding on an ass is seen with
> his right hand raised in blessing, as He enters the city
> through a porticullis gateway. He is met by singers, one of
> whom, standing in the gateway, holds palm branches in his
> hand. Other branches are to be seen strewn under the feet

of the ass by a youth who has climbed up into a tree, where he
is plucking the branches, and throwing them down. Over the
gateway on the wall of the city, are three singers, one of whom
holds a scroll on which are words and music. The words appear to be the opening of the Antiphon sung by Cantors and
Choir at the procession on Palm Sunday, the Cantors inside
the Church, the Choir outside. At the conclusion, the cross-
bearer knocks three times on the closed door, which is then
opened for the procession which moves up the Church singing
the "Ingrediente". The music on the scroll is not the plainsong,
"Gloria laus" melody, but the alto part of some polyphonic
setting of the words, written in Franconian notation.[35]

The York play indicates that the singing will be provided by a
children's chorus walking in the procession as the citizens go to
meet Jesus "with melodye" (XXV.264–65, 310), obviously a
detail reported first in the apocryphal *Gospel of Nicodemus*
which described "the children of the Hebrews" holding branches
and spreading "their garments beneath" Christ.[36] The *Ordo* of
1415 specifies "eight boys with palm branches singing *Benedictus*"
in addition to rich men and poor men.[37] The boys most likely
were pupils being trained in singing, probably at the cathedral,
for the text suggests that it will be "þe fayrest processioun / That
euere was sene in þis Jury" (XXV.311–12). In the example of
York glass cited above, those who follow Christ carry palms,
but they are all adults rather than boys. Nevertheless, we would
expect boys normally to have a prominent role in the Palm Sunday procession, and here we may expect that the action is actually designed to remind the audience specifically of a liturgical
event that would take place each year one week prior to Easter.
It is even not impossible that instruments were included in the
procession, though no solid evidence may be expected to be
forthcoming to support this view.

If we regard the Bakers' play of the *Last Supper* (Play XXVII)
to be the final play of the Ministry series,[38] the preparation for
the Passion actually overlaps the first play which can be identified as part of the Passion series—the *Conspiracy* (Play XXVI).
In any case, as the *Baptism of Christ* establishes one sacrament,
so the *Last Supper* fixes the form of another, the Eucharist,
which signifies the new order made possible by Christ's role as

the Lamb of God to be sacrificed on the cross. Prior to the meal, Jesus washes the feet of his disciples — a scene also shown in fourteenth-century glass now in the choir of York Minster. In the play, Mark will bring the water, and will also offer "a towell clene" (XXVII.39-42). As in the York glass, Jesus begins with Peter — an act which apparently in the play triggers James's question concerning primacy among the apostles. Unfortunately, the manuscript breaks off in the middle of Jesus' answer to James, and following the missing leaf in the Register the text indicates action in the midst of the meal. Judas has already received the bread or wafer, for Jesus is speaking to him, advising *"Quod facis fac cicius,/* þat þou schall do, do sone" (XXVII.90-91).

The York dramatic records indicate that the "lambe" which "is roste and redy dight" at line 7 was a stage prop that required mending in 1553 and 1557, while other props included "dyadems" which required "payntyng."[39] Presumably the apostles were seated at a table, with perhaps a ciborium and a chalice in addition to the "lambe" that surely took the form of the Agnus Dei. At Malvern, Judas is stealing a fish and preparing to place it under the tablecloth at the same time that he opens his mouth to receive the wafer.[40] In fourteenth-century York glass, Judas is alone on the side of the table toward the viewers,[41] a position that suggests the strong prejudice of the artists against having the villain's gaze meet the eyes of those who look at the representation of the scene. As in the account of the Last Supper in the *Meditations on the Life of Christ*, heavy emphasis is placed on the institution of the Eucharist, with the table setting and action designed to provide a direct link to the Canon of the Mass and Communion. The *Meditations* additionally explain that Christ "is the one whom you take in the sacrament of the altar made by Him today. He is the same one who was marvellously incarnated and born of the Virgin; for you He suffered death. And He is the one who, resuscitated and gloriously rising to heaven, sits on the right hand of God."[42] Following the Ministry plays, therefore, the events that will be dramatized are inevitable. As Jesus says in the *Last Supper*,

> My fadir saide it schall be soo,
> His bidding will I noȝt forbere. (XXVII.182-83)

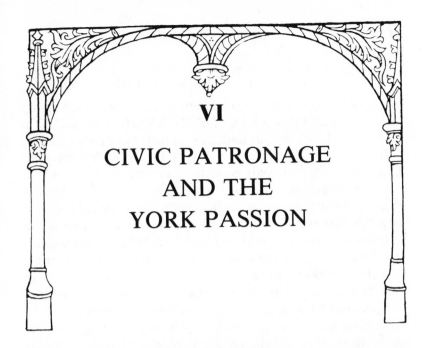

VI

CIVIC PATRONAGE
AND THE
YORK PASSION

When the York Realist's contribution toward the series of plays on the Passion was added,[1] a significant new aesthetic level was achieved by the cycle. It is doubtful, however, whether many of the original patrons of the York plays would have regarded this addition from a purely aesthetic standpoint; rather, the values by which the work of the York Realist would have been judged by his contemporaries were instead religious and practical. The new play texts were designed to augment the devotional life of the city and probably also to reduce the total number of pageants for the sake of efficiency in production. Nevertheless, it is true that the Realist's plays are indicative of more care for literary excellence than such (presumably earlier) dramas as the Skinners' *Entry into Jerusalem*, the Bakers' *Last Supper*, and the Pinners' *Crucifixio Christi*. As Jesse Byers Reese concludes after a thorough examination of the versification of the plays attributed to the York Realist, these plays contain extremely skillful alliterative verse and hence demonstrate that "we are certainly dealing with no 'feeble linguists,' no 'uncertain melodists,' no ' dull versifiers'."[2] In contrast to such inelegant lines as Mark's

> Maistir, we haue arayed full right
> Seruise þat semes for youre sopere.

>   Oure lambe is roste and redy dight,
>   As Moyses lawe will lely lere. (XXVII.5–8)

in the *Last Supper*, the splendid literary handling of each alliterative stanza in Plays XXVI, XXVIII–XXXIII, and XXXVI is
indeed worthy of serious notice as literary and dramatic art.

It is surely significant that the York Realist's work was done
at a time when civic patronage in York and elsewhere was so
strongly focused on the adornment of churches and the endowment of chantry chapels and other institutions regarded as appropriate outlets for charitable works. The aims and goals of the
substantial citizens of York were far from being totally mercan-
tile during the prosperous earlier part of the fifteenth century,
and these involved attitudes that extended up to the Reformation and beyond. The citizens' attention to the things of their
religion may be judged by the way in which the parish churches
were beautified with new painted glass and other adornments
designed to draw the church-goers' minds toward a meditative
experience of the Christian story. As noted above, the Minster
had received during the early part of the century a glorious East
Window where the emphasis was on the beginning and end of
history—the Creation and Judgment—both of which also provide the limits of the historical sweep of the York mystery cycle.
But the citizens themselves were more interested in their own
churches, and expended their funds generously to outfit them in
ways that could often rival the glories of the cathedral itself. For
example, between 1412 and 1427 All Saints, North Street,
received a new window with glass of the highest quality from an
affluent parishioner, Nicholas Blackburn, Sr., who had been
Lord Mayor in 1411/12, and his son, Nicholas Blackburn, Jr.[3]
The window, perhaps painted by John Chamber, Jr., who may
have been associated with the shop of John Thornton,[4] illustrates most clearly a dual desire to promote excellence in quality
and to make visible some important persons in the Christian
story. The three lights of this window show most prominently
John the Baptist with the Agnus Dei, the Blessed Virgin being
taught to read by St. Anne (to whom Nicholas Blackburn, Sr.,
apparently had a particular devotion[5]), and St. Christopher.

The focal point of Christian worship in the early fifteenth century is also here, for in a panel below the Virgin and St. Anne in the center light is a representation of the Trinity with Christ shown on the cross atoning for the sins of men. In a sense, when the window was in its former position in the North Wall, this panel invited the worshipper to look over at the larger Crucifixion in what was then the East Window over the main altar.[6] Christ's Crucifixion and the Mass which is a repetition of the sacrifice on the cross — these make possible the forgiveness of sins and open the way for the good Christian who faithfully performs the Corporal Acts of Mercy (illustrated in another window also given by the Blackburn family to All Saints, North Street, at a later date[7]) to enter into heavenly bliss at the Last Day.

The expense of such a window as the Blackburn window[8] at All Saints, North Street, like the expense of putting on the York plays, points not only to family honor and concern for personal salvation (the donors and their wives are present in the glass at the bottom of the Blackburn window, along with words requesting prayers for their souls[9]), but also to a more generous piety and desire of assisting others to acquaint themselves with the meaning of the Christian plan of redemption. In the window, the Virgin holds a Psalter, which is opened to Psalm 143: "D[omi]ne exaudi or[ati]onem mea[m] aurib[us] p[er]cipe ob[secrationem meam],"[10] which in the Authorized Version is translated "Hear my prayer, O Lord, give ear to my supplications." The Virgin, like the Blackburn family itself, is setting an example of prayer for all others to follow.

In York, the ecclesiastical center of the North, the influence nevertheless was more often the city rather than cathedral clergy which helped to orchestrate patronage of the religious arts. Indeed, rivalry between the city and the Minster would seem to have been the case. At All Saints, North Street, a vigorous program was undertaken to improve the church and its glass especially during the tenure of Father James Baguley (1413–40), when some of the very highest quality glass available at York was installed.[11] Elsewhere, of course, the citizens' contributions varied according to their means and the taste of the artists and workmen employed to do the work. But, with a large percentage of it still remaining, we can judge very little fifteenth-century glass to be bad, and some reaches a level of excellence that was rarely surpassed by glass painters elsewhere in England and on the continent during this period.

The early fifteenth century had meant, of course, some changes in both the technique of glass painting as it was practiced in York, and also in its design. The windows painted then, for example, illustrate a verisimilitude not normally found in the earlier glass from this city. Hence the panels of the great St. Martin window (c.1437) in St. Martin-le-Grand, Coney Street, show faces and other details no longer merely stylized but drawn in conformity with the principles of perspective painting which had been introduced by the Netherlands painters, though the scenes in the glass are nevertheless still enclosed under the magnificent canopies typical of the York school of glass painters. Christian iconography in this painting was not to be rejected, but to be revitalized. By breathing life back into the events associated with the life of Christ and the lives of the saints, they hoped to proclaim more effectively the truths which had previously been taught.

The plays written by the York Realist to replace earlier material in the Passion series at York also do not turn away from the traditional iconographic features of the story, though they share the glass painters' tendency toward realistic detail. Here too the purpose was to give new life to an older art form. These plays are indeed vibrantly alive, tending even to a kind of emotionalism that is the mark of successful popular drama. It might be thus suspected that there was a connection with the emphasis current in the sermons and art of the Franciscans,[12] and evidence suggests that this influence is more than indirect. While no one has demonstrated that the York Realist was a Franciscan (he was more likely a member of the city clergy), no perceptive person will deny the presence of the spirit of the *Meditations on the Life of Christ.*[13] This Franciscan work insists strongly not only upon iconographic features of the Passion, but also upon a detailed realistic display of the visual details which need to be imagined when contemplating this event in Christ's life. Specific attention will be given to the matter of realism in Chapter VII, below.

The plays, of course, were civic endeavors, with the various guilds of the city responsible for their individual plays.[14] Essentially the plays were under the control of the Corporation, as shown by the evidence in the *York Memorandum Book* and other civic records.[15] The effort involved in the performance of the plays was supported by all the citizens of the city, with appropriate fines for failure to participate. Thus, though the York Realist's aesthetic may indeed owe something to the Franciscans, his work must be considered primarily an art which embodies the substance of civic concern and lay piety. It is a drama that must first of all have pleased the Lord Mayor and the Council as well as the members of the various crafts who used his text as the basis for their pageants.

The York Realist's texts, then, are designed for use in a theatrical art directed at a popular audience of clergy and laymen alike. As in the case of York glass, those who are the viewers are invited by the iconography and by the presentation of fully imagined detail to participate in the scenes which are presented. They are invited to see what it would be like if they were themselves present at historical events such as the Passion. Such participation would be expected to produce a deeply felt piety, and it is a piety that leads the audience not only to think about but also to feel the suffering and death of Christ for men's sins. Here therefore are the sources of the emotionalism which permeates the contribution of the York Realist to the Passion sequence in the York cycle.

The portion of the York Passion for which the Realist is responsible thus utilizes realism as a *means* by which to achieve an effect—the acquainting of an audience with the suffering and death of Christ on the crosss. The iconography, however, functions as a way of pointing to that which could be apprehended intellectually—i.e., to the visual pattern and arrangement of symbols which penetrate to the most inmost meaning of the event. Thus both verisimilitude and iconography are necessary ingredients in the art of the Realist, whose goal was to produce a total response in the viewer. Such a response surely was what the pious pillars of the community wanted, and there is no reason to believe that they were less proud of the York Realist's work on the Passion sequence than they were of the glass which they installed in their churches.

II

This chapter will henceforth be limited to discussion of the plays which form a continuous line of dramatic development from the Agony and Betrayal to the condemnation of Christ. In these plays (XXVIII–XXXIII), which form a bridge between the conclusion of the Ministry series in the *Last Supper* and the *Road to Calvary*, the York Realist very clearly demonstrates the principles of his dramaturgy, which, as we have noted, is a kind that would have met with the strong approval of the affluent men who controlled the Corporation. This sequence of six plays — altogether more than 2500 lines of masterful alliterative verse — is not, of course, a self-contained unit, for it presents an action that depends for its effect on the plays that will immediately follow — three plays dramatizing the crucifixion and death of Christ, the last of which is also by the York Realist. The focus on the Crucifixion here, as in the Blackburn window with its crucified Christ in the Trinity panel, provides a basis for the perspective sketched forth in plays XXVIII–XXXIII.

The dramatic movement toward the Crucifixion had, of course, begun in earnest in Play XXVI when Judas, Pilate, and the chief priests conspired to have Jesus arrested. But after the completion of the events dramatized in the Bakers' play of the *Last Supper*, the York Realist turns his undivided attention to the presentation of an unbroken series of plays which together form a successful dramatic unit in an action which will result in apparent catastrophe and tragedy for Christ.

Play XXVIII, the *Agony and Betrayal*, is lacking some important lines in the first scene because of a missing leaf in the manuscript, and there are further problems of a textual nature,[16] but even in such a fragmentary form it is able to provide a most striking depiction of the disciples' weariness when confronted with a critical situation and of Christ's own very human fear of the future which will bring him rapidly to the cross. His "flessh is full dredand for drede . . ." (XXVIII.48). Christ's dread had received explanation in the *Meditations*, though in a passage which Nicholas Love failed to translate. The Franciscan author insists that insofar as Christ was human, he did not wish "to suffer the pain" and hence feared what was in store for him. "Therefore," he writes, "since He was a real man and placed in great anguish as a man, pity Him as intimately as possible."[17]

Unlike the Christ of the earlier Middle Ages who would go willingly off to the Crucifixion like a divine athlete entering a contest, the York Realist's hero in this play first stresses his *human* reluctance to do what he must do. In the Anglo-Saxon *Dream of the Rood*, Christ like a handsome young warrior-king had energetically hastened to the cross to mount upon it:

> Ongyrede hine þa geong hæleð, (þæt wæs god ælmihtig),
> strang ond stiðmod. Gestah he on gealgan heanne,
> modig on manigra gesyðe, þa he wolde mancyn lysan.[18]

(Then the young Lord—he was God Almighty—undressed himself, strong and steadfast. Bravely in the sight of many, he mounted the high gallows [the cross] so that he might redeem mankind.)

Before the eleventh century, West European iconography had simply failed to stress the human suffering of Christ in his Passion and Crucifixion,[19] since the current theological emphasis was then upon his divine role as the God-Man who came to overcome death through his Resurrection. And only in the twelfth century was this emphasis seriously challenged. As Sandro Sticca notes, Christ's sufferings take on a new importance in the theology of St. Anselm, whose *Cur Deus Homo* called attention to "the true significance of the humanity of Christ by stressing that the redemptive act took place on a human level."[20] A passage introduced by Nicholas Love into his translation of the *Meditations* explains:

> At the begynyng thou that desyrest to haue sorouful compassion thorugh sentence inward affection of the peynefull passion of Jhesu/thou must in thy mynde departe in maner for

the tyme the myghte of the godhede fro the kyndely Infirmyte of the manhede/though it so be in sothenes that the
god hede was neuer departed fro the manhede/For there
ben many soo blynded ghostly by vnresonable ymagynacion of the myȝte of the godhede in Jhesu, that they trowe
not that ony thynge myght be peyneful or sorouful to hym,
as to another comyn man that hath only the kynde of man,
and therfor haue they none compassion of the paynes that
he suffred, supposing that for as moche as he was
god/ther myȝt no thyng be ageynst his wil or dere hym:
but therfor here ayenst for to haue true ymagynacion and
inward [com]passion of the paynes and the passion of our
lord ihesu very god and man, we shal vnderstande/that as
his wille was to suffre the hardest dethe and moost
sorouful peynes for the redempticion of mankynde, so by
the same will he suspendeth in al his passion the vse and the
myght of the godhede fro the infirmyte of the manhede no
more takyng of for the tyme/than hath another tendir and
delicate man only after the kynde of man. . . .[21]

Such an assertion is commonplace after the twelfth century, and
represents a change in theology that eventually seeped down to
alter indeed the whole emphasis of Christian iconography.
What happened, of course, was that the Passion and Crucifixion
replaced the Resurrection as the central focus of Christ's
redemptive mission to mankind. As Émile Mâle notes, "By the
fifteenth century this celestial radiance [of an art which reflects
'all the luminous aspects of Christianity, . . . goodness and
gentleness and love'] has long since been extinguished. The majority of works left to us from the epoch are somber, art offering few images but those of sorrow and death. Jesus is no longer
teacher, but sufferer; or, rather, He offers His wounds and His
blood as the supreme teaching."[22]

Yet, in spite of the usual passivity of the Christ of the York
Realist, the older iconography of the Savior as a warrior still is
not entirely forgotton. In the midst of his Agony, Jesus prays:

þou fadir þat all formed hase with fode for to fill,
   I fele by my ferdnes my flessh wolde full fayne
Be torned *fro this turnement*. . . . (XXVIII.88–90; italics mine)

While Christ is hardly the eager warrior of *The Dream of the Rood*, the idea of the Passion and Crucifixion as a successful battle has curiously remained alive.[23] The idea is also encountered in the ancient notion of the *Arma Christi*. The weapons are, of course, the instruments of his suffering and death since "for the victor the weapons are symbols of triumph and authority."[24] Thus glass formerly in the East Window of St. Saviour's Church, York, shows these instruments on a heraldic shield[25] in a design appropriate for Christ's victorious tournament in which he conquers sin and death.

For the York Realist, therefore, Christ is not a rough-and-ready warrior hero but a civilized knight whose perfect humanity must overcome the imperfection which has manifested itself in the race of mankind. Christ is the second Adam[26] who has come to rectify the fall and to show men how to endure to the end in the face of unbelievable suffering. It is the suffering which is so vividly communicated in this scene, for the skillful handling of the alliterative verse leads him to a rich vocabulary at once lively and evocative. Jesus at the very beginning of the play, as we have noted above in Chapter I, admits that his "flesshe dyderis and daris for doute of [his] dede" and that his "enemyes will newly be neghand full nere" in order to threaten his "manhede" (XXVIII.2-4). The introduction of such Yorkshire words as *dyderis* (trembles, quakes) and *daris* (is frightened to the point of stupefaction)[27] gives the verse a curious forcefulness that makes the presentation of the Agony convincing as drama. Furthermore, the realistic setting forth of Christ's mental state in this scene opens the way for the emotionally charged plays which will follow—plays that will culminate, as his apostle Peter predicts, in the loss of his life when he is "Vnkyndely . . . crucified and naylyd to a tree" (XXVIII.26). The pattern is set: in each play iconographic features will be subjected to realistic elaboration and psychological probing in order to present them effectively to audiences. It is a pattern that must have appealed to the York city fathers who must have responded to his way of presenting such scenes.

As Christ in the *Agony and Betrayal* goes away from the disciples to pray, he steps up "to þe mounte" (XXVIII.84), which is surely an element of staging. The mount or hill is, of course, the Mount of Olives to which reference is made in the synoptic gospels. In iconography, however, the mount is often merely pictured as a mound; sometimes, as in the *St. Albans Psalter*, it is a raised hillock which Christ actually prays upon,[28] but more often it is a small raised mount (as in the *Hours of Catherine of Cleves*[29]) or rock (as in the Estouchville Triptych[30] and Jan Gossaert's painting[31]) before which Christ kneels. The York play would seem to indicate such an abbreviated hillock before which Christ might pray.

Here, away from the disciples who are overcome with fatigue in the garden, Christ tells us (XXVIII.50) that because of his dread he sweats "now both watir and bloode" — a literalistic interpretation which seems borrowed from *The Northern Passion*, a poem that has been identified as one of the York Realist's sources.[32] Then he begs his Father who is "bote of all bale and belder of blisse" (XXVIII.55) to allow him to be released from what he must do: "if it possible be this payne mygh I ouerpasse" (XXVIII.58). The "cup" which he would have "taken away from me" in the biblical text is not mentioned in the scene by the York Realist, nor does it appear in *The Northern Passion*.[33] Though the cup is often literally represented in iconography, usually with a Host suspended above it,[34] it is missing in the painted glass of c.1340–50 in a window in the choir of York Minster, and its importance in York art does not seem to have demanded inclusion of this detail in the *Bolton Hours* (c.1420) which show Christ kneeling in prayer and looking up to see the hand of God the Father emerging from the clouds.[35] It is thus quite probable that the York Realist did not have the cup in mind when he wrote the scene, though of course in production it might well have been added. The cup, if it had been used in the play, would surely have been a Eucharistic vessel. The stage directions of the N-town Plays, for example, tell us that "*An Aungel descendyth to jhesus and bryngyth to him A chalys with An host þer in.*"[36]

There is no question, however, about the presence in the York play of the ministering angel, who comes down at line 113. The angel delivers a message from God the Father to his Son to comfort him, though the Father will not release him from his obligation to die for the sins of all men ("For dedis þat man done has thy dede schall be dight, / And þou with turmentis be tulyd," XXVIII.117-18). All three of these iconographic details — the mount, the cup, and the angel — had appeared in the miniature in the twelfth-century *St. Albans Psalter*, and reappear together in many works of art through the fifteenth century (e.g., in Gossaert's *Agony in the Garden*). The York play has presented at least two — the mount and the angel — on stage.

The Agony is immediately followed in the same play by the Betrayal, in which the high priests, the soldiers, and Judas set out for the Garden of Gethsemane to arrest Christ. The scene is a common one in iconography. "Now," says Jesus, "will þis oure be neghand full nere / That schall certefie all þe soth þat I haue saide" (XXVIII.245-46). Judas brashly greets his Master with an "All hayll" — a salutation implying betrayal as late as the time of Shakespeare — and asks to kiss him, "For all my loue and my likyng is holy vppon ʒou layde" (XXVIII.251). Through this hypocritical "kissing is mans sone betrayed" (XXVIII.253). A supernatural light then apparently surrounds Jesus, or else the soldiers are struck by some strange sense of his divinity which is now revealed. In any case, the soldiers are amazed, and probably also fall to the ground, as in *John* 18.6 and in a Carolingian ivory in the British Museum.[37] This is a detail not often encountered in art,[38] and appears also only in the N-town cycle[39] among the other English cycles.

Malchus, the overly zealous soldier named in *John* 18.10, is the man whose ear was cut off by Peter's sword. The York play follows the Harleian manuscript of *The Northern Passion* (l. 563) in having Malchus be a lantern bearer, but this is hardly unique: Malchus also appears, for example, as a lantern bearer in fifteenth-century painted glass in St. Martin-cum-Gregory where the lantern appears fallen between his feet, and in continental illustrations such as those in the *Belles Heures* of the Duke of Berry and the *Hours of Catherine of Cleves*.[40] Jesus, of course, since he has chosen the way of submission — he is the anti-type of the lamb which had been sent by God as a substitute for Isaac in the play of *Abraham and Issaac*[41] — will heal Malchus's ear and go quickly with the irreverent gang that has arrested him.

Here begins the demonstration of Christ's *patience*—a patience which will sympathetically be set forth from this point onward through his death in the *Mortificacio Christi*—while his enemies and tormentors engage in spectacular displays of vituperation and irrational behavior.

Such irrational behavior, of course, provides the York Realist with an opportunity for indulging both in more realistic detail and in caricature. The liveliness of his presentation in the plays which depict the trial and torture of Christ provides a sharp contrast between unstable antagonists and the God-Man who stands for the very principle of stability—the supporting power of divinity—that upholds the universe. Christ's role in these plays may seem static, but it is in fact the focal point for all the action. Furthermore, everything that happens is directed toward the end which inevitably must be the Crucifixion.

Christ is portrayed as encountering a series of trials, each building toward his outrageously unjust conviction at the conclusion of Play XXXIII. These trials are well documented in both continental and English iconography,[42] though the artists show more evidence surely of being excited by the more sensational scenes of the Buffeting, Flagellation, and Mocking. York art itself gives Christ before Herod in glass of c. 1420–30, and an early fifteenth-century woodcut shows him before Pilate, who is washing his hands. A copy by Barnett of lost glass from the York Minster Chapter House also shows the latter scene, and this may now be seen in the nave clerestory.[43] In the *Hours of Catherine of Cleves*, Jesus is shown before Caiaphas, before Pilate, who is washing his hands, and before Herod.[44] In each of the miniatures, Jesus' posture is the same: his face is emblematic of patience, his eyes looking down, his wrists tied and his hands covered. His feet are bare. In the rich *Hours of Etienne Chevalier* by Jean Fouquet, precisely these features appear again, with the exception of the sleeves that completely cover Christ's hands.[45] The York plays clearly call for a similar representation of Christ in these trial scenes, for his demeanor here is tailored to heighten the contrast between those around him and the innocent victim whose silence so infuriates his inquisitors. "He lokis like a lambe" (XXX.273), Caiaphas insists to Pilate when he brings Christ before him to place charges of treason, witchcraft, and other wrong-doing. But, as in an initial illuminated by Herman Scheerre in the early fifteenth century, the accuser standing beside Christ would seem to be the one set apart by his indecorous and antic behavior.[46]

Against the background of these trials, the York Realist presents the stories of two erring apostles, Peter and Judas Iscariot. These two had been set off against each other as a pair of opposites at least as early as the first recorded Passion Play from Montecassino, which dramatizes Peter's denials and repentance in Scene v and Judas's return of the thirty pieces and his suicide in Scene vi.[47] Peter's three denials, predicted by Christ before his arrest (XXVIII.147-52), are dramatized in Play XXIX while Jesus is being brought before Caiaphas. After Peter's second assertion that "I sawe hym neuere are" (XXIX.129), the York Realist introduces Malchus again (the biblical text merely names those "that stood by") to insist that this man indeed was not only with Jesus at the time of the arrest, but also was the disciple who had "swapped of my nere" (XXIX.142). Curiously, there seems to be no cock crowing to bring Peter to repentance;[48] instead, Christ himself, as he is led into the playing area, reproaches him for his faithlessness (XXIX.162-65). Peter's genuine repentance is then to be contrasted with the false repentance in Play XXXII when despairing Judas, feeling he has sinned so deeply that he can never be redeemed, returns the money to the high priests. Here Judas is certainly humanized, and the audience must indeed have felt his great sorrow as he begged Pilate to "Haue mercy on my maistir trewe" (XXXII.237). Though the audience knows what terrible end is in store for Judas, his suicide is not presented on stage in the York play.

The relationship between Peter and Judas is clear: these two opposites again point out the two paths that men might follow in their lives — one representing true repentance and forgiveness, and the other representing despair and remorse but not true repentance. (Shakespeare's Macbeth is, of course, an accurate reflection of the way of Judas: once he has killed the king, he feels sufficient anxiety and remorse, but never makes any real effort to repent truly and to return to a state of innocence through forgiveness.) In the Passion plays in the York cycle, Judas and Peter look forward to that famous pair of thieves on the cross: the bad thief on Christ's left, and on his right the good thief, whose penitent words induce the dying man-God to promise that, "Sen þou fro thy foly will falle,/With me schall dwelle nowe þis day,/In paradise place principall" (XXXVI.210–12).

The scene with Pilate and his wife Procula also is introduced into the midst of the Passion series by the York Realist. J. W. Robinson comments that the scene in which Pilate goes to bed is one which, like the scene in which Caiaphas goes to bed in Play XXIX, "may be explained by referring to the York Realist's habit of working out the events of the Passion story in their natural sequence and logical detail."[49] The going-to-bed episode may be unique, but it should be noted that Procula's presence in the Passion Play goes back to the earliest stage which is still extant — the Montecassino play.[50] The significance of the scene in the York play is discussed by Rosemary Woolf, who isolates the opening words spoken by the devil to Procula ("O woman, be wise and ware, and wonne in þi witte," XXX.167) and then suggests that these words have "the ring of a temptation." She continues: "the York dramatist obviously had in mind the parallelism between Eve and Procula noted in the *Glossa ordinaria*, namely that just as the devil through a woman brought death to man, so he sought by a woman to retain the *imperium mortis*, of which he might be deprived by Christ's death."[51] The figure of Procula is here an ironic shadowing of the Blessed Virgin, who is called the Second Eve and whose presence and lamentation at the cross will be dramatized in the *Mortificacio Christi*.

Even more lively than the scene between Pilate and his sensual wife are the episodes of torture, both psychological and physical, to which Christ is subjected. In these scenes, however, the liveliness is directed specifically toward enlisting the audience's sympathy for the divine victim, the man of sorrows who is made to suffer insults and blows at the hands of the officious soldiers, who appear to have been dressed in military armor as in a miniature by Fouquet.[52] Examples of armed soldiers appear in fourteenth- and fifteenth-century glass in the Minster and in All Saints, North Street, in scenes such as the Crucifixion and Resurrection. In the

York plays, there is no hint that the Realist sympathizes in any way with these torturers. Like the prominent citizens of York who controlled these plays, he must have represented the conventional piety of the time. Such piety would see these torturers only as an opportunity in drama to underline the sufferings of Jesus in such a way that many in the audience might respond with piety rather than with rowdiness.[53] Unquestionably, the response was intended to be conditioned by the knowledge that, as a York book of hours (c.1420) in the York Minster Library proclaims in a prayer, "lorde iesu cryste, leuand god sone / . . . set [his] deyd, [his] cros, and [his] passione / Be-twixt [the] dome, and my saul, for deyd þat I haue don, / Now [and] at my endying þat I be noght fordon."[54] Hence we may see more clearly why such city fathers as Nicholas Blackburn, Sr., would be as likely to support the plays as he would be to endow (as Blackburn did in 1424) a popular daily chantry Mass in the Chapel of St. Anne on Foss Bridge, or to support the activities of the Corpus Christi Guild.[55]

The pattern of physical torture is set in the Buffeting, which takes place in the presence of the high priests in Play XXIX. The soldiers are given opportunity to teach Christ to bow obediently and to behave appropriately before the ecclesiastical authorities. Ironically, the inappropriate behavior at this point is assigned to the soldiers, whose speeches intentionally lack any glimmer of illumination of knowledge of what they are really doing. There is even haggling over the stool or chair upon which Christ ought to sit, for example. Despite the fact that the usual iconographic features of this scene include a stool or chair upon which Christ sits (e.g., in an initial in the *Bolton Hours*, fol. 62), the text here fails to make clear whether the stool is ever given to him. As in the Martyrdom Window in York Minster, the total impression of the soldiers' treatment of Christ is unquestionably horror and shame. When the third soldier begins hitting him, he shouts, "Playes faire in feere, and þer is one and þer is — ij; / I schall fande to feste it with a faire flappe — / And there is — iij; and there is — iiij" (XXIX.362-64). They are *playing* with Christ as a cat plays with a wounded and helpless bird. Kolve has pointed out, furthermore, how the soldiers' actions may be analyzed in terms of *game*.[56] The game that they consciously

play is "popse" (XXIX.355), variously known in the Middle
Ages as Hot Cockles, papse, *"the bobbid game,"*[57] etc. It was a
game similar to the modern Blind Man's Buff. The connection
between this game and Buffeting was, however, conventional.
G. R. Owst quotes John Bromyard's *Summa Predicantium*, which
associates "the manner of the Jews who buffeted Christ when
blindfolded, saying—'Prophesy, who is that smote thee'" with
"the manner of those who, *in still playing that game*, smite
someone on the head smartly while his face is hidden, but laugh
at him, when he raises his head to see, as though they had done
nothing to him."[58] Another example, roughly contemporary
with the work of the York Realist, is also cited from MS.
Bodleian 649, fol. 82:

> A common game in use nowadays is that which the soldiers
> played with Christ at his Passion: it is called *the bobbid
> game*. In this game, one of the company will be *blindfold*
> and set in a prone position; then those standing by will hit
> him on the head and say—
>
> > *"A bobbid, a bobbid, a biliried*:
> > Smyte not her, bot thu smyte a gode!"
>
> And as often as the former may fail to guess correctly *and
> rede amys*, he has to play a fresh game. And so, until *he
> rede him that smote him*, he will be *blindfold stille and
> hold in* for the post of player.[59]

As further corroboration, the visual arts in England and in
countries with close ties with English culture also seem to depict
the Buffeting in this way, though of course in all cases the artists
allow for the fact that the torturers here are Jews and not Roman
soldiers—a fact that the York Realist alters in his drama in order
to portray them as soldiers throughout the whole sequence of
plays from the Betrayal and Buffeting until the Mocking in Play
XXXIII. A contemporary English alabaster cited by W. L.
Hildburgh shows a veiled Christ and tormentors hitting him
with fist, cudgel, and club.[60] A very similar veil covers Christ's
head in the *Hours of Catherine of Cleves*, though there the
game is just at the point of breaking up: the tormentors are beginning to substitute rude sounds for blows. One man vigorously

blows what appears to be a kind of cornett, and even in the border someone hits a pan with a stick.[61]

Kolve incorrectly asserts that when the soldiers "have tired of their game of papse, they vary it with another, reminiscent of a drinking ceremony, 'Wassaille, Wassaylle',"[62] but the shouting and noise-making are rather symptomatic of their game proving unsatisfactory: because Christ refuses to play their game—he is a spoil-sport[63] whom they therefore label as a "layke" or lack-wit because he "likis noȝt þis" (XXIX.377)—they are not able to continue. The game falls into anarchy, and the tormentors comment anew on Christ's foolishness which is proven to their satisfaction by his refusal to play—a refusal that successfully defeats their demonic game.

John Plummer has aptly described how in the miniature in the *Hours of Catherine of Cleves* the figure of Christ, in spite of "the indignities inflicted upon Him, . . . sits in quiet majesty. . . ." The figure is enthroned and symmetrical, and gives an impression of stability. "In contrast," Plummer writes, "the four tormenting figures around him are aggressively active and correspondingly eccentric in position, asymmetrical in posture and irregular in outline and feature."[64] In the York Buffeting, the soldiers show a futile determination to gain a response from Christ; the irregular orchestration of blows and untuned sounds is set against the dignified silence of the Lord. Christ is here a model of the virtue of Patience. Indeed, this entire scene, like the York Passion's scenes of trials and torturing which follow, seems clearly influenced by the representation of the virtue of Patience in medieval iconography.

In an illustration in a ninth-century *Psychomachia* manuscript,[65] Patientia stands amid the threatening figures of the Vices. And as late as the sixteenth century, Patientia still is visualized, in the engraving from a series of Virtues formerly attributed to Brueghel, as quietly enduring amid the threatening representation of an upside-down world of human depravity and malevolence. So Christ's suffering at the hands of his torturers somehow had become associated in men's minds with this Virtue in particular. Hence a depiction of the Flagellation—more violent than the Buffeting—appears in conjunction with Patientia on the Shrine of the Three Kings at Cologne Cathedral.[66]

Informing the medieval idea of Patience is also the Old Testament figure of Job, who often appears in conjunction with representations of this Virtue.[67] Job is, of course, not only a model of patience, but also a figure of Christ's sufferings and Passion. St. Jerome had written: "Job dolens interpretatur Jesus Christus, qui dolores nostros portavit."[68] The demonic princes of the church and of this world would brag about their reservoir of power which they apparently believe places them above law and morality; Jesus, whose sovereignty is genuine in the world, glories in being submissive. Like Job, he accepts the affliction which comes to him. The sores which are opened up over every part of his body in the Flagellation are then to be compared to Job's boils. A twelfth-century manuscript asks, "For did not Our Lord also sit *in stercore* when He appeared in human form in the den of our iniquity? Through His Passion He has scraped off the poison of our iniquity."[69]

Through all his anguish in Plays XXIX–XXXIII, the most striking element is perhaps Jesus' silence. Beyond a few simple and brief denials, he speaks only twice to his accusers: once to Caiaphas (XXIX.312ff) and once to Pilate (XXXIII.300–07). In presenting an essentially silent Savior, the dramatist, as Rosemary Woolf has noted, has borrowed from the *Meditations* a Christ who does not answer back when accused of everything from witchcraft to sedition:

> The author of *Meditationes* conceives Christ's silence as a sign of his patience and humility: though the gospels record Christ speaking, yet for the purpose of devising a devout meditation the author felt free to rely upon Isaiah liii.7: 'He was oppressed, and he was afflicted, yet he opened not his mouth: he is brought as a lamb to the slaughter, and as a sheep before her shearers is dumb, so he openeth not his mouth.' In the mystery cycles this idea is part of the effect but not the whole. Far from Christ's silence being solely a manifestation of his unquestioned submission to human suffering, it becomes rather a sublime expression of his divinity; where elevated language could only fail, silence becomes a magnificent symbol of the inexpressible.[70]

As another reminder of the dignified and silent Christ's divinity, the York Realist introduces into Play XXXIII an extended episode borrowed from the apocryphal *Gospel of Nicodemus*, in which the banners bow to him automatically[71] ("þis werke þat we haue wrought it was not oure will," the banner bearers insist, XXXIII.183). Even when the strongest men available are brought to hold them, the banners still bow (XXXIII.204–67). Pilate himself – a composite character of good and bad[72] – finds now that he "myght noȝt abstene/To wirschip hym in wark and in witte" (XXXIII.274–75). In the light of what appears to be a miracle and of the priests' continuing accusations, Pilate demands that Christ should "Speke, and excuse þe if þou can" (XXXIII.299). When Jesus answers, he only comments on idle words, for which men shall be held accountable at the Last Day (XXXIII.300–07).

But hostile words will shortly be replaced by hostile blows as Pilate, threatened now in his insistence on sovereignty by someone who claims to be king of the Jews, orders his knights to "Skelpe hym with scourges and with skathes hym scorne./ Wrayste and wrynge hym to, for wo to he be wepyng" (XXXIII. 337–38). The word *skathes*, from the Old Norse *skathe*, means "hurt, harm, damage."[73] He will now indeed be beaten with scourges, whips of the kind shown in one of the panels of the St. Martin window in St. Martin-le-Grand and in the Penancers' window in the nave of the Minster.[74] He will be beaten until he has suffered harm and hurt over his whole body, as in a miniature in the *Bolton Hours* (fol.57ᵛ). But when the Flagellation is completed, he will reveal his true character through his appearance even more clearly to the audience, though Pilate, despite his curiosity and his order that the men "Wrayste" him, will never be able to penetrate to the truth about him. To the audience at York, this event shows indeed how Christ is the antitype of Job. During the beating, Christ speaks no word of complaint. The wounds which the blows make on his naked body – in the play apparently represented by a white leather suit such as had also been used to display the "nude" Adam and Eve in their innocence[75] – will present an appearance very like Job with his boils over his whole body.[76] In a devotional image from St. Saviour's, York (now in All Saints, Pavement), the scourged and nude Christ, his hands and feet manacled, appears seated.

The depiction of the Flagellation in the play by the York Realist is clearly in many ways similar to what is pictured in the visual arts. But there are some problems too. Normally Christ is bound to a pillar – an item of considerable significance in York, one would think, since a piece of it was given to the Minster in 1418 – as in most examples in art and in the other three extant Middle English cycles.[77] Nevertheless, no column seems to be mentioned in the text. Yet if such a detail were for some reason omitted from the production of the York play, an opportunity for accurate iconographic tableau would be passed up. The column, it is true, is very stylized in Barnett's copy of an original panel formerly in the Chapter House, but this was an example of thirteenth-century glass and it may not have been possible to copy exactly the design of the early glass at the time when Barnett did his work. Nevertheless, one of the scourges is original, and we may believe that the placement of the torturers on each side of a Christ tied to the column with a rope is accurate. In the *Hours of Catherine of Cleves*, two men are fastening the binding to Christ's arms and feet and lashing him to the pillar, while a third prepares to strike him in the face with his fist. A fourth man holds a scourge above his head in such a way that it extends beyond the frame of the miniature into the border: he is surely bent upon hitting the Lord with as much force as he can muster.[78]

In the York Flagellation scene, the soldiers' brutality quickly becomes dominant. They mercilessly strike the fainting Jesus, whom they scornfully accuse of napping ("We sall wakken hym with wynde of oure whippes," the third soldier insists, XXXIII.365), and then set forth to beat every part of his body systematically. They name the parts as they proceed; "hippes" (l. 367), "haunch" (l. 368), "lippis" (l. 370), "paunch" (l. 371). At line 375, the second soldier pulls "at his pilche" or leather coat – calling attention perhaps to the white leather suit or body stocking possibly worn by the actor playing Christ to present nudity or near-nudity in a modest manner, but also surely pointing out the wounded and bleeding skin of Christ. "Thus youre cloke sall we cloute to clence you and clere ʒou," the third soldier sneers (XXXIII.376), unconscious of the irony of his statement. The irony would not have been lost on the audience, however. Christ is indeed the one who through the pain of this ordeal is in fact cleansing and clearing all those who will be his followers for the remainder of history.

The Flagellation fails to stir Christ to any response other than pa-
tient suffering, and after he loses consciousness for a few moments
("He swounes or sweltes," XXXIII.383), action moves quickly to
the Mocking in which the soldiers "will kyndely hym croune with a
brere" and clothe him in "purpure and palle" (XXXIII.389–90). As
the fourth soldier explains, "þis worthy wede sall he were, / For
scorne" (XXXIII.391–92). He is given "a rede / So rounde" to serve
as "his septure" (XXXIII.403–05). The soldiers kneel before him in
mockery, as they do in medieval art and drama from the time of the
early twelfth-century mosaics at S. Angelo in Formis and the
Montecassino Passion Play.[79] Their *"Aue,* riall roy and *rex
judeorum"* (XXXIII.408) spills over into a series of "hails" that
echo the "hails" of Christ's admirers in the *Entry into Jerusalem.*[80]
During the "hails" of the soldiers, presumably at least one of them
(the second soldier) does not kneel; most likely he flaps Christ
about the head with a stave as the others mock him. The fourth
soldier's "Hayll, freyke without forse þe to fende" (XXXIII.414)
would seem to be in response to such humiliating hitting or some
other similar act which Jesus does nothing to deflect. These
soldiers surely appear as frightening and as dreadful as those men
who surround Jesus in the famous *Christ Mocked* by Hieronymus
Bosch.[81] The York Realist cannot call upon such surrealistic details
as the spiked dog collar which one of Bosch's men wears,
presumably to show that, as the *Meditations* indicate, he was "truly
. . . surrounded by many terrible and ferocious dogs."[82] But the
Realist nevertheless utilizes the lively realism at his disposal to
make the scene believable as drama. The raucous scene then ends in
a way designed to appeal to the audience for whom the plays were
written — an audience that was at least in part attuned to a desire to
receive spiritual blessing from seeing the plays. The Mocking ends
with the first soldier's ironic request to Jesus for thanks and for
blessing on their deeds:

> We, harlott, heve vp thy hande,
> And vs all þat þe wirschip are wirkand
>   Thanke vs, þer ill mot þou þryve. (XXXIII.417–19)

Thus the tumult concludes, and Christ is returned to Pilate, who
will wash his hands of his death when the high priests and the
people continue to demand his crucifixion.

III

The plays depicting the events between the Last Supper and the Crucifixion written for the York cycle by a dramatist whom we know as the York Realist embody a serious attempt to set forth the Passion vividly and in a manner which would prove effective before a popular audience. Their spirituality is marked by those characteristics which have been linked with the religious perspective of rich merchants and others who generously gave windows of painted glass and other objects of religious art to churches, cathedrals, and chantry chapels in the early fifteenth century. There is an emotionalism present—an emotionalism which characterized the Christianity of Northern Europe especially from the fourteenth century through the early part of the sixteenth century. The concern of the men who made up the Corporation was to provide plays which would draw upon this emotionalism and which would make men *feel* as deeply as possible the spiritual reality of the Passion and Crucifixion. The result is an emphasis that has been found offensive by more recent historical periods; nevertheless, the desire for personal identification with the sufferings of Christ was then very real. The tone of at least a portion of the York Realist's work has something in common with a fourteenth-century poem in Harley MS. 2316 in which the speaker, remembering that his "leman swete," Christ, has died for his sins "on rode tre," now wishes that the love of Christ may be rooted in his heart "as was ʒe spere in-to [his] side, / whan [he] suffredis ded for me."[83]

The whole design of the Passion series in the York cycle shows attention to the dramatic ordering of events, with the movement of the action focused on the central scene of the Christian story— the crucifixion and death of the sacrificial Lamb of God. The successful utilization of realistic detail to make the iconographic features of the events come to life is indicative of immense dramatic skill, which, along with the masterful versification, ought to make the York Realist one of the major writers of the Middle English period. But whatever the modern assessment of his work, it is clear that his contribution to the York Passion was what the city fathers of York wanted, for his plays continued to be played presumably for more than a hundred years – until in 1569 the Protestant authorities forced the mysteries to end in the city of York. In that year Matthew Hutton, whose effigy is still to be seen in the Minster in the south choir aisle, complained that though the Corpus Christi play "was plausible 40 yeares agoe, and wold now also of the ignorant sort be well liked: yet now in this happie time of the gospell, I knowe the learned will mislike it and how the state will beare with it I knowe not."[84]

1. Cain and Abel. Great East Window, York Minster.

2. The Fall. Great East Window, York Minster.

3. Expulsion (above) and Adam and Eve laboring after the Fall (below). York Psalter, MS. Hunter 229, Glasgow University Library.

4. Sacrifice of Isaac. York Psalter,
MS. Hunter 229,
Glasgow University Library.

9. Corpus Christi. Painted glass from St. John's Church,
Ousebridge, York, and now in York Minster.

10. Crucifixion (detail). Restored painted glass
in York Minster Nave.

11. Christ being placed on the cross. Painted glass now
in Church of All Saints, Pavement, York.

12. Pentecost. Painted glass in York Minster Nave.

13. Supper at Emmaus. Painted glass now in church
of All Saints, Pavement, York.

14. Resurrection. Bolton Hours, York Minster Library MS. Add. 2.

15. Ascension. Bolton Hours, York Minster Library MS. Add. 2.

16. Corporal Acts of Mercy: Feeding the Hungry. Painted glass
in Church of All Saints, North Street, York.

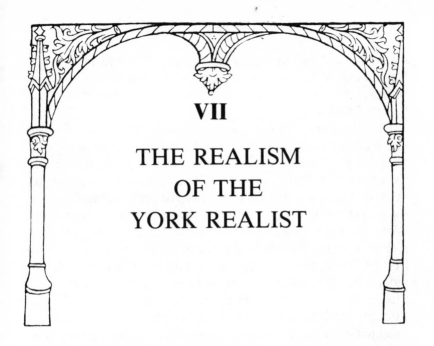

VII

THE REALISM
OF THE
YORK REALIST

The style of the gifted anonymous dramatist whom scholars now identify as the York Realist was recognized long ago by Charles Mills Gayley, who spoke of his work as belonging to a "realistic period" and noted that the dramatist himself is distinguished "by his observation of life, his reproduction of manners, his dialogue, and plasticity of his technique: whether in presentation of the comic, or of the tragic and horrible, aspect of his narrative."[1] More recently, J. W. Robinson presented evidence to illustrate more specifically the nature of the playwright's concern for detail, for dramatic use of dialogue, and for realistic presentation of human behavior.[2] In the discussion that has followed the publication of Robinson's article almost two decades ago, however, even the term *realism* has been questioned with regard to its appropriateness for late medieval drama.[3] Nevertheless, though there are some ways in which his interpretations need qualification, an argument still can be made for retaining *realism* as the best word to describe one aspect of the work of the York Realist, particularly in those plays which he contributed to the Passion series. It is urgent, however, that we understand precisely what we mean by *realism*, and that this understanding should be carefully balanced with attention to the traditional and iconographic elements in the Realist's plays, for if we may borrow some words by Rosemary Woolf out of context, these scenes "should not be . . . explained solely in terms of realism."[4]

In the previous chapter it was suggested that the York Realist, like many of the skilled artists and painters who were his contemporaries, believed primarily that he was giving new life to the symbolic pictorial narrative of the Passion. From the standpoint of aesthetic experience as well as of philosophical inquiry, the previous century had meant increased interest in *particulars*. While the painters and the York Realist perhaps did not completely share the thoroughgoing phenomenalism of the nominalists at Oxford, they nevertheless no longer tended to follow the older practice of eliminating the arbitrary individual detail from their work. Seemingly irrelevant details often provide the means through which an illusion of reality may be impressed upon the imagination of the audience. This tendency in art is perceptively identified by Erwin Panofsky as a "modernistic rebellion" among Northern artists who craved "for volume and space as opposed to two dimensional patterns, for light and color as opposed to line, for concrete, particularized reality as opposed to abstract, generalized formulae." This rebellion, according to Panofsky, is "comparable indeed to the *philosophia moderna* of those nominalists who found the quality of real existence only in things 'individual by virtue of themselves and by nothing else'."[5] There is a turning to immediate experience, to detail, to individuality as sources for an affective art.

Thus, for example, in the York Realist's trial of Jesus before Herod, the monarch is individualized and at the same time is given a wonderful liveliness through his indecorous behavior, which is set forth in a unique manner. The king even invents his own language—"*Seruicia primet,*/Such losellis and lurdaynes as þou, loo,/*Respicias timet.*/What þe deuyll and his dame schall Y now doo?" (XXXI.243–46)—as he combines being offended (at Jesus' disregard for his royalty) with attempting to have fun at the Savior's expense. Thereby Herod, who assumes that Jesus is mad or a fool, illustrates the ultimate foolishness of those who reject salvation. In this way the York Realist, like the

Northern painters, brings together such elaboration of specific detail in a realistic manner with the system of symbolism and meaning with which certain scenes in Christian history had been imbued for centuries. In the work of the York Realist, iconography and realistic detail co-exist.

Another instance which illustrates the relationship between detail and meaning occurs when the York Pilate's attendant urges him to "wasshe whill þe watir is hote" (XXXIII.443). Robinson is properly impressed by this detail. "Other medieval dramatists (and more learned exegetes, too)," he insists, "would not normally concern themselves with the temperature of the water in which Pilate washed his hands — the allegorical meaning, perhaps, but not the temperature."[6] Yet in both philosophy and art of the early fifteenth century, the tendency of the age was toward depiction of such seemingly irrelevant details as the concern of Pilate's attendant and the temperature of the water. As Meyrick H. Carré notes, "One tendency of the new school of thinkers was the inclination to seek for reality in the individual thing in preference to the universal entity. Associated with this trend there appeared increased emphasis upon intuition or sensory apprehension in knowledge."[7] While painting could never concern itself directly with such a sensory experience as the temperature of the water, artists too were capable of showing great sensitivity through visual details. Thus in a miniature in the splendid *Hours of Catherine of Cleves*, dated 1430–40, the attendant pouring water over Pilate's hands is also shown to be very solicitous of his master's comfort, for he has a towel draped over his shoulder in readiness. In spite of the fact that both his hands are presently occupied with pouring the water, he will have the towel ready for Pilate when he needs it.[8] Surely the towel in the book of hours is the visual analogue of the beadle's care about the temperature of the water in the play. However, in neither instance is the symbolic meaning of Pilate's act of washing abrogated.[9] Indeed, the vividness with which the symbolic act is dramatized is designed to draw attention to it and hence to underline its meaning.

Hence the York Realist in his concern for vivid details succeeded in filling out scenes and broadening his understanding of characters.

For example, even a villain such as Judas appears in the York
Passion as something more than a "flat" character or symbolic
representation of man's evil nature. Of course he is still the archetypal betrayer, but he is also a human being who *feels* envy
and greed, then unfortunately reacts in such a manner that he
will *act* on the basis of such feelings. Therefore he is plunged
convincingly into tragedy and finally into a despair that will lead
him ultimately to suicide and damnation. The scene in which
Judas meets Caiaphas and Annas will curiously take place at
Pilate's mansion, to which he has trouble gaining entrance. The
Porter decides that he does not like Judas' appearance — "Thy
glyfftyng is so grymly þou gars my harte growe" (XXVI.158) — and
the lively exchange which follows draws heavily upon particular-
izing details. Even after the betrayer had indicated that he has come
to keep "youre dugeperes" from possible injury (XXVI.181–83),
the Porter with the typical officiousness of a bureaucrat must
first consult with his lords before Judas may be let in. Then,
utilizing material from the popular sermon tradition, the York
Realist gives Judas a *motive* for betraying Jesus. He wants the
thirty pence he would have stolen had the precious ointment
brought by Mary Magdalene been sold,[10] for as treasurer for the
disciples he had made a practice of diverting a tithe to himself:
"The tente parte þat stale I ay still" (XXVI.138).

   Finally, in a triumph of realism, the York Realist arranges his
portrayal of Judas' betrayal agreement so that this character is
made to play a role which considerably narrows the distance between him and his audience's experience. Like a merchant, he
offers a bargain to the trio Caiaphas, Annas, and Pilate. They
begin questioning Judas closely about his offer in preparation
for haggling over the price, and finally Pilate asks, "Now what
schall we pay?" (XXVI.229). Of course they agree at once that
Judas' price, only thirty pence, is indeed a great bargain. The
eagerness with which they accept Judas' fee gives a moving impression of something most valuable sold for a ridiculously small
price. (In the early fifteenth century, thirty pence was not, of
course, the infinitesimal sum that it would be today. York records show that in 1396 Robert Paton was paid twelve pence for
working [presumably with his assistants] as a carpenter "for

pageant building." That same year "the painting for the pageants" cost two shillings.[11] In 1501, when the York Realist's plays were still being played in York, the Coventry accounts show that two shillings sixpence purchased five yards of blue buckram.[12]) The horror and foolishness of what Judas is doing are not suppressed, but rather the dimensions of the drama are expanded so that the scene with its bargaining may more effectively capture the attention of the members of the audience, many of whom were themselves tradesmen or merchants. A new scope has surely been added to the story of Judas' betrayal through the introduction of realistic details which make the biblical event come to life as a dramatic experience designed to affect a particular audience.

The extent of the York Realist's attention to realistic detail and his use of such detail may be judged by comparison of the York scene in which Judas sells his Lord with the same scene in the Montecassino Passion. In the earlier liturgical drama from Montecassino, Judas merely makes arrangements for the betrayal in thirty lines of formalized verse.[13] The Montecassino Judas, who is purely evil, is not individualized as a character, and his actions seem to be little more than what would minimally be needed to transfer the scene of betrayal from the miniature in the *Codex Purpureus Rossanensis* or from the sculpture at Modena Cathedral into dramatic form.[14] The betrayer simply appears at the synagogue where he meets Caiaphas, explains that he too sees Jesus as a threat, and offers to betray him. Caiaphas responds with the money. While the aesthetic impact of a drama such as the Montecassino Passion can be very powerful when presented before an audience prepared to appreciate it, it is not popular drama and would surely have seemed inappropriate for a crowd of flourishing tradesmen in a fifteenth-century city such as York. The York Realist, on the other hand, deliberately sets out to flesh out the bare story and to make it come to life. He is interested in the appearance of reality—an appearance of reality which will help to bring home to the audience the truths told in the story. Thus his work may be compared to the accomplishments of the Northern painters whose experiments with perspective assisted them to create a life-like quality. Such concern with perspective and a life-like quality has been identified also in the York glass painters such as John Thornton of Coventry.

In contrast to the liturgical drama and earlier vernacular plays, the work of the York Realist stands apart from that medieval aesthetic which, informed by *philosophical* realism, had encouraged the artist to attempt to capture the essential meaning of a scene or event without drawing upon unnecessary or unwarranted details. For this dramatist as for nominalists such as William of Ockham, the key to reality is through "immediate present experience."[15] However, the York Realist refused to discard traditional iconography in his depiction of scenes from the Passion of Christ. He wants to have it both ways: he utilizes particulars since these give life to the play, while at the same time, as will be shown below, he also relies heavily on traditional ways of communicating through iconography. Hence he inventively presents the sensual Procula amorously flaunting herself in Play XXX, though, as we know, she is actually included in the drama for reasons which extend beyond realism for its own sake. As we have seen, she had been present in dramatic representations of this scene as early as the Montecassino play,[16] and now in the work of the York Realist represents individualized human concupiscence allied with external forces of evil against the Savior of men. Through his realism, the York Realist is able in this scene to elaborate upon the bare outline of events as told in their source, the apocryphal *Gospel of Nicodemus*. The elaboration is not frivolous, for it is designed to present the story with a greater sense of vividness and to relate its meaning more effectively to the lives of the members of the audience. Hence the York Realist sets out to create a more emotionally charged drama than had hitherto been presented at York. The final effect of this drama is not to focus attention only on the particulars, but rather to point to the truths of the Christian story as these are to be made applicable to the lives of all those who look upon the spectacle.

In the York Passion, the work of the Realist combines both its realism and its iconography toward producing a desired emotional response. The culmination of the Passion sequence in the event of the Crucifixion is orchestrated so that its appeal will be both to the head and the heart — but especially to the heart. Essentially this is not a drama written to support the optimistically rational theology of St. Thomas Aquinas, but rather, as the previous chapter has suggested, it shows real affinity with the popular exposition of Christianity as expounded by the Franciscans. The York Realist would seem to believe that religious drama ought not to stop when it has told its audience "*about*" the Passion; he wishes further to draw them into "direct acquaintance with" a re-enactment of the historical event.[17] Thus apprehended, it involves a series of events toward which no viewer could be expected to remain coolly unemotional.

The high point of the Passion series comes, of course, at the Crucifixion, which received perhaps its most vivid prose description in the *Meditations on the Life of Christ*. In the *Meditations*, each detail of Christ's treatment is given minute scrutiny.[18] Such careful attention to particulars also marks the plays by the York Realist. Unfortunately, except for a few lines at the beginning of Play XXXIV, the Shearmen's *Road to Calvary*, neither the approach to the site of the cross nor the *Crucifixio Christi* (Play XXXV) are by the York Realist. When the Realist picks up the story in the excellent *Mortificacio Christi*, he is able to do full justice to this final drama in the Passion series. Here at last is the end of the process which was begun when Judas agreed with the high priests and Pilate to betray his Master. At the beginning of the play, Christ is hanging on the cross, but not as an isolated figure. The whole scene of the Crucifixion is here spread out before the audience, with spoken dialogue and visual effect combining to create a vivid spectacle designed to impress itself upon more than the mere intellects of those who are watching.

The *Mortificacio Christi* opens with the terrible liveliness of those who have condemned Christ and who now stand by to watch and jeer. Pilate, concerned about his sovereignty, speaks first: those who rebel against his authority may see what their reward will be if they will only look at the men on the crosses. He is, nevertheless, sorry about Jesus who has been crucified because of the malice and envy of the high priests rather than because of any guilt. The two priests, however, have no such doubts: they mock Jesus for the statements he had made and for the miracles he had performed before his arrest. "If þou be funne / To be Goddis sonne, / We schalle be bonne / To trowe on þe trewlye ilkone," the sneering Caiaphas tells him (XXXVI.101–04). But Christ on the cross *is* the suffering Son of God who patiently looks out from the perspective of the cross upon a turbulent and sinful world. The contrast between his enemies and the dying Lord emphasizes the pain of hanging on the cross as well as his forgiving attitude toward all men. Everyone is implicitly invited to become acquainted with the physical suffering of his crucifixion, which he is enduring so that all men who are repentant may be rescued from their misdeeds.[19]

The presentation of realistic detail in the Crucifixion thus, as in the fashion of showing this scene among the fifteenth-century Northern painters, performs the function of stimulating an emotional response. The realism does not have its end in itself, but in the desire to make the audience *feel* what is being presented in the playing area, for only when the Passion and Crucifixion are felt can the iconography of the tableau have its desired effect. Such an effect would have been inconceivable, of course, in the early Christian centuries, the period when Christian iconography was slowly being developed as the sacred science of luminous and talismanic figures which point to the divine realities.

As we know, only after the eleventh and twelfth centuries did the Crucifixion generally become the soteriological center of the Christian story. Thus for the new order founded by St. Francis of Assisi in the thirteenth century the cross was available as the emotionally-charged symbol of forgiveness which represented what was believed to be the central fact of Christian existence. By the end of the Middle Ages, as Émile Mâle has complained, *suffering* would seem to have replaced *love* as the central term which might be used to describe what is at the heart of religious art.[20] Christ, by suffering on the cross, presents men with the gift of salvation; as Jesus tells them in the York play, "On roode am I ragged and rente, / þou synfull sawle, for thy sake; / For thy misse amendis wille I make" (XXXVI.120–22).

The anguish that is evidenced in the York *Mortificacio Christi* is completely missing from earlier representations of the Crucifixion such as the previously noted fifth-century ivory in the British Museum which contrasts the death of Judas on the left with a stylized Christ on the cross at the right. Similarly, Anglo-Saxon ivories showing the Crucifixion stress neither the pain of this most inhumane form of execution, nor the visible effects of the Flagellation.[21] All this had long changed by the time of the completion of the fourteenth-century window which depicts the Crucifixion in the west end of the nave (south aisle) of York Minster (plate 10). In this window, given to the Minster by Thomas de Beneston in 1338–39 (and unfortunately very clumsily restored in the eighteenth century), Christ's arms are painfully extended upward to the points on the cross where they are attached. Small mourning angels fly about the victim, whose suffering appears here to be much in evidence.[22] Yet the York Minster window does not reach the level of affective display that was achieved in the fifteenth century in, for example, the *Hours of Catherine of Cleves*, which contains a miniature[23] representing the Savior, his wounds still bleeding profusely, at the time of his death. On each side of Christ, the two thieves, brutally tied with their arms stretched over the cross-pieces of their crosses, frame the central event, which is calculated to touch the emotions through its pathos. Even some of the angelic and animal figures in the borders of this illumination show sorrow or anguish.

This kind of realism in which the smallest details become of intense interest and the source of emotional response is often, as F. P. Pickering has shown, the result of visualizing imagery in the most literalistic way.[24] The source of Crucifixion imagery is often the psalms, which were drawn upon to fill out the lack of information about Christ's death in the Gospels. In contrast to the simple representation of Jesus in the *orans* position adopted in pre-eleventh century art, later art as well as the York *Crucifixio Christi* and *Mortificacio Christi* stress the most painful details — details which are frequently inspired by the way in which the Crucifixion was foreshadowed in Old Testament texts. In the first of these two plays, which is not written by the Realist though his hand may be traced in it perhaps as a reviser, the torturers attempt to place Christ on the cross while it is on the ground, but they find that the holes in the cross are drilled too far apart ("It failis a foote and more," the third soldier announces, XXXV.107). As in many examples in the arts (e.g., the famous painting by Gerard David, a miniature in the *Holkham Bible Picture Book*, fol. 31^V, and an alabaster noticed by Hildburgh), they apply a rope to stretch Christ's body to fit the cross—an action that pulls his sinews "asoundre" (XXXV.132); the scene[25] is one that is depicted in York art in a panel of c.1370 now in All Saints, Pavement (plate 11). In this example, the men are driving the nails into the hands and feet with hammers following the stretching of Jesus' body. With his body taut on the cross so that the ribs are seen, we are to be reminded of Psalm 22—"all my bones are out of joint. . . . For dogs have compassed me: the assembly of the wicked have inclosed me: they pierced my hands and my feet" (*A V*). But the figure of Christ on the cross now becomes at once more grotesque and more vivid through another dimension of this realism, including its literalizing of Psalms 57 and 69. As Pickering notes, even the symbol of the harp, which we associate with the psalmist David, becomes also associated with Christ and then literalized: Christ's body is stretched like the strings of this musical instrument, with the nails functioning as the tuning pegs.[26] Christ has become the harp (*cithara*) mentioned in the psalm, and his pain is also paradoxically the source of harmony for men and women who rightly meditate upon his suffering. For this reason the depictions in the visual arts began more and more to stress the pain and the suffering as something the believer ought to empathize with in the most profound way.[27] A fourteenth-century poem exclaims: "swete be þe nalys,/and swete be þe tre,/and sweter be þe birdyn þat hangis vppon the!"[28] Such an emphasis upon sweetness, however, did not deny the reality of the details of the Passion and Crucifixion as these are presented, for example, in the illustrations in the painted glass of York Minster or in the illuminations of the *Hours of Catherine of Cleves*.

The final stage in the development must surely be the central panel of the Isenheim Altarpiece by Matthias Grünewald early in the sixteenth century. At his death, the body of Grünewald's Christ is literally covered with sores from the ill treatment he has received. Thorns stick in his flesh from the crown of thorns which is still in place on his head. The terror of death as the termination of suffering is here mirrored in a manner that goes far beyond what must have been presented in the York *Mortificacio Christi*. Nevertheless, the York play, too, was obviously in performance tending in the direction of such realism as we find in Grünewald. The scene depicted on stage must have been emotionally stirring.

The York Passion indeed is in the spirit of the *Meditations*, for it urges the Christian spectator to utilize the scenes which he sees as an aid to meditation. He is to meditate on the overwhelming affliction felt by the Lord. He is to have "hyhe compassion" for the torments which he witnesses, for he will see Christ "so tormented/that fro the sole of the foote, in to the hyhest parte of the hede/there was in hym none hole place, ne membre withoute passion."[29] As Joseph of Arimathea says in the *Mortificacio Christi* when he approaches to take down the body, "All mankynde may marke in his mynde/To see here þis sorowfull sight . . ." (XXXVI.365–66).

The audience's attention is carefully focused on the event and its significance when the York Realist dramatizes the Reproaches of Christ to mankind ("Þus for thy goode/I schedde my bloode./Manne, mende thy moode,/For full bittir þi blisse mon I by" (XXXVI.127–30). The Reproaches or *improperia* as they appear in the York play are, of course, liturgical in origin; as a form they are, in fact, "extremely ancient," having appeared in England as early as the *Regularis concordia* in the tenth century.[30] In the hands of the York Realist, their conventional form actually increases their dramatic effectiveness, for at this point the audience receives more powerfully than elsewhere the impression that this is what it was actually like when Christ was crucified.

Similarly traditional in the *Mortificacio Christi* is the Virgin's lament or *planctus*. Like the Reproaches, the *planctus* is characterized by the York Realist's concern for appropriateness and tact. Rosemary Woolf notes (p. 265) that the "author allows the elaborate and harmonious stanza form to impose a shape upon the content of distress, so that the Virgin does not appear distracted and uncontrolled but has rather the reserves of dignity befitting her pre-eminence." The Virgin remembers how "full louely" Christ "laye/In [her] wombe" (XXXVI.133–34), and bewails the fact that this day she must be separated from him. She thinks of Jesus on the cross as "þis blossome so bright" which is unhappily grafted to the tree of the cross, and complains that she has been smitten by a "swerde of sorowe" (XXXVI.137–38, 159). At the moment of his death, she tells him that her "harte is heuy as leede" before she comes suddenly to the realization that he is no longer living (XXXVI.262–64).

The striking emotionalism of the York Realist's presentation of the death of Christ is continued in his depiction of the Deposition. This indeed appears to be a scene that is intentionally sensational. Joseph of Arimathea and Nicodemus slowly and sorrowfully take down Christ's body after the suffering is completed.

> Betwene vs take we hym doune
> And laie hym on lenthe on þis lande. (XXXVI.378–79)

Yet, in contrast to the Towneley Crucifixion's presentation of the mechanics of the Deposition, little attention seems to be wasted on such matters here. If Nicodemus pulled the nails which hold the body to the cross, as in the painted glass from St. Saviour's Church, York (now in All Saints, Pavement), in an English alabaster now in the Victoria and Albert Museum, and in the miniature in the *Très-Belles Heures de Notre Dame*,[31] there is at least no indication for him to do so in the text of the York play, though in performance he may well have performed this function. The emphasis is on the manner in which the two men take Christ from the cross and lift him down between them, as in another alabaster sculpture also in the Victoria and Albert Museum.[32] As they lift him down, Joseph and Nicodemus show off the broken body of Christ and form a tableau which, if we may judge from the painting by Roger van der Weyden[33] or the miniature in the *Belles Heures* of the Duke of Berry,[34] must have been felt deeply by sensitive members of the audience. This way of presenting the Deposition goes back in the West to the *St. Albans Psalter*, where apparently for the first time the "incident itself . . . furnishes only a kind of substructure or pretext for the staging of a grandiose lamentation over the crucified Saviour in the Golgotha setting. Nicodemus seems to be less concerned with carrying out his work and completing the descent of the deceased than with presenting Christ's body and holding it in a position which affords to the mourners the best opportunity of showing their affection and grief."[35] In the York *Mortificacio Christi*, the mourners are members of the audience who have been drawn into the sorrow which is represented, for the Virgin Mary and others have left the stage at line 273. The scene is designed to bring tears to all eyes.

The handling of this scene in the York play has something in common with the details and the feeling of a passage in the York *Hours of the Cross* from a manuscript book of hours in the York Minster Library.[36] "At þe tyme of euen-sang þai tok hym fro þe rod . . . ," the text explains, then continues until the passage culminates in a statement linking the Deposition with one's own moral condition ("lord for þat ilk schame þat þu doun was tane/lat neuer my saul wit deydly syn be schlayne"). Following is the *incipit* of the Latin text from which the English is translated — a text that concludes with the *Adoramus te* which contains the *Responsorium* "Qui[a] per sanctam crucem tuam redimisti mundum."[37] In the York *Hours*, of course, the emotional effect of the scene would be dependent upon the quality of the individual's piety, while in the York play the paradox of a death designed to give men life is dramatized fully in an attempt to insure that all might not fail to feel the sorrow and meaning of this event. It is to be noted, for example, that once Joseph and Nicodemus have laid the body on the ground, they then raise it up once more before they take it to the grave which Joseph has prepared. Here is an opportunity for a visual effect beyond the reach of the ritualized York *Hours* — and it is an opportunity which is not missed.

As the vehicle for visual display, the York play's Deposition scene cannot be unrelated to another display of Christ's wounded and crucified body — the *Corpus Christi*. Indeed, the York Realist has arranged for the showing of Christ in a pose similar to this familiar design as it was seen in a number of painted glass windows at York.[38] Furthermore, the Realist's purpose in showing off the body cannot be dissociated from the religious purpose behind the Corpus Christi windows,[39] nor is it unrelated to the Feast of Corpus Christi, which, of course, provided the occasion for the procession with the host and the York cycle of plays. At the Deposition scene, therefore, the York Realist has in a sense summed up the entire Passion and Crucifixion. Thus was the audience reminded of the centrality of the sacrifice of Christ on the cross within the pattern of Christian history.

Of particular interest is the way in which the body of Christ is represented in the Corpus Christi subject, for the figure in painted glass may be taken as evidence of details the medieval audience expected to see. The glass from St. John's, Ousebridge, now in the north transept of York Minster, presents a Christ who has endured much suffering (plate 9). The wounds are vividly depicted, and also include bleeding bruises all over his body from the flagellation ordered by Pilate. In any case, as noted above, it cannot be denied that both the windows and the Deposition scene in the play allow for showing Christ's body in approximately the same posture and generally for the same purpose.

The audience in the Deposition scene of the *Mortificacio Christi* is clearly being invited to meditate on the whole meaning of Christ's Passion. Basic to the York Realist's understanding of the event is, of course, his belief that Christ in his Passion and Crucifixion gave his body for the salvation of the world. Such also is the message of the liturgy of the Feast of Corpus Christi. This liturgy contains many references implicitly linking Christ's body, sacrificed for men, with the continuing practice of the sacrifice of the Mass.[40] The showing of the body in the *Mortificacio Christi* by Joseph of Arimathea and Nicodemus as they take him from the cross and again after he has been laid upon the ground may thus be regarded as a realistic presentation of the sacrificed human and yet divine body—a body which is present in essence in the host at Mass and which is also associated with the forgiveness of sin. The doctrine which links Christ's sacrifice with divine forgiveness is very clearly illustrated in a fourteenth-century illumination from a Carmelite Missal: the trinitarian *Corpus Christi* is seen above, with a priest baptizing an infant below—i.e., performing a rite associated with removing the stains of sin.[41] And as

John Thoresby, archbishop of York, wrote in 1357, "the sacrement of the auter [is] cristes owen bodi in likeness of brede . . ." ("Eucharistia est unum corpus Christi," the official Latin proclaimed).[42] The play, like the rite, takes men back to the original event, *but unlike the liturgical observance*, it does so by encouraging men to use their imaginations when they place themselves at the foot of the cross on stage. Instead of asserting, as in the rite of the Eucharist, that the *reality* but not the appearance of the Crucifixion is present, the drama plays with appearances. Stage illusion is thus consciously manipulated so that people may see the appropriate details—bleeding hands, feet, and side as well as the bloody marks of the torture and flagellation which Christ had previously suffered. The York Realist invites his audience to suspend its disbelief and thereby to discover experientially what it would have been like to look upon the historical event. This could never have been the case in the earlier liturgical drama where there is no attempt to combine realism with the symbolic action of the play.

The importance of a meditational experience of the kind encouraged by the York Realist in his contributions to the York Passion had been stressed in the *Meditations on the Life of Christ*, which (in Nicholas Love's translation) insists:

> who soo desyreth with thappostle Poule to be Joyeful in the crosse of oure lord ihesu crist / and in the blessid passion / he must with hely meditacion theryn for the grete mysteryes and al the processe therof yf they were inwardly consydered with alle the inward mynde and beholdyng of mannes soule / as I fully trowe they shold brynge that beholder in to a newe state of grace. For to hym that wold serche the passion of oure lorde with all his herte and alle his inward affection there sholde come many deuoute felynges and sterynges that he neuer supposed before. (Sig. N3^{V})

The Franciscan emphasis on an existential acquaintance with the realities of Christian life is here, and it helps to explain the York Realist's purpose in presenting realistic detail, carefully observed manners, and more psychologically accurate characterization than previous drama in the Middle Ages. As an artist, he seeks to drive home the meaning of the Passion in a way that impresses itself upon the whole man and not merely his intellect. The result is an art which, like the preaching of the friars, turns realistic detail[43] to emotional effect — with a tendency to induce tears. A fourteenth-century Middle English lyric sets forth the approved response:

> IHesu my god, ihesu my kyng,
> Þou axist me noon oþir þing,
> but trewe loue and herte ȝernyng,
> And loue teeris with swete mornyng.[44]

The realism of the early Netherlands painters was similarly able to bring tears to the eyes of pious beholders. A cursory look at a book of hours such as the *Hours of Catherine of Cleves* provokes admiration for the workmanship, the vivid and lifelike colors, the ingenuity of the borders, and so forth. But closer examination of the subjects illustrated in the illuminations demonstrates the extent to which the book exploited themes designed to make man remember his fallen nature and his mortality. The representations of the Passion, however, show a single unfallen man who *for our sake* allows himself to be sacrificed as an innocent victim. Here is an art designed to be wept over. Panofsky thus comments with good reason that

> there was a peculiar piety which seemed to distinguish the *intent* of Flemish painting from the more humanistic — and, in a sense, more formalistic — spirit of Italian art . . . Michelangelo is said to have remarked, to the dismay of the saintly Vittoria Colonna, that Flemish paintings *would bring tears to the eyes of the devout* [italics mine], though these were mostly "women, young girls, clerics, nuns, and gentlefolk without much understanding for the true harmony of art."[45]

As the inheritors of Italian Renaissance formalism in art, we thus need to adjust our understanding of the realistic painters of the North, who did not strive for their realism for realism's sake.
 The work of the York Realist also demonstrates that there was in the period following 1415 in the North of England a similar concern which in intent wished to provide assistance to the imaginations of the men and women in the audience in order

to bring them to an existential understanding of and relationship with the divine realities presented through the paradoxical *true illusion* of the play. This is a conclusion that is not contradicted by the external evidence. The Franciscan William Melton was formerly given credit for successfully encouraging in 1426 the separation of the plays from the Feast day of Corpus Christi, though this separation did not in fact take place until c.1476.[46] However, in spite of his concern that persons not lose the benefit of attendance at the services that day on account of the "indulgences granted to them in that matter by Pope Urban IV of happy memory," he nevertheless also specifically approved the playing of the plays. As the entry in the *York Memorandum Book* notes, Melton, "coming to this city, has commended the said play to the people in several of his sermons, by affirming that it was good in itself and most laudable."[47] As a man trained in theology at Oxford (the *York Memorandum Book* identifies him as "sacre pagine professor") and known as an effective preacher,[48] Melton most likely would have approved of any drama intended to bring an audience to an aesthetic experience and understanding of the Passion. Surely Melton was a man less interested in "the true harmony of art" than in inspiring people to respond existentially and emotionally to the scenes presented by the plays. Thus it is more than likely that he would have been sincerely respectful toward an art form that encouraged pious tears. (To be sure, hysterical tears, such as the "boisterous weeping" of Margery Kempe, were another matter; Melton is reported to have refused to admit her to a series of sermons which he gave at Lynn unless she could control herself and refrain from such a distracting display.[49])

The conscious purpose of the York plays was thus not to provide psychological release into dramatic game or entertainment for its own sake. Indeed, such a response would seem to come under the categories condemned by the friar Melton when he spoke of rowdy citizens and foreigners to the city who "attend not only to the play on that same feast, but also greatly to feastings, drunkenness, clamours, gossipings, and other wantonness."[50] The plays, however, were deliberately designed to impress feelingly upon the people the spectacle of the Christian story.

The realism of the York Realist may be defined, therefore, as a tendency intended to bring to life the meaning of the Christian story as formerly presented through a more strictly symbolic art. It is part of a larger impulse toward perspective and illusion in the arts of the fifteenth century, and it even in a sense looks forward to Coleridge's "willing suspension of disbelief" as a dictum applied to the way the audience is meant to respond to the action on stage. Audiences are encouraged to look upon the play as at a meditational aid and, through the use of their imagination, to acquaint themselves experientially with the important facts and historical events of Christianity. In this drama, the symbolism of the earlier periods is not rejected, but is enveloped in a presentation that seems at once more modern and more emotional than anything which had come before.

VIII

FROM *TRISTIA*
TO *GAUDIUM*

I

The thirty-seventh play in the Register is the *Harrowing of Hell*.[1]
This play opens with a tableau closely related to the conventional
Image of Pity as Christ's soul (Anima Christi) rises from the
grave and begs the audience to

> be meke to me,
> And haue thy maker in þi mynde,
> And thynke howe I haue tholid for þe
> With pereles paynes for to be pyned. (XXXVII.1–4)

The expected response to this tableau surely involves the penitent
feelings and perhaps even the tears which were, as we have seen,
characteristic of civic piety in the fifteenth century in England.[2]
The play thus begins in sorrow—an emotion that is intended to
spring up spontaneously in the hearts of the spectators. But the
play is not static in its presentation of sorrow.

Within the York cycle, the *Harrowing* follows the *Mortificacio
Christi* with its moving Deposition scene. Joseph of Arimathea
and Nicodemus place the body of Christ in a tomb, as we have

seen, and anoint him. The careful display of the body, as we have established, is calculated to evoke the pious tears which are expected to flow again at the sight of Christ's soul rising from the grave at the beginning of the *Harrowing*. In the Deposition scene, the stress is of course upon making the experience of Christ's death come alive imaginatively for audiences, who are invited to discover what it would have been like if they had had the opportunity to witness their Savior's agony, death, and burial historically. Yet, at the end of the Deposition, there is a very distinct movement away from woe as a response and toward an expectation of bliss. As Joseph of Arimathea and Nicodemus indicate by their example, a more thorough understanding of the Crucifixion will evoke joy rather than sorrow. Hence it should not be found surprising that the York *Harrowing of Hell*, which also appears in an adapted form in the *Extraccio animarum* (Play XXV) of the Towneley cycle,[3] should reproduce the movement from *tristia* to *gaudium* which traditionally characterized the Lenten liturgy[4] and which is particularly accentuated in the services for Holy Saturday. Here the Exodus theme is strong: Christ delivered from hell the souls of the righteous who preceded him in history just as God had delivered the people of Israel from Egypt.[5] So also will Christ deliver the souls of his followers from the jaws of the leviathan on the last day of history. Yet, though in the Holy Saturday service the rejoicing has begun because the supreme act of sacrifice has been successfully completed on the cross on the previous day, the sorrow which is the starting point is never really forgotten. As the *Pange lingua* implies, sorrow links together the disobedience associated with the first tree of temptation and the perfect obedience of the good Son on the tree of the cross.[6] The experiencing of sorrow by the pious man hence tends to detach him from the folly of human selfishness and to reconcile him with the source and object of all rejoicing.

From the standpoint of imagery, the York *Harrowing* gives illustration to the movement from *tristia* to *gaudium* through images of light and darkness. Light is of course closely associated with Christ's act of redemption in the liturgy,[7] and therefore explains the first soldier's statement in the Towneley *Processus Talentorum* that the face of Christ on the cross "shoyn as any glas"

(XXIV.83). When his soul rises from the grave in order to go to the rescue of Adam, Eve, and the others who have been confined in hell, the York play gives the following lines to the father of the race:

> Nowe see I signe of solace seere,
>   A glorious gleme to make vs gladde,
> Wherfore I hope oure helpe is nere
>   And sone schall sesse oure sorowes sadde. (XXXVII.41–44)

Eve recognizes the light as the same as that which had originally shone on them "In paradise full playne" (XXXVII.48), and Isaiah appropriately echoes the text of *Isaiah* 9.2: "I spake of folke in mirke walkand/And saide a light schulde on þame lende" (XXXVII.53–54). Christ is the bringer of light, without which there can be no joy.

The pattern which is established in the York *Harrowing* (and in the Towneley *Extraccio animarum*) is hence first of all dependent upon the theology and iconography of the Passion, which must establish Christ's victory and triumph before the deeds chronicled in the harrowing story can be presented. The "contrast between eschatological and human history" noted by O. B. Hardison, Jr., is to the point here, for indeed on the *human* level tears are the appropriate response to the events of Good Friday, while on the *eschatological* level "Christ has already achieved His victory over the *adversarius*."[8] Therefore John Speirs' comment[9] that the harrowing in the Towneley cycle "enacts the victory that follows [a] temporary eclipse" is eschatologically inaccurate. The battle indeed has already taken place, and thus here there is no real "contest between light and darkness." All that remains in the harrowing episode is a mock battle and a ceremonious rescue of souls.

The harrowing episode also certainly does not involve any "new form" or any "proof of the accuracy of Hocart's observation: 'Thus the old beliefs which began before our earliest written records continue to supply Christianity with its imagery'."[10] The imagery of light and other details of symbolism in the *Harrowing* may be traced over an extended period in the iconography of medieval art. Hence the figure of the victorious Christ standing by a set of broken gates and/or symbolically stepping upon the devil (at the same time that he is reaching out to draw Adam from Limbo) had appeared centuries earlier in art and indeed had first evidenced itself in England before the Conquest.[11] This scene is depicted in a miniature in an Anglo-Saxon Psalter (MS. Tiberius C. VI, fol. 14) now in the British Library and also in a mid-eleventh-century sculpture at Bristol Cathedral.[12] While the only warrant in the Bible for the harrowing is a passage in the Epistle to the Ephesians which asserts that Christ "also descended first into the lower parts of the earth" (4.9), Caxton's translation of Jacobus de Voragine's *Golden Legend* seems accurately to indicate that the manner in which "Jhesus cryst drewe the holy faders oute of helle" was well known to everyone.[13] All doubts concerning the authenticity of this event, which had been set forth in St. Augustine and the apocryphal *Gospel of Nicodemus*,[14] were set to rest in the popular mind by the definitive statement in the Apostles' Creed: "I believe . . . in Jesus Christ . . . who . . . was crucified, dead and buried: He descended into hell. . . ." Specifically, the iconography of the harrowing found its sources in the book of *Job*, in the Psalms attributed to King David, and, as we have seen, in the Old Testament prophecies in *Isaiah*.[15] When the representation of the scene took shape as drama – a development that owes a great deal to the traditions of art[16] – the playwright as well as the director of the play and the actors must have remembered the mood of the Holy Saturday service which commemorates the event in the liturgy. Thus, the York *Harrowing* involves the handling and shaping of absolutely conventional materials in ways which are consistent with the traditional manner of responding to these materials as set forth in the liturgy of the Church.

As noted above, the paradox of the Crucifixion is crucial for such a presentation of the *Harrowing* in the York cycle. Defeat and execution are to be identified with triumph. Hence when V. A. Kolve comments that "the decisive *action*" in the harrowing plays "always turns on whether or not the gate of hell will hold" as Christ knocks and cries, "*Attolite portas principes*,"[17] he is wrong: the decisive action has *already* taken place, for it is the Crucifixion which has established Christ's victory. Again, close attention to imagery will demonstrate the manner in which the York *Harrowing* establishes a movement toward *gaudium*.

In a passage quoted by Kolve (p. 195) from York Play XXVIII, the *Agony and Betrayal*, Christ comments that his "flessh wolde full fayne / Be torned fro this turnement . . ." (XXVIII.89–91). Christ is thus a knight preparing for battle—a battle which in the later Middle Ages ensues on the cross and not in the pit of hell.[18] The iconographic representation of his arms therefore illustrates within a heraldic shield the instruments—the crown of thorns, the nails, the cross, the sponge, the spear, etc.—by which the battle is won.[19] What had appeared to the Blessed Virgin on the human level as a defeat had been in fact a most glorious victory. If, as King David indicates in the York *Harrowing*, Christ is already "mekill of myght / And stronge in ilke a stoure, / In batailes ferse to fight / And worthy to wynne honnoure" (XXXVII.129–32), it is because he has already proved himself on the cross. On the cross he has overcome Death and has demonstrated himself to be a "comely conquerour" (XXXIX.86–87). In this battle, therefore, Christ is a knight whose cross may be thought of as his palfrey and whose goal is to release man's soul from bondage to Death. At his death, Christ paradoxically wins victory over death and ends the domination of Satan over souls. Hence, separated from his body which "bidis in graue" (XXXVII.23), he may be expected to come to the kingdom of darkness as a bearer of light and joy and carrying a vexillum—a staff with a pennant of victory and with a cross at the top. Such is the case in the representation of the harrowing in one of the panels of late fourteenth-century glass formerly in St. Saviour's and now in All Saints, Pavement, York.[20] (A similar vexillum or staff with pennant and cross, again symbolic of Christ's victory over Death, appears in the *Hortulanus* scene in another panel in the same window in All Saints, Pavement.) Thus, when Christ, having won the victory on the cross, arrives at the gates of hell, no great struggle is forthcoming. Promise of any such conflict is as anticlimactic as Satan's "we are like to haue were" in the Towneley *Judicium* (Play XXX.113). As Christ says in *The Descent into Hell* in the N-town cycle, "Aȝens me it wore but wast / to holdyn or to stondyn fast / helle logge may not last / Aȝens · þe kynge of glorye" (XXXIII.1010–13).[21]

It is true that a somewhat different view of the events of the Crucifixion and harrowing had prevailed in the Anglo-Saxon period. *The Dream of the Rood* could envision a Christ energetically mounting the cross in preparation for his struggle with the powers of darkness — a struggle that is vividly portrayed in the description of the harrowing in the Old English *Christ and Satan*. But by the late Middle Ages, there would be no battle between Christ and Satan that goes on until dawn, when the Lord's strength is finally made manifest. In the play performed at York in the fifteenth century, the battle is already a victory for Christ when he appears and announces at the beginning of the action of the harrowing that, having won back Adam and Eve and the others through his death on the cross, he will now merely pay a visit to Limbo "to vnbynde" them (XXXVII.8) and to bring them to Paradise.

The element of anticlimax in the York *Harrowing* — an element which leaves the way open for farcical treatment of the pretensions of the demons and devils — has its basis in some additional theological factors. After the twelfth century, the new emphasis on the Passion and Crucifixion as central in Christ's mission to mankind meant that even in popular literature the harrowing must not any longer be an intense conflict in any way uncertain in regard to its outcome. What matter are the manner in which men come to sympathize with the sorrows and sufferings of the Lord as he provides "satisfaction" to the Father for the sins of men, and thereafter the way in which they are invited to participate in the joy of the release of souls in bondage. But the earlier theories concerning the Redemption remain important for an understanding of the play.

The older theories hold that Christ somehow deceives Satan, who thinks he is a mere man and hence legally his prey. Christ, who is without guilt, thus is able to offer himself as ransom for those who have waited in Limbo. Alan H. Nelson explains: "In putting Christ to death, Satan oversteps the limits of his power, and thus forfeits his rights over the souls of mankind."[22] The Savior is a kind of divine angler who "is able to draw out leviathan with a hook" (*Job* 41.1). Hence, Gregory of Nyssa writes that the devil is a ravenous fish who tries to gulp down the bait which is Christ, but underneath the humanity (which is all that Satan is able to recognize) is the hook of his divinity. This image was later popularized by St. Gregory the Great. The immensely influential *Sententiae* of Peter Lombard, who speaks of Christ's cross as a trap baited by Christ's blood and of Satan as the mouse caught in the trap,[23] also helped to keep similar theology alive and popular well into the period when the York play was written. Thus, the *Harrowing* as played at York contains a scene in which Christ, when confronting Satan, refers to "Mi fadir" (XXXVII.226), whom the audience, educated with regard to the eschatological realities, recognizes as his Father in heaven. But Satan, reacting on a human or less than human level, responds with a sneer:

> Thy fadir knewe I wele be sight,
> He was a write his mette to wynne. . . . (XXVII.229-30)

Christ's humanity deceives Satan still, though he is flabbergasted that this son of a carpenter has so much power. As Jesus explains, he has deliberately hidden his "Godhede" in order to ransom man's soul (his motive is "hartely loue") and "to make [Satan] mased and madde" (XXXVII.245-52). Accordingly, now that Christ is in hell, the demonic master of the place cannot against him enforce his will, though previously all human souls had been forfeit to him. Satan has unknowingly accepted the ransom of Christ, who has through his divinity broken the gates of hell; and darkness can have no more dominion over the people of God.

Christ, standing before the gates of hell and calling for them to open, quotes from the twenty-fourth psalm, which includes a famous passage that was sometimes read as part of the Palm Sunday liturgy:

> *Attollite portas, principes,*
>   Oppen vppe, ȝe princes of paynes sere,
> *Et eleuamini eternales,*
>   Youre yendles ȝatis þat ȝe haue here. (XXXVII.122-24)

When the gates fail to open, Christ in the York text again speaks:

> *Principes, portas tollite,*
>   Vndo youre ȝatis, ȝe princis of pryde,
> *Et introibit rex glorie,*
>   Þe kyng of blisse comes in þis tyde. (XXXVII.181-84)

In each of these instances, a response by Satan, who fails to understand the eschatological meaning of Christ's words, is immediately followed in the York text by the words of King David, who indeed does recognize the psalm as his own prophecy uttered long ago ("Þat may þou in my Sawter see, / For þat poynte prophicied," XXXVII.187–88).

The third and final speech of Christ before the gates, however, takes a different form in the York play:

> Þis steede schall stonde no lenger stoken:
>   Opynne vppe, and latte my pepul passe. (193–94)

Presumably Christ has, as in the medieval rite for the consecration of a church in which words from Psalm 24.7–10 are used,[24] struck the gates with his staff each time he has called out the words "*Attolite portas, principes*" or "*Principes, portas tollite.*" The gates shatter or break open when he speaks for the third time. Now the devil, called Rybald in the Towneley version, laments: "oure baill is brokynne, / And brosten are alle oure bandis of bras" (XXXVII.195–96).

The gates themselves also have their principal source in Psalm 24, as Rosemary Woolf has noted; they had appeared in the imagery of accounts of the harrowing since at least the time of Tertullian.[25] In the visual arts, the gates are to be seen in Western Europe at least as early as the eighth century.[26] The representation of the harrowing in the panel of painted glass now in All Saints, Pavement, typically shows the broken gates beneath Christ's feet. Broken gates with metal hinges appear, along with a demon under the gates, in the glass of Great Malvern Priory Church, Worcestershire.[27] In the York play, a devil's report, to be passed on to Lucifer, is that "alle is vnlokynne" (XXXVII.197), while a revision in the Towneley play obviously describes the breaking of the gates at the moment when they give way: "oure yates begyn to crak! / In sonder, I trow, they go . . ." (XXV.209–10). But the devils' woe is a cause for rejoicing among the members of the audience.

The pinning of the devil under the broken gates, as in the Great Malvern glass, is iconographic shorthand for the sequence which follows the entry of Christ into Limbo in the drama. The York play as a result contains a debate — a kind of verbal triumph for Christ through logic and rhetoric—culminating in the sinking of Satan into hell's pit (cf. Towneley, XXV.360). Satan's agility in argument will be recognized as akin to Iago's in Shakespeare's *Othello*; hence, he is excellent at tactics but is lacking in the sound strategy which is needed to win the war. Satan thus is no match for Christ, who has brought the light of his divinity into hell itself. The divine soul of Christ, who is at once God and man, asserts its superiority over the demon's pretended power. The prince of demons is told that he "schall be feste, / þat þou schalte flitte not ferre" (XXXVII.335-36). The York play follows the Apocalypse in having Michael do the actual binding of Satan, whereupon Christ orders him to go down "Into [his] selle where þou schalte sitte" (XXXVII.339-42).

In the staging of the play, the entire architecture of hell can be ascertained fairly accurately by internal evidence, though it is also useful to examine representations of the scene of the harrowing in the visual arts. Most prominent in the scene is the hell mouth, out of which the souls of Adam and Eve and the others are drawn, as in the restored fifteenth-century wall painting in the parish church at Pickering, Yorkshire, in the fourteenth-century wall painting at Chalgrove, Oxfordshire, or in an English alabaster now in the Victoria and Albert Museum.[28] Hell mouth is certainly also the pit into which Satan vanishes. The hell mouth, visualized in terms of the jaws of the leviathan mentioned in *Job* 41.1, must surely have had some smoke issuing forth during the early productions of the play of the *Harrowing*. At Coventry in 1557, as noted above, an expenditure of four pence is recorded for "kepyng of fyer at hell mouthe."[29] Writing of French drama, Grace Frank notes the possible presence of a cauldron located at the base of the neck of the beast whose head contains the entry to hell; the cauldron seems "responsible for the flames and smoke of which we hear so much in the medieval drama."[30] Such a device indeed might have been utilized in order to create a properly spectacular hell mouth at York.

Beyond the hell mouth, then, is lower hell where the wicked souls of Cain, Judas, Ahitophel, "And alle of þare assente" suffer eternally (XXXVII.306-10). Here is *tristia* from which no release is possible. Though in later medieval representations of hell such as the miniature in the *Holkham Bible Picture Book* (fol. 34ʳ), the lower region of hell is illustrated through the symbolism of a blast furnace, no such elaborate setting seems to be called for in the play of the *Harrowing* at York. However, the battlements represented in the *Holkham Bible Picture Book* miniature are surely not entirely absent from the pageant staging of the York play, which calls for "watches" of demons "on þe wall" (XXXVII.140). The impression is given that hell is like a castle which is defended by a gate and walls. One of the devils is porter of hell gate — a role which may be identified elsewhere in the Towneley cycle (Towneley, XXX.371ff) and also in an earlier non-cycle *Harrowing*.[31] Presumably, Limbo, the "special space" where Adam, Eve, and the others are kept, is in the York *Harrowing* like the castle yard, with the hell mouth appearing in place of the keep.[32] The audience is asked to imagine this whole area inside the gates as the place of darkness, from which Christ will rescue those who have for as much as "Foure thowsande and sex hundereth ȝere" (XXXVII.39) awaited his coming.

Those who have been sitting in darkness even at the mouth of hell include primarily Adam and Eve, the primordial ancestors of the race, as well as Moses, Isaiah, David, John the Baptist, and others who had awaited Christ's act of redemption on the cross. In iconography, it is Adam whom Christ grasps by the forearm when he harrows hell, as in the alabaster in the Victoria and Albert Museum. One text of the Chester *Harrowing* specifies: "Tunc Jesus accipiet Adam per manum."[33] In the wall painting at Pickering, Adam seems to be handing an apple in unchewed state to Christ as he is led forth. Eve follows, and then the other patriarchs.[34] The alabaster in the Victoria and Albert Museum shows all with hands joined in prayer (*junctis manibus*), illustrating the new gesture for praying introduced in the thirteenth century. Similar gestures are to be understood in the York *Harrowing* play as well as in the Towneley adaption of this drama. The joy of the ransomed souls is gracious and proper as it is expressed through all their acts and words when they are drawn from darkness and brought into the eternal light of Paradise.

In the York play, the final speech of Christ to the good souls accompanies a blessing:

Mi blissing haue ʒe all on rawe,
  I schall be with youe wher ʒe wende,
And all þat lelly luffes my lawe,
  Þai schall be blissid withowten ende. (XXXVII.401–04)

Here again is a significant detail specifically recorded in the painted glass now in the West Window of All Saints, Pavement, where Christ is seen with his hand raised in benediction upon the first persons ever to receive salvation. Such a blessing by the Savior is also recorded in Virgil's account of the harrowing in Dante's *Inferno* (4.61).

With a blessing, therefore, Christ sets his ransomed people free from bondage, while at the same time he has bound the chief of devils, Satan. In contrast to the decorum of Adam, Eve, and the patriarchs, the demons, who in appearance must have resembled the devils in the painted glass in St. Michael, Spurriergate, York, have moved with erratic movements and have evidenced irrational words and deeds which at once are comic and threatening. Hell is the inverse of all that is stable and good. Even the language of the demons is topsy-turvy. Though these creatures have power in the world, before Christ they cannot hope for anything other than defeat. Indeed, they will not even have the opportunity to do battle with Christ: "with hym may ye not fyght,/ffor he is king and conqueroure," says David in the Towneley version (XXV.128–29). All their hope of victory is lost, for they had already suffered defeat when Christ died on the cross. Here indeed is cause for rejoicing.

The most significant difference between the York play and the Towneley adaptation involves the introduction of the archangel Michael in the York *Harrowing*. It is possible that Michael was not present in the York play in the early history of this drama, for his name does not appear in the *Ordo* of 1415 or in Burton's second list; hence it is likely that Michael may have been added to the drama after the text had been borrowed and adapted for production elsewhere, probably in West Yorkshire — a borrowing which would later be incorporated into the Towneley manuscript. Yet, as Martial Rose notes, the angel Michael commonly leads the souls up to Paradise in other medieval treatments of this episode.[35] In the Chester cycle, for example, Jesus orders

Michael to "lead these men singinge/to blys that lasteth ever" (XVII.211-12). Caxton's translation of the *Golden Legend* explains that "He receyued the sowles of sayntes and brought theim in to the parodys of exaltacon and joye" (fol. cclxxxii). In the English translation of the *Gospel of Nicodemus* known to the authors of the York play, Christ is said to have taken Adam by the hand and then "with Michael he bad him ga." Whereupon, "þai toke þe way with gud entent/vntyll Paradyse full thra. Michael rasayued þam sone/þat war to him bikend,/In blys he has þam done/þat lastes withouten end."[36] The scene dissolves into perfect joy.

Michael's role as a rescuer of souls is, of course, very well established in iconography apart from the above passage from the *Gospel of Nicodemus*. In a miniature in the *Hours of Catherine of Cleves*, which may possibly be roughly contemporary with the possible additions to the York version of the Harrowing, this archangel, shown leading five souls out of a terrifying hell mouth, is grasping one of them by the forearm just as Christ had done in representations of the Harrowing.[37] Below, in the border, a fowler is setting snares for birds—a reference to Psalm 91.3: "Surely he shall deliver thee from the snares of the fowler . . ." (*AV*). As Christ notes in the opening lines of the York *Harrowing* play, the "feende þame [i.e., men and women] wanne with trayne" (XXXVII.9). David, who quotes Psalm 16.10, reminds us that Christ has promised not to leave the souls of the righteous "In depe helle where dampned schall goo" (XXXVII.376-77). Through his deception of Satan, Christ indeed has become ransom for these souls in Limbo.

The souls of the righteous, as they move up to the staging prepared as a representation of Paradise, walk in orderly procession singing *Laus tibi cum gloria*, which (like the *Te Deum* with which the Towneley play ends) signifies the expression of joy and the culmination of the movement toward *gaudium*. In the meanwhile, the soul of Christ must return to the sepulchre to await his Resurrection. The mock siege is completed, the castle of hell has fallen to the powers of light, and the way is made open for righteous souls to enter into a more happy abode after death.

In the *Harrowing* which appears in the York cycle, dramatization is given to the aftermath of Christ's victory on the cross. The iconography of the play is entirely traditional, and it provides a bridge between the Crucifixion and the process of redemption. By breaking down the gates of hell and releasing man's first parents and the prophets from Limbo, Christ asserts his newly-won power to set men free from guilt and death. Indeed, he is now able to return them to the primordial innocence at the same time that he makes possible their hope of bliss. Thus, as noted above, the *Harrowing* looks back to the Exodus play, which dramatized the manner in which the people of the Lord crossed the Red Sea as they escaped from bondage—a bondage which for them had been like death. Hence, it is no accident that Jesus, standing before the gates of hell, should demand that Satan "Opynne vppe, and latte my pepul passe" (XXXVII.194), for these words echo exactly God's words "lette my pepull passe" in Play XI, line 124, of the York cycle. At the same time, the iconography of the York *Harrowing* looks forward to the Last Judgment, when the blessed will be given the joyful gift of eternal bliss which was made possible by the victory on the cross—i.e., by Christ's act of dying for the sins of all men. Like the Towneley play which is ultimately based on it, the York *Harrowing* sets forth the movement from *tristia* to *gaudium*, for the sorrowful sight of Christ crucified is transformed in them into the spectacle of the victorious Lord whose triumph over sin and death is also an invitation to all men "on molde" to participate in the supreme joy which will ultimately be experienced in Paradise.

II

The close connection between the Harrowing and the Resurrection in iconography suggests that these two episodes may well be bracketed together for study, since both underline the expression of joy and praise overcoming the sorrow and lamentation of Christ's followers at the same time that his enemies are immobilized and overcome. The relationship seems to be well established in a poem of triumph by William Dunbar entitled

"On the Resurrection of Christ":

> Done is a battell on the dragon blak,
> Our campioun Chryst confountet hes his force;
> The yettis of hell ar brokin with a crak,
> The signe triumphall rasit is of the croce,
> The divillis trymmillis with hiddous voce,
> The saulis ar borrowit and to the blis can go,
> Chryst with his blud our ransonis dois indoce:
> *Surrexit Dominus de sepulchro.*

> . . .

> The fo is chasit, the battell is done ceis,
> The presone brokin, the jevellouris fleit and flemit;
> The weir is gon, confermit is the peis,
> The fetteris lowsit and the dungeoun temit,
> The ransoun maid, the presoneris redemit;
> The feild is win, ourcumin is the fo,
> Dispulit of the tresur that he yemit:
> *Surrexit Dominus de sepulchro.*[38]

Christ's victory will, of course, be certified in the Resurrection, which will take place on the third day in spite of precautions that are taken by Pilate and the high priests, Caiaphas and Annas, whose scepticism prevents them in the York play from believing the testimony of the Centurion—a ringing acclamation of the marvels that accompanied the death of Jesus. Indeed, Christ's earthly enemies will prove as ineffectual as his hellish enemies were demonstrated to be.

The Resurrection, which in the York play takes place in mime—perhaps because it is a devotional image too holy for the addition of dialogue—was actually a fairly popular subject in local art. Curiously, in spite of the immense importance of the Resurrection theme in early Christian thought, the scene does not appear at all in catacomb art, for example.[39] Indeed, it only becomes widespread in the art of the thirteenth century,[40] the date of the earliest York example, a miniature in the York psalter in the British Library (MS. Add. 54,179, fol. 59). Above, the Resurrection scene includes Christ with a cross staff emerging from a tomb, while his grave clothes are draped over the tomb's edge. Angels appear at each end of the sepulchre, but no soldiers are in sight. Below, Jonah is pictured emerging from the whale,[41] a scene which would appear typologically to suggest the Harrowing as well as the Resurrection. More nearly contemporary with the York play, of course, is the illumination in the *Bolton Hours* (fol. 37) where Christ is shown with vexillum and with right hand raised in blessing (plate 14). His wounds from the torture and execution during his Passion and Crucifixion are all prominently displayed. Two of the soldiers seem to be sleeping, but two others are not; one of these in particular gives evidence of amazement — the kind of reaction that is recorded by the soldiers in the York play in their report to Pilate:

> We wer so ferde downe ganne we falle
> And dared for drede. (XXXVIII.369-70)

The source of this reaction, which is also recorded in painted glass from the fifteenth century now in the Chapter House[42] as well as in other English examples such as the illuminations in the *Abingdon Missal* (MS. Digby 227, fol. 13) dated 1461,[43] the *Holkham Bible Picture Book* (fol. 34^V), and two alabasters published by W. L. Hildburgh,[44] can be traced. M. D. Anderson's suggestion that this iconography shows "the influence of the plays" on the visual arts[45] will be rejected when it is recognized that the artists were in fact instead drawing on a tradition which has its source in the apocryphal *Acts of Pilate*.[46] This work reports the words of the soldiers, who explain that they became "sore afraid and lay as dead men" when they saw an angel come to remove the stone from the sepulchre; that their eyes were not closed in sleep according to this account is indicated by their knowledge of the coming of the three women at the tomb, though in their amazed state they can only look on fearfully without taking any action.[47]

At the Resurrection in the York play, "melodie" of superb quality is appropriately heard. The music is the *Christus resurgens*, which here is a respond from the York rite presumably.[48] The singer is an angel, whose role is indicated in a sixteenth-century stage direction in the margin of the Register. It would be interesting to know whether this actor-singer also played the role of the angel who is identified in the *Ordo* in a hand later than 1415 as a "youth" wearing a white alb who speaks to the holy women.[49] The angel here is the one to whom the famous *Quem queritis* speech (translated, of course, into English) is given:

3e mournand women in youre þought,
Here in þis place whome have 3e sought? (XXXVIII.235–36)

The scene has shifted to one of very great traditional significance — the appearance of the three Marys at the tomb with their "anoynementis faire and clere/þat we haue broght/To noynte his wondis on sides sere . . ." (XXXVIII.213–15). This is the tableau of lamenting women whose words paradoxically reflect the joy of Easter morning — a tableau that is justly famous for the dramatic treatment given to it in the monastic rite and music drama from Anglo-Saxon times through the twelfth-century Fleury Playbook with its masterful *Visitatio Sepulchri*.[50] The angel in the York play points out the grave cloth or "sudary," familiar from the Fleury play where it is also included as a stage property, and tells the women that Christ is alive and may "be foune in Galilé/In flesshe and fell" (XXXVIII.243–44, 249–50).

In visualizing the Resurrection play at York, the actors may have drawn on one additional detail that would have further emphasized the triumph of Christ in rising from the tomb. We know that in the Chester cycle Jesus stepped forth from the tomb onto the back of one or more of the soldiers. As the first soldier complains,

He sett his foote upon my backe
that everye lythe beganne to cracke. (Chester, XVIII.274–75)

This detail has been noted by Hildburgh in English alabasters,[51] and is also included prominently on a destroyed roof boss in York Minster and in a panel in the Great West Window, both examples of fourteenth-century York work.[52] The window, painted in the workshop of Master Robert, also shows a very revealing design on a shield belonging to one of the soldiers: it contains the face of a devil. Christ with his vexillum, rising from the tomb and casting his grave clothes over the side, would surely have displayed his wounds which are the emblems of his victory and would have mimed the sign of blessing that we frequently encounter in art. The suffering has not been forgotten, but he

has transcended all human pain at the same time that he has
overcome all symbols of earthly power, represented here by the
soldiers sent by Pilate. Sorrow has been definitively transformed
into joy since, as the scene implies, those who are onlookers
watching the play or devoutly gazing at the art will be allowed to
join the souls of the blessed who have been released from hell in
the Harrowing. The poem "On the Resurrection of Christ" by
Dunbar explains how this may be so when the poet writes:

> He for our saik that sufferit to be slane,
> And lyk a lamb in sacrifice wes dicht,
> Is lyk a lyone rissin up agane,
> And as a gyane raxit him on hicht,
>
> •   •   •
>
> The blisfull day depairtit fro the nycht:
> *Surrexit Dominus de sepulchro.*[53]

IX

PILGRIMAGE
AND
TRANSCENDENCE

I

The thrust of the plays which follow the Resurrection in the York cycle — the Winedrawers' *Appearance of Christ to Mary Magdalene* (Play XXXIX), the Woolpackers' *Travellers to Emmaus* (Play XL), the Scriveners' *Doubting Thomas* (Play XLI), the Tailors' *Ascension* (Play XLII), and the Potters' *Pentecost* (Play XLIII) — continues to trace the pattern of *tristia* to *gaudium*, from sadness to joy established in the Harrowing and Resurrection dramas. Thus, for example, the laments of Mary Magdalene — laments which actually begin in the context of the Resurrection play itself (XXXVIII.270-87) — punctuate the opening of the dramatization of the *Hortulanus* scene in Play XXXIX, where she suggests that the death of beloved Christ has created the greatest woe ever felt by a human being. Symbolically, to be sure, she represents the hope of salvation here seemingly frustrated by the disappearance of the One who ought to be instrumental in that salvation. Hence Jesus' words to her at the moment when he reveals himself command her to "of mournyng amende thy moode . . ." (l. 62). The result of the revelation of his presence will then cause her joy to return, as we would expect.

But even in the *Ascension*, Peter, speaking before the reap-
pearance of Jesus, comments on the heaviness which the apostles
all feel — "Oure heuynes and oure mournyng" which Christ had
promised "to joie turned schuld be" (XLII.19-20). With respect
to this theme, the summing up comes in the speech of the third
apostle in the *Pentecost* play following their new experience of
the Holy Spirit:

> Euen als he saide schulde to vs come
>   So has bene schewid vnto oure sight:
> *'Tristicia impleuit cor vestrum'* —
>   Firste sorowe in herte he vs hight;
> *'Sed conuertetur in gaudium'.*
>   Sen saide he þat he schulde be light.
> Nowe þat he said vs, all and summe,
>   Is mefid emange vs thurgh his myght. (XLIII.145-52)

Rooted in iconographic tableaux, however, the repetition of
theme does not appear to be symptomatic of unsatisfactory
structure or design in the plays. The plays are, after all, episodic
in nature, providing what to the modern viewer must at first
seem a fragmentary vision of the critical events of human
history seen from the standpoint of the Christian story. Each
play at York was presented apparently by a different set of actors under the immediate sponsorship of a different guild.
Hence, in the post-Resurrection plays alone, Jesus would have
been played by four separate actors, while five different
pageants would have presented discontinuous views of the
sacred settings where Christ appeared to his followers, ascended
into heaven, and, as he had promised, sent the gift of the Holy
Spirit to the apostles and Mary. F. C. Gardiner rightly notes the
importance of the line "For prossesse of plaies þat precis in
plight" (XL.192): "Still rooted in the ritualizing impulse of
religious drama, this York play sees in the other episodes *a context of successive moments of insight*."[1] Each image and each
verbal exchange between the characters hence function separately
within a total context, which through accretion produces the impression of a pilgrimage of the soul at the same time that the
plays are presented along their processional route.[2]

Since the scenes of the drama must be drawn from among those which normally lent themselves to being visualized, the dramatists, guilds, and actors could hardly be expected to "invent" matter for presentation, nor was it possible even to be innovative with regard to the action, characterization, or theme. Even the structure of the drama is fixed by iconographic and exegetical traditions. Nevertheless, the result is hardly lacking in genuine dramatic interest, for, as Robert Edwards has pointed out, "the Christian dramatist receives [plot, character, etc.] from his history, and his work consequently tends toward spectacle that expresses mystery rather than rational demonstration."[3] *Mystery* — this is the source of the joy which is being offered again and again in these plays, and it is beyond the comprehension of mere human reason and beyond the grasp of mechanically innovative plot. To adapt a tag from Milton, the civic plays such as those presented at York were for their purposes better teaching than the philosophy of Aquinas. And they did more than teach: they participated imaginatively in the mystery itself.

Participation of this kind in the drama as a devotional experience is actually posited on taking the human condition from its current state — a state which involves the alienation inevitable among fallen men — and insisting upon beginning the pilgrimage which will open up that condition to the joy of heavenly bliss. The apostle Thomas represents this condition when, in his scepticism, he insists that his fellow apostles are merely telling foolish "tales" as they inform him that Jesus "is resen agayne" (XLI.134-36). He will believe only the evidence of his senses — sight and touch — and rejects the testimony of the others, though at the same time he is mourning very deeply the loss of Christ: "On grounde nowe," he complains, "may I gang vngladde / Boþe even and morne" (XLI.99-100). The appearance of Christ to him (in a scene that is perhaps to be visualized much like the example in painted glass at All Saints, North Street, York[4]) thus serves to break down his scepticism and his consequent alienation, while the scene as presented in the drama serves directly to penetrate the barrier of unbelief and lack of trust between the audience and the divine Being signified by the actor playing the role of Christ.

"Blissed be þey euere," Jesus explains, "Þat trowis haly in my
rising right, / And saw it neuere" (XLI.190–92).

For Mary Magdalene in her despair, however, the loss of
Christ and the consequent loss of order in her life are even more
significant. She is, we remember, the former prostitute whose
life was changed from its instability to a controlled desire for
God;[5] she is at first fallen, as all of us are *fallen* in our human
condition, but she is given *hope* through the *focus and direction*
which divine love promises her. In a sense she is the representative
of the holy *eros* or desire which presses to break through to the
mysteries of Being and to be united with him.[6] Thus she is representative of the condition of the Church, illustrated from early
times as a feminine figure (Sponsa) consistent with the
allegorical reading of the *Song of Songs*. In the Bene-
dicktbeuern Passion Play, Mary Magdalene demonstrates her
early alienated state when she goes to the merchant to buy
cosmetics and in the song "Chramer, gip die varwe mier" asks
for merchandise that will make her attractive to men; following
her conversion, her personal attractiveness will not matter any
longer to her, for she has transcended all earthly love. Now she
will need no paint to cover her true identity, for by losing herself
she can at last find herself. And the self that she discovers is a
creature essentially on pilgrimage to the place of eternal bliss
where she may be joined forever with the Bridegroom.

But the pilgrimage has its moments of despair for the Magdalen,
and these come at the Crucifixion of the one whom she perceives
as central to her existence. With the other holy women, she goes
to the tomb to anoint the body – an unhappy and seemingly
futile pilgrimage. Even the announcement of the angel at the
tomb fails to reassure her, and her meditation on the Passion
overwhelms her again. "Þer is nothing to þat we mete / May
make me blithe," she announces (XXXVIII.286–87). This mood
is, of course, continued in the *Hortulanus* scene, where the darkness of her despair is comparable to that of an exile banished
and losing hope. Her emotional and spiritual stability shaken,
she nevertheless continues to seek at least a sight of Jesus (or, if
that is impossible, a message from him). It is at this moment
that Jesus in fact does appear before her in disguise. Earlier art,

as in the embroidery of the Syon cope in the Victoria and Albert Museum, presented him in a loose gown with wounds displayed and with the vexillum supported by his left hand. This iconography is extant at York, as in the glass in a Chapter House window or at All Saints, Pavement.[7] Late iconography, however, tended often to provide a motive for the Magdalen's inability to recognize her best friend and Savior: he was, as in the restored panel of fifteenth-century glass in the choir of York Minster, in fact holding a spade. In the seventeenth-century, Torre described the scene as containing "a little Image of our Lord, in white wTH a spade . . . like a Gardiner And in the sepulcre lye the Linnen Cloaths. And an Angell in white by them bearing a Cross Erected. . . . On the other side kneels Mary Magdalen habited purple."[8] Similar iconography with Christ appearing as the gardener appears in the *Holkham Bible Picture Book*, on an English alabaster noted by Hildburgh,[9] and on a misericord at Lincoln.[10] It will be remembered that the spade plays an important function in the iconography of the Fall, with Adam normally shown digging in the earth after the Expulsion. Christ, as the second Adam, following his great work of redemption therefore is shown with Adam's instrument, the spade. But the giving of the full gardener's costume as well as the spade to the risen Christ also, of course, illustrates once again the late medieval tendency to literalize scenes and symbols.

Christ is, as the Magdalen says, the "comely conquerour" whose "loue is swetter þanne þe mede [i.e., honey]" (XXXIX.86–89). With this image of transcendence, the focus of her earthly pilgrimage has returned along with her joy:

> Alle for joie me likes to synge,
>   Myne herte is gladder þanne þe glee,
> And all for joie of thy risyng
>   That suffered dede vpponne a tree.
> Of luffe nowe is þou crouned kyng,
>   Is none so trewe levand more free.
> Thy loue passis all erthely thyng,
>   Lorde, blissed motte þou euere bee! (XXXIX.134–41)

Christ's blessing upon her, he sends her forth on a journey to "Galilé" where she will report her transcendent experience to her friends and relatives there.

But the experience of transcendence is not the Magdalen's alone, for through *play* it is shared with the audience, which likewise is invited to see itself as "pilgrims and strangers in this world."[11] Jesus has reviewed to Mary Magdalene his role as a lover-knight who went into battle to redeem man's soul — a role which he has explained in terms of the armor and weapons he used on the cross — and he has asked her to write these details in her heart.[12] Through the drama, the audience will receive an imaginative view of the historical event that also provides hope for modern-day pilgrims who share the joy and hope of the Magdalen.

The understanding of pilgrimage in relation to transcendence is made particularly clear in the *Travellers to Emmaus*, which dramatizes the spatial relationship between mortal men and the mystery of Being. According to a sermon formerly attributed to St. Bernard, contemporary men resemble the two early followers in their initial blindness to transcendence since

> we are mortal, we dwell in exile, and we are not strong enough to seize that blessedness-to-be-praised, because of its multitude of glory. Who can even breathe among those joys of over-flowing jubilation which will be given in the fatherland, when that little moment of sweetness, which now he shows us in the way, in the pilgrim country, will inebriate the whole mind and grip the whole breadth of the heart with new delights? Thus . . . "Their eyes were held fast," because the Lord was in the dress of a pilgrim.[13]

The "dress of a pilgrim" in the later Middle Ages was, however, very distinctive, and indeed is important for establishing the iconography of this play. Just as the play identifies "Emax" (Emmaus) as "þis castell beside vs" (XL.14) on the basis of the word *castellum* in the Vulgate, so too the stranger, Jesus, is understood through the same biblical text (*Luke* 24) as *peregrinus*. Indeed, when we look at examples in art as early as the mosaics at Ravenna, Jesus already appears in the garb of the pilgrim of the day.[14] In the fourteenth through early sixteenth centuries, the Savior and also the two followers who do not recognize their master are all dressed in the contemporary garb of pilgrims, as in English miniatures from the fourteenth century[15] and in York glass from 1420–30 now in the Chapter House.[16] This glass shows two separate scenes, the first of which is the journey with all three bare-footed figures wearing the pilgrim's hat of the type associated with St. James and Compostella as well as carrying the traditional pilgrim's staff. Therefore the hat, with its scallop shell, and other aspects of the pilgrim's garb may best perhaps be examined in the larger representations of St. James, a number of which survive in York art contemporary with the plays.[17] But the meaning here is of the utmost significance: as pilgrims in the world, we are to look toward the example of the early followers of Christ and toward the means of experiencing the transcendent set forth in the sacred stories.

In the York Chapter House glass, the journey to Emmaus is followed by another panel showing the supper at Emmaus, where Christ, seated between the others (identified in the York play and the York records as Cleophas and St. Luke[18]), is giving the bread which he has broken to them. Another example of York glass, a late fourteenth-century panel formerly in St. Saviour's and now in All Saints, Pavement (plate 13), shows Christ in pilgrim's hat with its scallop shell and wearing a jacket; before him on the table are a chalice and bread,[19] which of course suggest the Eucharistic overtones present in this meal shared with the two men who long for the Christ who they feel is not any longer among them. It is through the breaking of the bread that they will know him; in the York play, his words echo words from the Mass:

Nowe blisse I þis brede þat brought is on þe borde.
Fraste þeron faithfully, my frendis, you to feede. (XL.157–58)

But at the moment of recognition Jesus vanishes from among them—a stage device that may have been quite spectacular.[20] The tableau indeed suggests the hieratic function of ritual, revealing the divine presence in the bread and wine on the table where Jesus has indeed himself been present in a symbolic and also real offering of himself. In the Mass, the elements of bread and wine thus have the purpose of linking those who even look on them to the transcendent deity whose mystery thus becomes a means of spiritual sustenance for persons journeying through life. In the liturgical play at Padua in the thirteenth century, the action of the *Peregrinus* had thus concluded in a very interesting way: following the vanishing of Jesus, "wafers are thrown from the roof of the church and all who can, catch them."[21] The Padua play, like the York play later, hence was designed to link the biblical event with the Eucharist. For the York drama, the linkage would seem to have been very significant indeed since the day of performance was the Feast of Corpus Christi—a day devoted to honoring the establishment of the Eucharist—though the connection between the drama and the *theology* of this feast (as distinct from its popular celebration) probably should not be overemphasized.

II

At the Ascension in the York cycle, Jesus proclaims that his earthly "jornay" has come to its end, and announces to his disciples and to his mother that he will now go to prepare "a stede" (i.e., 'a place') for them where they may forever dwell with him (XLII.153, 169-72). His prayer to his Father follows:

> Sende doune a clowde, fadir, forthy
> I come to þe my fadir deere. (XLII.173-74)

The prayer will, of course, be immediately answered, and he ascends in the manner depicted in most English art of the later Middle Ages.[22] The depiction in the *Bolton Hours* (fol. 37) may be taken as reasonably typical: across the top of the miniature are three rows of stylized folds representing the cloud into which Jesus was taken up; only his feet and the bottom of his robe are visible beneath this cloud (plate 15). Below, standing at each side, are the disciples and the Virgin, all standing with hands upraised. In early sixteenth-century glass, possibly painted by John Petty, in York Minster, the figures below the ascending Christ kneel, while glass now in All Saints, Pavement, of four-teenth-century date distinguishes the Virgin from the apostles by means of her crown.[23] The latter example is particularly interesting because the imprint of Christ's feet on the ground is shown—a detail that appears even more prominently in the unusual roof boss formerly in York Minster (the present boss is a copy based on a careful drawing made in the early nineteenth century).[24]

Following the Ascension, the disciples and Mary are spoken to by two angels, presumably two of the four angels reported to have borne the cloud into which Jesus stepped.[25] The first chides those below for continuing to look toward heaven, for, he promises, Jesus will come again at the Doom, at which time he "Who wele has wrought full gladde may be" while he "Who ill has leved [will be] full sore dredand" (XLII.223–24). The second angel insists that the disciples should "preche" the news about Christ, with the understanding that the faithful shall have their reward in heaven at the end of their life's journey while those who refuse grace will have pain everlasting.

But the Ascension is not the end of the Christian story, for one additional scene will be needed to certify the promise of God's grace to his followers. This scene will be Pentecost, when the Holy Spirit, usually represented by a dove as in the sixteenth-century glass possibly by John Petty (plate 12) in the nave of York Minster,[26] comes down. But the play also speaks of light as bright as the sun (XLIII.115), and hence some kind of device to produce tongues of fire as in the mid-fourteenth-century glass in the choir of the cathedral[27] may also have been used. In the lost Bedern Chapel glass, Torre reported both a dove and three "long rays of golden light" coming down upon the Virgin and the apostles.[28] In the *Fitzwilliam Missal* (Fitzwilliam Museum MS. 34, p. 201), the Virgin is kneeling in the center of the scene—a detail which illustrates her central role for the whole Church that is founded upon this occasion of Pentecost.

The experience of transcendence which Mary's Son offers is indeed to be carried on to succeeding generations by the Church, for which this experience will be sufficient protection against all the vicissitudes of the earthly pilgrimage. In the York plays which follow the Resurrection, the insights which are at the heart of the scenes show not only that sorrow rightly ought to be transformed to joy when the divine realities are understood, but also that earthly life, perceived in terms of pilgrimage, will ultimately conclude in the bliss of eternity which is the end of man's long exile—an exile which in turn originated in the Expulsion from Paradise in primordial time.

X

THE VIRGIN MARY

The Blessed Virgin Mary, whose cult flourished strongly in the period immediately before the Reformation in England, was the object of veneration particularly in cities such as York, where devotion to her was deeply imbedded in civic piety. Civic devotion, of course, gave much attention to her participation in the Infancy, Passion, and Resurrection scenes, but her role in the Christian story was also regarded apart from such episodes involving her Son. She was at once the model of womanhood — and, indeed, of the condition of being human — and the mediatrix through whom the deity might be approached, since it was felt that the Son could hardly deny the requests of his beloved mother. In York wills before the Reformation, she is almost always included in invocations directed to God, as in the almost standard formula "I give my soul to God Almighty and his mother Mary and all the saints." The statement in the codicil of the will of Nicholas Blackburn, Sr., is even more revealing, for it extends the extent of Marian devotion to special veneration for her early life and her mother, Anne:

> I Nicholas Blakburn, elder, citizeen and marchaund of
> York, besekes Almyghty Godd, als any erthly man kan or
> may, in saule and mynde, to graunt me myght and grace so

to dyspose and ordeyne with the resideu of ye gudes y^t he
has gyffen me here in y^{is} werlde, yat it may be pleasanns
and lovyng to hym soveranly, and his blissed moder Saynt
Mary, and hir blissed moder Sancte Anne, and all y^e
Halowes in heven, and help and releve unto ye heel of my
saule and Margrete my wyffe, our faders and our moders,
our brethir and our sisters, our childer and all our frendes,
and all ye saules of yam, yat I have hadd of any thyng in
yis werld undeserved, and all Crysten saules.[1]

Blackburn's will, probated 10 April 1432, also provides for the
endowment of the chantry chapel dedicated to St. Anne[2] which
has been noted above in Chapter VI. The devotional context in
this instance is clarified also by another previously noted dona-
tion made by Blackburn—the window containing the panel
which prominently displays St. Anne teaching the Virgin to read
in a tableau that obviously was a favorite scene in devotion
directed to the early life of Mary.[3]

Unlike the N-town plays which dramatize Mary's early life, the
York cycle lacks emphasis on the Virigin's childhood—a lack of
emphasis that does not suggest lack of devotion to the mother of
the Redeemer. The visual arts in York, however, hardly ignore the
early life, and York glass even today contains evidence of the
strong strain of Marian devotion at this northern ecclesiastical
capital. By stressing Mary's early life as well as her later accomplishments, her cult could give attention to her tenderness and
her perfect expression of charity, which are qualities that would
seem essential for the mediatrix who in her goodness and humility
intercedes for men at the throne of heaven.

In York art, certain Nativity scenes also underline her tenderness—scenes, for example, which show her as *Maria lactans*,
feeding her Child from her breast.[4] Thus she is shown with her
Son at her breast in a Chapter House carving from c.1280 as
well as in a York Minster roof boss which was destroyed by fire
in the nineteenth century (the replacement substitutes a bottle
for the exposed breast!). Mary is an exemplar of Charity, and in
the *Speculum Humanae Salvationis* she sometimes thus with
iconographic correctness bares her breast as a sign of her mercy.[5]
Such would therefore also be the meaning implied in the painted

cloth given by Thomas Robson to Holy Trinity Priory in 1519; his will describes the image on this cloth as "of Our Lady, with her Son sowkyn on hir breste, with a similitude of a preste knelyng."[6] In a compilation of Middle English poetic meditations, an anonymous author wrote:

> Þanne, lady, praye for vs
> To þi sone, swete Ihesus,
> In þat ilke carful cas,
> þat he for-ȝyue vs oure trespas.
> Ȝif he be hard to for-ȝyue
> And graunte grace þat we may lyue,
> Prey hym for þat ilke loue
> Þat drow him doun from heuene aboue
> To souke of þi swete tete,
> Þat he wolde oure peynes bete;
> ffor oure synne al-þey be sterne,
> Þin askyng wil he þe not werne.[7]

The function which she performs in mediating between sinful man and her Son is, for late medieval religion, very important, for as Queen of Heaven she represents a principle of mercy by which the sternness of Christ the Judge is balanced.

At the Last Judgment, therefore, Mary is often seen in English art actively interceding for the souls of men and women at the bar of justice. This may not have been stressed in the extant York play of *Doomsday*, but obviously Mary's role was very popular in ordinary civic devotion. Thus, for example, a woodcut in the printed *York Hours* shows her at Christ's right during the Judgment when she is begging for mercy upon the souls of those devoted to her cult.[8] An alabaster in the Victoria and Albert Museum shows her placing a rosary on the beam of the scales to help a soul, and the same motif also appeared widely in wall paintings.[9] In all her humility, Mary nevertheless exerts tremendous power over God himself, for she is, after all, *Theotokos*, the Mother of God, as the Church Council at Ephesus had proclaimed in 431 A.D. Furthermore, in her concern for the followers of her Son, she is also the mother of the Church.[10] As a mother, she is the blessed one who radiates concern for the people. Her function is immediately opposed to the destructive principle in the universe. Mary is perfectly creative, the *magna mater* to whom the medieval citizens of York felt devoted more than to the other saints.

From the standpoint of strictly orthodox theology, Mary was not to receive worship in the sense that God is worshipped. Nevertheless, as the agent of divine intervention, she was in fact invoked very frequently indeed, and for that matter in fifteenth-century York it would have been difficult to distinguish between the *latria* owed to God and the *hyperdulia* permitted to her.[11] For example, in the York *Coronation of the Virgin*, Jesus speaks of the "Wirschippe" which the "aungellis bright" shall direct to Mary as the Queen of Heaven (XLVI.95). As the angel indicates when he comes to tell her of her coming death in the York Drapers' *Death of Mary*, she is "myghtfull Marie, Godis modir so mylde":

> Hayle be þou, roote of all reste, hayle be þou, ryall.
>   Hayle floure and frewte noȝt fadid nor filyd,
> Haile, salue to all synnefull. . . . (XLIV.2–4)

It is not surprising that, at least after about 1430,[12] Mary's image in York churches was ubiquitous, appearing in painted images of alabaster or wood before which the citizens provided wax lights, and also in painted glass and wall paintings as well as other depictions of generally devotional intent. Wills, the fabric rolls of the Minster, and other documents record her presence in the visual arts everywhere. She was everywhere present as a reminder that, in the words of a fifteenth-century poet, she might be invoked as a defender against ultimate doom:

> O mary meik, we the beseik,
> Befor þe Iuge quhen sall meit,
> Off thy prayer we þe require,
> Defend ws fra our fa
> On dreidful domesday.[13]

The practice of such invocations in the fifteenth century would tend to find extension in certain forms, particularly involving the specific use of devotional images everywhere at hand. These images participated in the reality of the one represented, it was believed, and hence a prayer said before a statue would tend to be regarded as particularly efficacious. Indeed, as we know, there was not really a firm line normally drawn between the image and the reality behind the image; as in the Eucharist itself, the visible form tended to provide a channel of communication that would relieve the isolation of the praying Christian and would assist him to overcome his alienation.[14]

Protestant reaction against devotion of this kind should not, therefore, surprise us. While neither Luther nor Calvin completely condemned the veneration of Mary, their followers nevertheless often strongly attacked those devotional practices which focused upon her. The visual representations that illustrated her suffered heavily in England in the Reformation, as we know. The most striking example of iconoclasm aimed at Marian representations is perhaps the vandalism effected in Henry VIII's time in the Lady Chapel at Ely where an entire cycle of Marian scenes in sculpture was smashed.[15] In the plays, Protestant objections to Marian subjects may also be noted. At York, the Creation to Doom cycle was presented in 1548 and again in 1561 and thereafter without the Death of the Virgin, the Assumption, and the Coronation.[16] In the case of the Towneley manuscript, the Marian plays were apparently removed from the playbook — a destructive act that also took with it, for example, an important part of the Towneley *Judicium*.[17] Nevertheless, in spite of some iconoclastic feeling among some Lollards,[18] England as a whole and York in particular were far removed in the period before the Reformation from the wave of sentiment that would question the validity of the cult of Mary. In the fourteenth and fifteenth centuries, her importance was almost universally admitted. Hence, for example, when the Mercers' guild was established in 1356–57, this organization, which was to be so important for the history of the city and of the plays, was founded "in honour of our Lord Jesus Christ *and the blessed Mary*."[19]

Very logically, therefore, the patrons of the York plays arranged for the dramatization of those scenes which illustrate the remarkable death and subsequent history of the Virgin — events regarded as having particular significance for all Christian men

and women who themselves would someday stand before the
bar of justice at the feet of the Judge at the great Doom. These
events in the York plays would appear to have been drawn from
the *Golden Legend* and similar sources, all of them ultimately
dependent upon the apocryphal *Transitus Mariae* attributed to
Melito.[20] Also it should be noted that the scenes in the plays are
for the most part those that had been shown normally in depictions in the visual arts over a period of several centuries. In the
twelfth-century *York Psalter* now at the University of Glasgow,
the angel's appearance to Mary with the palm is followed by her
announcement of the angel's message to the apostles. Next she is
shown on her death bed, with St. Peter holding the palm at its
foot; beside the bed is Jesus giving her his blessing, while a
chorus of angels sings from the upper right hand corner. The
scene is followed by her funeral, with the interruption of the
procession by the hostile Jew, named Fergus in the York dramatic records. The next illustration shows her burial by the
apostles (above) and the carrying of her body to heaven by angels (below), a scene which is not perfectly consistent with the
accounts in such sources as the *Transitus Mariae*.

The brilliantly colored miniatures in the early *York Psalter*,
however, are probably not sufficiently close to the period when
the plays were produced to throw much light on actual matters
of iconography or potential production. Later depictions, both
at York and elsewhere in English art, would rather seem to provide better guides to our understanding of the York plays on the
subjects of the death, assumption, and coronation of the Virgin.
More valuable, therefore, would seem to be the mid-fourteenth-
century panels now in the choir clerestory windows in York
Minster.[21] These show first the coming of the angel to Mary with
the palm described in the play as "oute of paradise" (XLIV.15)
and as a token sent to her by Christ to indicate that she will soon
be crowned Queen of Heaven. Here, as sometimes in the Annunciation scenes, the Virgin has been reading a book (presumably a prayer book) when the angel comes to her. Above, the
hand of the deity reaches down in blessing upon the aged
Virgin, who is said in some accounts to have been sixty years of
age at her death. It is, of course, her death that the angel, identified in the York play as Gabriel, will announce to Mary.

The next panel in the series shows the death of the Virgin among the eleven apostles, who have miraculously been snatched up and brought into her presence (Thomas remains missing). In the York play, the number of men is also eleven, including eight apostles and three Jews who appear to be Mary's kinfolk, in addition to two virgins who are in attendance.[22] Jesus also appears in order to reassure her and urge her not to fear; he will protect her at her death from the devil, who according to the 1415 *Ordo* appeared on stage with one of his demonic followers.[23] The painted glass shows Christ appearing at her bedside and holding her soul, represented as a small naked creature which he has received from her — an exact duplication in the visual arts of the description of her death in the *Golden Legend*, which explains that Mary's soul "went forth out of her body, and flew upward in the arms of her Son."[24] The dramatization in the York play, however, seems to follow a slightly different account, though it is possible that details are merely arranged from the standpoint of practical stagecraft since here also Mary specifically gives up her soul to her Son:

> Mi sely saule I þe sende
>   To heuene þat is highest on heghte,
>   To þe, sone myne þat moste is of myght,
> Ressayue it here into þyne hende. (XLIV.171-74)

In the play, Jesus will now send his angels, of whom there are four, to take up both her "Body and sawle" (l. 189) to heaven where she will be placed beside "þe high trinité" (l. 181). It is perhaps curious that the *Golden Legend*'s handling of her burial in the Valley of Josaphat, which ought to be required to clarify the action of the following plays, is omitted. But unquestionably the sorrow of the apostles is implied, as in the panel of York glass which shows them all weeping or otherwise expressing their mourning. Yet this is a scene which ultimately is joyful and appropriately concluded with music; in the case of the York play, the music is the antiphon *Ave regina celorum*. The curious fifteenth-century stage direction "*Cum vno diabolo*" here may mean because of its placement that one of the demons actually joins in the otherwise angelic song — a song which asserts Mary's power over heaven and also, as empress of hell, over the regions of darkness.

In the series of panels of York glass, the death of the Virgin is followed by her funeral, which shows the apostles carrying the bier and a small figure attempting to overturn "the tabernacle of him who brought disturbance upon us and upon our people. . . ."[25] His hands wither and stick to the bier "so that," the *Golden Legend* says, "he hung therefrom by the hands, and, being grievously tormented, wailed and lamented."[26] His discomfiture is very evident in his facial expression in the York glass. This lively scene is one which was presented in a separate play in the early fifteenth century, when it was performed by actors playing the roles of four apostles, the impious Fergus, and two of his cohorts as well as an angel.[27] The latter supernatural figure would have been assigned to strike the two additional Jews miraculously blind, if we are to believe that the playwright followed the account in the *Golden Legend*.

Unfortunately, *Fergus*, the play that dramatized the funeral of the Virgin, was never entered in the Register. The reason may be that it was seldom performed in the latter part of the century when the Register was compiled, but from the evidence which remains we may be certain that we are missing here a unique and fascinating play. Certainly the opportunities for exploiting the scene theatrically are present. We might like to know, for example, if the play shared the sensationalism of some other depictions in the visual arts—e.g., in the wall paintings at Eton College Chapel where the impious Jew's hands cling miraculously to the bier, while he himself has fallen to the ground.[28] The inscription associated with this scene at Eton reads: "Judaeus · quidam · feretrum beate virginis tangere · <   > credidit liberatur."[29] At Chalgrove, another wall painting seems, in spite of its damaged state, to show St. Peter sprinkling the penitent and kneeling Jew with an aspergillum, whereupon the penitent takes the heavenly palm and goes to his cohorts to heal them also if they will believe.[30]

In the 1415 *Ordo*, the play (identified in Burton's later list as "Portacio corporis marie"[31]) was noted as presented by the "Lynweuers," but since this word is inked over an erasure it points to practice as late as 1476 when this guild did indeed take over Fergus.[32] In the early part of the fifteenth century, the Masons presumably were responsible for the play, since a

Goldsmith's petition entered in the *York Memorandum Book* in 1431-32 notes their dissatisfaction with its subject matter:

> . . . the Masons of this city have been accustomed to mur-
> mur among themselves about their pageant in the Corpus
> Christi Play in which Fergus was beaten because the subject
> of this pageant is not contained in the sacred scripture and
> used to produce more noise and laughter than devotion.
> And whenever quarrels, disagreements, and fights used to
> arise among the people from this, they have rarely or never
> been able to produce their pageant and to play in daylight
> as the preceding pageants do. Therefore, these Masons
> have been striving with great need to be relieved from this
> pageant of theirs and assigned to another which is in har-
> mony with sacred scripture, and which they will be able to
> produce and play in daylight.[33]

It is not known what happened to *Fergus* between this date, when presumably the Masons were relieved of their responsibility and given the scene of *Herod* which, as recent scholarship has shown, was apparently joined to the *Magi* scene, and 1476, when the Linenweavers agreed "perpetually to kepe, bryngforth, and plaie or to make to be plaied yerely vpon Corpus Christi day a pageant and play Called ffergus at þair propir Costes and expenses. . . ."[34] We may guess that this guild was also not happy about presenting *Fergus*, since the dramatic records provide evidence of fines and arrangements by which the guild would help to support other pageants when *Fergus* was not presented. In 1485, the play is "laide apart," but does not disappear entirely from the records until 1518.[35] The Linenweavers apparently continued to be responsible for the play for at least more than forty years, while at the same time it would appear to have been played but seldom.

The records seem to indicate that *Fergus*, while dramatizing the story of the funeral of the Virgin, involved more than its share of comic elaboration, to the extent that the "noise and laughter" reported in 1431-32 were regarded as distracting from the devotional purpose of the plays at York. In other words, the audience response to the play was often inappropriate — not the "religious laughter" that the Corporaton desired to promote, we would imagine. A previously unnoticed piece of evidence to support the theory of comic elaboration of this scene in the York plays appears in the visual arts in a border of a fourteenth-century window in the Minster nave. David O'Connor and Jeremy Haselock have identified the comic monkey funeral in the Pilgrimage Window (c.1320–30, plate 8) as a parody of the Virgin's funeral procession.[36] Here a monkey leads the procession with hand bells, while the monkey crucifer follows; four monkeys carry the bier, which is also being attacked by the smaller figure of a monkey who parodies the actions of Fergus. While the only extant dramatization of the funeral of the Virgin (in the N-town plays) gives no evidence of unusually comic elaboration of the story,[37] the York play of *Fergus* would nevertheless appear to have been lively indeed — and perhaps very lacking in the reverence which the plays were ultimately intended to promote. We may even wonder about the nature of the beating which the character Fergus is reported to have received: was this a case in which the audience participated, beating the actor playing the role? If so, we can see clearly why the Masons wanted to be quit of the play and why the Linenweavers were apparently so reluctant to produce it in spite of their promise to stage it perpetually.

Careful study of the iconographic background of *Fergus* has led one student to suggest that one line of its text (or, it may be added, the entire text of a short liturgical piece) may be known. Mark Sullivan comments:

> Music is necessary to the plot and symbolism of the play. In the *Ludus Coventriae*, the angelic choir sings "*in celo*," echoing the singing of the "Alleluia" of Peter and the apostles so that "the erthe and the eyer" are filled with "melodye." The Jewish reaction to this music provides the initial motive for them to consider attacking the funeral procession. But the music begins with Peter's singing of a line from Psalm 113: "Exiit israel de egipto · domus iacob de populo barbaro." This line, followed by the apostles singing the second verse — "Ffacta est iudea sanctificacio eius israel potestas eius" — includes the incipit of the psalm that appears not only in the *Ludus* version of the story, but also in Melito, the *Golden Legend*, and the *Blickling Homilies*.

The first line of the psalm reflects Mary's own exodus from this world, and is the only line we can reasonably feel certain to have been included in the York *Fergus* play.[38]

Music for this liturgical excerpt would have been readily available, since it was included as an item in the burial service in the Sarum Missal.[39]

Music is much more important for the two plays which follow, the Weavers' *Assumption* and the *Coronation of the Virgin*, assigned in the Register to the Hostelers or Innholders. The first of these plays is unique in English drama since it contains the text and music for angelic songs that introduce and conclude Thomas's vision of the Assumption.[40] Strongly underlined here is the iconographic importance of music in the depiction of this scene.

The *Golden Legend* had indicated that Thomas was not with the other apostles at the time of Mary's death and burial, and, in keeping with his character, "refused to believe" until "the girdle wherewith her body had been begirt fell unopened into his hands, that he might understand that she had been assumed entire."[41] In the play, however, he has not yet met the other apostles since he is returning from India when he comes to the "Vale of Josophat in Jury" where he sits on a bank to rest (XLV.97–104). At this point he has the vision of Mary surrounded by the twelve singing angels which has its ultimate source in the more complete legend told in the apocryphal *Transitus Mariae*. As Carolyn Wall notes in an article on the York play, however, we need not assume that the playwright was directly familiar with the *Transitus* source since the legend was widely known in England by the fifteenth century.[42] Thomas's vision of Mary's soul being taken up to heaven and his receipt of her girdle are curiously brought together with a scene of the burial of the Virgin (with the small figure of the impious Jew included) on the Syon cope, which is early fourteenth-century in date. Thomas's vision of her Assumption is also apparently intended on a roof boss at Peterborough Cathedral, where she holds a belt that she presumably will throw down to him.[43] An alabaster in the Walters Art Gallery, Baltimore, shows Thomas receiving the girdle from the Virgin, who is being taken up into heaven and crowned.[44]

The *Assumption* would appear to be a fairly late addition on the basis of the musical style in the compositions included, and surely when the drama is compared with the description in the *Ordo* of 1415 the evidence seems to point toward the transformation of an ordinary Assumption play into a more elaborate vision of St. Thomas, who was, to be sure, present in the earlier version and, in a manner perhaps consistent with the *Ordo*, is sent forth at the end to preach again in India. The staging of Play XLV would not seem to have been very complex, though of course the use of machinery would have been technologically feasible. The pageant wagon of the Assumption was used for the entry of Henry VII at York in 1486, and here the available machinery was used for both descent and return as "our lady" came down from heaven first to "welcome the king" before thereafter ascending "ayene into heven wit angell sang and yer schall it snaw by craft tobe made of waffrons in maner of Snaw."[45] But the pageant utilized may well have been that used not for this play but for the next, the *Coronation of the Virgin*, which repeats the Assumption — an event that will require music and singing as she ascends from below to a higher level symbolic of heaven.

The early support of the Coronation play by the mayor[46] would seem to suggest special attention to the *Coronation of the Virgin*, probably an expansion of the drama described in the *Ordo* of 1415. Until the Innholders took over the play (sometime before 1468-69), this production must indeed have been splendid in order to be consistent with the important office of the mayor who was the chief magistrate of the city. But even later the city was willing to subsidize this play, in 1484 giving two shillings toward its production. Yet in 1433 the city had contributed *twenty* shillings toward the play for the players — a considerable sum, equal to the amount paid on Corpus Christi day to the Minstrels, who may also have participated in this drama of the Coronation.[47]

In the visual arts, both the Assumption and the Coronation were popular throughout England during the late Middle Ages, and York was no exception in this regard. In spite of fierce Protestant hostility we may be surprised that so much remains as evidence of this popularity. Though the Protestant clergy and officials were determined to cleanse York Minster and the parish

churches of York of both elaborate ceremonial and Catholic imagery,[48] some surprising examples were allowed to remain. In
spite of the zeal of such men as Dean Matthew Hutton, therefore, a boss showing the Assumption remained (probably in damaged state) in the doorway of the choir screen in the Minster. This
very delicately carved fifteenth-century work shows the Virgin
with her arms crossed standing in the midst of a mandorla surrounded by clouds and being borne up by four angels. In fifteenth-century glass in St. Mary Bishophill, Junior, Mary is
shown crowned and wearing an ermine mantle. The Coronation
of the Virgin seems to have fared even better than the Assumption, for many York examples remain, and these include painted
glass and a pendant boss on the choir screen in the Minster as
well as painted glass in several York churches. The most interesting of these surely is the panel of painted glass in Holy Trinity,
Goodramgate, where God is shown as three persons crowned
and in human form, all united under one ermine mantle as an
indication of the unity of the Trinity. The Father originally held
the Virgin's crown, apparently, and other restoration has altered
some additional aspects of the design, as in the case of the
Virgin's head which had at some point been knocked out and
which has been restored.[49] The York play, which seems to have
included only Jesus among the persons of the Trinity, would
therefore have been closer in design to several other examples in
York art which show merely the Son crowning his mother, who
is often seated in a rich chair, as in the glass in the Great West
Window. However, we may note that both the Father and the
Son appear in the sixteenth-century fragment which represents a
revision of the Innholders' play in the Register.[50] While angels
commonly appear in the Assumption, their presence in the Coronation is less usual, but they do appear, emerging from the
clouds between Christ and the Blessed Virgin (seated and
crowned) in the *Bolton Hours* (fol. 37^V). Thus had been the case
in the play as it was described in the 1415 *Ordo*, which identified
a group of angelic singers.

The Marian plays in the York cycle hence conclude with the
scene of the Coronation of the Virgin, who becomes Queen of
Heaven and mediatrix between man and God. For alienated

man on the pilgrimage of life, she represents the hope of salvation, which without her would seem too often beyond the grasp
of fallen men and women. Thus the Coronation itself, whether
pictured on a morse on a cope (the fabric rolls of York Minster
record eight examples), on a Gospel Book cover, or in painted
glass or alabaster, represents the urge of civic piety to achieve an
experience of transcendent religion. In the York plays, the scene
which illustrates the Coronation is appropriately preparatory to
the Last Judgment itself, when mercy will be given to those who
have performed the Corporal Acts of Mercy and damnation will
be given to those who have failed to live lives of charity. The
Virgin has at once been the perfect model of charity and the
mother of the Church. This is wonderfully set forth near the
close of the York play when Christ announces to her:

> Before all oþere creatours
>   I schall þe giffe both grace and might,
> In heuene and erþe to sende socoures
>   To all þat seruis þe day and nyght. . . . (XLVI.145–48)

XI

THE LAST JUDGMENT

In the earlier version of the York Mercers' play of *Doomsday* as described in Burton's *Ordo* of 1415, Mary, Queen of Heaven, is on stage with her Son:

> Iesus Maria xij apostoli iiij^{or} angeli cum tubis et iiij^{or} cum corona lancea et ij flagellis iiij^{or} spiritus boni et iiij^{or} spiritus maligni et vj diaboli.[1]

As the previous chapter indicates, Mary's presence at the Last Judgment would hardly be unique, for she was widely regarded as *virgo mediatrix* – a role given substance through reference to typology and popularized by works such as the *Speculum Humanae Salvationis*.[2] Very likely in the play presented in 1415 she was interceding actively for souls, as was the case in frequent representations in the visual arts.[3] A continental woodcut in the printed *York Hours* of the early sixteenth century shows the Virgin prominently at Christ's side in supplication, while St. Michael instead of weighing evil and good deeds merely uses his sword to threaten those who are excluded from mercy.[4] In the York plays, however, the Virgin may possibly have dropped out of this pageant by 1433, for there is no record of her role in either dramatic records or play text then or thereafter. As Peter

Meredith has warned us, of course, we cannot even assume that the description of the Mercers' play in the *Ordo* referred to anything like the same play that was being produced as shortly thereafter as 1433, the year the remarkable indenture discovered in 1971 by Johnston and Rogerson (née Dorrell) was drawn up.[5]

But the presence of Mary in the 1415 *Ordo* nevertheless identifies an important concern of the Mercers in their concluding spectacle of the York cycle even after this character was dropped from the play. Mary above all represents mercy extended to the whole body of Christ—i.e., to the Church—and indeed the quality of *mercy* is the principle that is at the heart of the theatrical display. To be sure, the time of the Last Judgment precludes the abrogation of what has already been established in history: the time of mercy is past. Grace can now be extended only to the good souls since it is the end of history and of time. For the elect, this day may be fearful, but it is ultimately the day when mercy is given. Nevertheless, for those watching the play *it is still the time of mercy*, and their lifetimes will be the space in which they may so order their souls that they may at the Last Day be among the blessed. Herein the play urges an immediate response, since delay in the spiritual life, especially in an age of high mortality and swift death, might cut persons off from the highly desired mercy of God. Hence it is that the acceptance of God's mercy is vital to each person in the present, and for late medieval piety this must be done according to the precepts set forth in *Matthew* 25.

Mercy is therefore dependent upon doing deeds of charity. Such deeds, of course, could include more than assistance to the poor, though the poor and the similarly disadvantaged were often the beneficiaries of charity. The evidence of wills is important here. In her will in 1474, for example, Joan Warde left money to be distributed to prisoners, while Henry de Brighton, a chaplain, in 1427 left thirteen shillings and sixpence "for distribution among prisoners and lepers in York City and suburbs." Henry de Bolton, a cooper, in 1404 left one pound "for distribution to the most needy and poor on my burial day."[6] But charity was indeed commonly understood in a much broader sense, so that even the presentation of the cycle plays on the feast of Corpus

Christi would count as a charitable deed, as also would the foundation of chantry chapels and the endowment of lights before images of saints.[7]

In the passage from *Matthew* 25 that is paraphrased by Christ in the York *Doomsday* as an explanation for the division of good souls from bad, charitable deeds are codified according to six categories that were widely recognized in the late Middle Ages. These categories are, of course, collectively identified as the Corporal Acts of Mercy, normally with a seventh act included—the burial of the dead. (The seventh Corporal Act is retained only in the N-town cycle, but may be seen in various examples in the visual arts, including the restored wall painting at Pickering in North Yorkshire.) In the York play, Jesus explains that feeding the hungry, giving drink to the thirsty, clothing the naked, succoring prisoners, giving shelter to the homeless and to pilgrims, and visiting the sick are obligatory acts which are done to fellow men in Christ's name:

> Mi blissid childir, I schall ʒou saye
>   What tyme þis dede was to me done:
> When any þat nede hadde, nyght or day,
>   Askid ʒou helpe and hadde it sone. (XLVII.309–12)

At the Last Judgment, those who had failed to do the charitable Acts of Mercy would themselves be turned away from the ultimate source of mercy and would be consigned to hell's pit.

As noted above in Chapter VI, the Corporal Acts of Mercy are represented in an important window in All Saints, North Street, a church which was located in a section of York where many affluent merchants lived in the early fifteenth century. Indeed, this glass, installed c.1420, is typical of the windows inserted in this church during a period of prosperity for the York merchants, for it was of the very highest quality and the finest design.[8] While no direct connection can be established between the window and the York *Doomsday* play, the concerns which inform each are very obviously similar, for the Acts of Mercy presented in the glass are the basis for the extension of mercy to the saved at the Last Day. It is very significant to note that in the window in each case the charitable man is dressed in the garb of an affluent merchant (in one panel he wears an ermine collar) who distributes alms to prisoners, gives bread to the hungry, and so forth. In an important sense these acts are also placed over against another window, also containing the highest quality of glass—the Fifteen Signs of Doomsday window in the same church. The legendary signs of the end of time are not given illustration, of course, in the York play, though elsewhere in the English cycle plays they do indeed play a part.[9] But as a warning of the end, the Fifteen Signs of Doomsday in the All Saints glass serve to point to the potential for eschatological disaster for those who will not live their lives as persons expecting to face the Judge at the Last Day. When we look back to the Corporal Acts window, we now will see it as setting forth the manner of life which will lead to a satisfactory encounter with the Judge and to the joy of eternal life.

The vividness with which the Corporal Acts window sets forth its scenes has caused it to be one of the most admired examples of early fifteenth-century painted glass from a parish church in England. Such vividness would also have been expected from the York Doomsday play, and hence it is worthwhile to give very close attention to the design and subject matter of the glass. In the panel which shows giving drink to the thirsty, the merchant is shown pouring from a flagon in a cup, while a servant is bringing more to drink from the man's house. Six persons are receiving drink, and of these one is a cripple (center, below) who wears knee pads and uses small hand crutches which he utilizes for mobility. This man, like a standing figure above him, holds out his cup to be filled by the charitable man. In the panel which shows giving shelter to the homeless, one of the standing men also is crippled and is using crutches. This figure is grasping a strap which is attached to the old man with a staff who stands in the center of the panel where he is being welcomed by the host. In the scene that illustrates feeding the hungry (plate 16), a servant is distributing a large basket full of bread to those who are standing about, and in the panel showing visiting the prisoners the charitable man has given food and drink and is now about to give them some money. Visiting the sick presents a different view of charity, for the person who is visited is obviously not poor: even his bedspread is very richly embroidered — a sign that charity was to be given to all in need, both rich and poor, by all who were able to do so. Everything in the window is drawn with great care for detail, and we note such aspects as the unique faces and the attention obviously placed on items that are included (e.g., the basket which holds the bread, the bedspread mentioned above, etc.). The preference for this kind of precision should make us doubtful of any interpretation that would make the Mercers' play in the York cycle vague or lacking in the specific details which would create a more sharply visualized play. The play therefore ought not to be judged solely by the surviving text in the Register, which gives the state of the Mercers' play in the latter part of the fifteenth century and in the sixteenth century before the suppression of the Corpus Christi drama. Though the incomplete Towneley *text* is more lively, the York play *as staged* may hardly have seemed ineffective as theater and as spectacle.

The first sixty-four lines of the York *Doomsday* are entirely devoted to God the Father's summary of the history of the race and of his merciful act in sending his "sone with full blithe moode / Till erþe, to salue þame of þare sare" (XLVII.27-28). The Son's duty was to "reste on roode" in order to buy his people "with his body bare":

For þame he shedde his harte-bloode —
    What kyndinesse myght [God] do þame mare? (XLVII.30-32)

The key lines are surely the ones in which the Father explains that men have "founde me *full of mercye, / Full of grace and forgiffenesse*" (XLVII.41-42; italics mine), though unfortunately the race has not always responded appropriately to his offer of such mercy, grace, and forgiveness. Indeed, because the world is now so wicked, the Father will order historical time to come to an ending: he will send his angels "To blawe þer bemys, þat all may here / The tyme is comen I will make ende" (XLVII.63-64).

Presumably God's speech is spoken from a structure at the top of the pageant wagon, perhaps in the sixteenth century from what is identified as the "trenette hus" in an inventory of 1526,

which of course refers to the new pageant created for the play by
Thomas Drawswerd between 1501 and 1507.[10] The Father would
seem to have appeared above with the Son and Holy Spirit, perhaps in the non-realistic but popular design that utilized the figure
of Christ on the cross with his wounds displayed prominently
immediately before the Father.[11] The Father's lines suggest such
a display, and there is additionally the presence of this motif on
the seal of the Mercers' guild from 1435. The seal, which shows
a ship on each side (and we remember that York, situated on the
Ouse River, was a seaport with direct connections to the Flemish
ports in the fifteenth century), illustrates the Father seated
above the water with both hands raised (his right hand is giving
his blessing) while before him is the smaller figure of Christ on
the cross.[12] Presumably, if my conjecture is correct, the
Mercers' pageant wagon, both before and after Drawswerd's new
pageant was completed, was given an upper level for a *tableau vi-
vant* which would show forth the very emblem of the sponsoring
guild. After Drawswerd's new pageant was introduced in
c.1507, the figure of the Son may well have been carved in alabaster and painted in order to approximate the proportions that
are observed with regard to the size of the figures in the Trinity
scenes showing Christ on the cross. Such a Trinity scene almost
surely appeared in any case on the banners listed in the 1433 indenture and identified as "j Baner of rede bukeram bett with
golde with þe Trinite and with ostret feders and With j lange
Stremer Item iiij Smale baners with Trinite in þam and Roset."[13]

In contrast to the depiction of the Last Judgment in the Great
East Window in York Minster—a window which shows, above,
the story of the early history of the race as a prelude to the more
elaborate series of panels illustrating the matter of the end of
time—the York Mercers' play practically ignores the *Apocalypse*
with its complex narrative of events to come at the conclusion of
the age. Instead, with its heavy reliance on *Matthew* 25, the play
was fairly typical of the ways in which the Doom was most commonly pictured in the visual arts. Indeed, every visual aspect of
the York play would seem to find its parallel in painting or
sculpture from the fifteenth century. At its most simple, the
scene would show, as in an illustration in the *Bolton Hours* of

c.1420, a large Christ (with prominent wounds) sitting on a rainbow. An angel at each side blows a beam or trumpet, and below
St. Peter admits the good souls to the heavenly city while the
souls of the wicked are entering a gaping hell mouth.[14] Another
York illumination of approximately the same date, an initial in
York Minster Library XVI.K.6, fol. 31, also gives graphic representation to the wounds from the flagellation which remain
visible. The chapel of the Mercers' guild appropriately contained
a similar Judgment scene painted on a cloth at the high altar; the
records of the guild indicate that the cloth depicted "our Lorde
syttyng on the rayne bowe."[15]

That the Judgment scene was very often regarded as central is
indicated not only by the placement of the painted cloth in the
Mercers' chapel, but also by the common location of the scene
in many other churches both at York and elsewhere. In the eighteenth century, Thomas Gent reported, for example, that the
central subject in the East Window over the high altar of Christ
Church, King Square, was the Last Judgment,[16] and we know
from the remains of wall paintings throughout the country that
the scene was very popularly placed above the chancel arch.[17]
The symbolism here is very obvious and also quite relevant to
the placement of the Doomsday play at the conclusion of the
Corpus Christi cycle. As E. W. Tristram has noted, this is even
to be regarded in the visual arts as the "normal position" of the
scene, since the chancel arch "symbolized the division between
this world and the next."[18] Durandus had understood the cruci-
form church to be arranged with the chancel signifying the
"head," keeping in mind the symbolism of Christ as head of the
Church, while the transepts represent the arms and the nave represents the body, which also suggests the symbolism of the
Church as the body of Christ.[19] The chancel, as the space where
the Eucharist was consecrated — a space associated with the
common intersection of eternity and time in the rite — was therefore to be recognized in terms of the end of the earthly journey
of man; metonymically it was a space that lay on the other side
of the Judgment — the scene that hence was appropriately painted
above the arch separating the chancel from the remainder of the
building. The congregation of a parish church thus would look

upon the painted scene of the Judgment when looking toward the East — the direction in which the Second Coming was to appear and also therefore the direction toward which the church building itself was oriented.

Those who have devoted themselves to the seven deadly sins instead of the Corporal Acts of Mercy — an opposition which is directly represented in a Last Judgment wall painting at Trotton, Sussex — must, it is assumed, look upon the scene with terror. A hell mouth was always present, it would seem, in the visual arts as in the York Judgment play. And behind the hell mouth was, as we have seen, always a place of torture, with its cauldron (or, later, a blast furnace) for souls; this place might be really present in the scene, or it might be imagined. The famous early York Doom-stone shows such torture,[20] and the linkage between this treatment of souls and the location behind the mouth of hell is something almost ubiquitous in the arts. The Mercers apparently had a hell mouth which was either separate from their pageant wagon or attached to it.[21] The "helle mouthe" is given separate listing in the 1433 indenture, and also is mentioned in the 1526 inventory, though in each case the information from the dramatic records does not supply an unequivocal answer to the question of whether or not it was attached to or detached from the wagon. However, the 1526 entry, which as noted above in Chapter II lists only a "hell dure," may provide basis for the conjecture that no separate pageant was intended. In a number of examples in the visual arts, the evil souls being thrust through this bad entrance are being rounded up by having a chain pulled around them as a group; the demons are clearly enjoying it all, as in the painting at the Church of St. Thomas of Canterbury, Salisbury, where the restored wall painting shows a king and a queen as well as a high ecclesiastic among the damned.[22] In the York play, the first bad soul complains immediately upon his resurrection about the "hydous horne" of the angels and cries out in despair that he and the other wicked souls are doomed on account of their "wikkid werkis" (XLVII.115, 129). He and his fellows must now endure "wikkid peynes" forever and ever as they "In helle . . . dwelle with feendes blake, / Wher neuer schall be redempcioune" (XLVII. 136, 143–44). The second bad soul then actually notes that wicked fiends stand by to carry them off and torture them, and in their predicament their weeping will not assist them in any way to escape what they have deserved.

Hell is not a pleasant place. Behind the entrance of this place, according to a source cited by G. R. Owst, "is stynke, and ther is all derkenes. . . . There is horribull sygh3t off develes, dragons, wormes and serpentys to turment them. Ther is sygh3ynge and sorowynge, wepynge and weylynge, hideous cryynge, grugeynge and murnynge, hunger and thyrste irremediable, wyth gnagyng off tethe wyth-owte ende."[23]

At York in 1463, the souls, both good and bad, were given a "now pagand yat was mayd for ye sallys to ryse owtof."[24] The 1415 *Ordo* had noted four good and four bad souls, but by 1433 the number had apparently been reduced to two for each category—a number which, it would seem, was not increased thereafter. Thus the new pageant of 1463 could be quite small and easily transported; its frame was of fir but was further filled out with lathe, and the whole was covered with five yards of "now canvays."[25] Johnston and Rogerson speculate that the pageant was without wheels and was made in the shape of a coffin, but careful examination of examples in the visual arts from England during the period reasonably contemporary with the play will provide no absolute confidence with regard to the precise design.[26]

The evil souls were most likely given leather suits somewhat similar to the ones provided for Adam and Eve to simulate nudity. These would be the items listed in the important 1433 inventory as "Array for ij euell saules þat is to say ij Sirkes ij paire hoses ij vesenes and ij Chauelers [and] Array for ij gode saules þat ys to say ij Sirkes ij paire hoses ij vesernes and ij Cheuelers."[27] ("Sirkes" are shirts, "vesernes" are masks, and "Cheuelers" are wigs.) Undoubtedly these sets of garments for the good and bad souls differed in color as a means of differentiating between the recipients of mercy and of damnation.

In the York play, the role of the devils who descend upon the damned is much smaller than that of those in the Towneley play, which though based on the text of York's play nevertheless is expanded to include among other recognizable demons the unforgettable Tutivillus, whose principal task is to gather up in a sack those words misspoken or mumbled at Mass.²⁸ The York *Dooms-day* has three devils, each of whom speaks only four lines. Never-theless visually their role at York should not be underestimated in spite of the seemingly bland speeches assigned to them. Merely painting "ye dellwys gere" cost the Mercers twelve pence, paid "to Richard pantur" who did the work, in 1463.²⁹ In 1415, there had been six devils, but these were reduced to three already by 1433 when the indenture indicates that their garments were com-pleted by six masks — two for each devil in the play — described as "vj deuelles faces in iij Vesernes."³⁰ In 1526, however, when York was less prosperous than it had been a century before, two devils perhaps sufficed, if we are to believe the inventory of that year which mentions only "ij dewell cottes" and "ij dewell heddes."³¹

The reason for a larger number of angels than devils in the York *Doomsday* is, however, rather puzzling unless we see that the division of the race into saved and damned is here intended actually to place more emphasis on God's mercy than on the harshness of his judgment. The *Ordo* of 1415 had named four angels with trumpets (reduced later to two, as in the Register and in the inventories of 1433 and 1526) and four carrying signs of the Passion (identified as the crown of thorns, the lance, and two scourges). By 1433, the number of angels had increased to include presumably, in addition to the two angels with the trumpets, seven great and four smaller ones "gilted" holding signs of the Passion, and the "ix smaler Aungels payntid rede to renne aboute in þe heuen."³² The Register, which is dated ap-proximately a generation later than the indenture, has speaking roles for three angels only, and two of these are the ones who blow their beams or trumpets to call souls "to þis grette assise" (XLVII.94). The third angel in this group is surely the most in-teresting of those with speaking roles. Though limited to eight lines of dialogue, he is the angel previously noted in Chapter VIII, above — the popular St. Michael, the traditional enemy of the great dragon Satan and the angel who participates directly in the psychostasis.³³ In glass of c.1330 in St. Michael-le-Belfrey, York, he is weighing souls (one of the pans of the scales contains a seated demon of small size), and the same act is recorded in mid-fifteenth-century glass in St. Mary Bishophill Junior.³⁴ But in the Towneley play, he is simply identified as the angel with a sword, while in art he may sometimes be seen merely carrying this sword, with which he separates the good souls from the bad.[35] In the wall painting at St. Thomas, Salisbury, St. Michael with his sword escorts the good souls toward the gate of heaven. The York Mass for the Dead likewise stresses this role in the Offertorium which prays that the souls of the faithful may not be held in the inferno but may be led by St. Michael into holy light.[36] And this is the function that he performs in the York Doomsday play when he orders the souls not to stand together, for he can only escort the blessed to heaven: "parte you in two! / All sam schall ȝe noght be in blisse . . ." (XLVII.169–70). The good shall indeed be placed on the "right hande," while the "weryed wightis" shall be on God's "lefte hande as none of his" (XLVII.173–76).

The angels which carry the symbols of the Passion — emblems of Christ's mercy which he has extended to the world — would seem in 1433 to have included both actors and puppets, with the former perhaps also functioning as singers to produce the music after line 216 and at the close of the play — a close which also brings to an end the entire cycle of pageants at York with a harmony appropriate for the bliss that is entered into by the good souls. However, the 1433 list is problematical, and hence it may even be argued that all of these were puppets rather than human actors. It is well known that puppets were widely used in the Middle Ages,[37] and there is no way of distinguishing between sets of costumes and the carved and clothed figures that could easily have been prepared by the carvers of the city of York. While it would be most attractive to see the angels as combining male actors — men *and boys* — with puppets, we simply cannot be certain on the basis of the evidence available. Nevertheless, the text in the Register indicates very specifically which signs of the Passion were included: scourges, the cross, the crown of thorns, a spear, and a Jew spitting.[38] Finally, the "grete" angel noted in the 1433 indenture as having "a fane of laton and a crosse of Iren in his hede gilted" is surely different from the other angels in this group. The gilt iron cross is likely to have been similar to such an item on the head of the fifteenth-century angel in the tracery of a window at Lavenham, Kent.[39] By 1526, in any case, the list of angels was much reduced in number.

The 1526 inventory indicates the reduction or possibly the elimi-
nation of the smallest angels reported in 1433. The later inventory is again extremely ambiguous, but the evidence would seem
to argue again for simplification and some reduction of com-
plexity in the spectacle presented on the new pageant wagon
which had been built by Drawswerd. The 1433 indenture, as we
have noted, explicitly lists the eleven "smaler Aungels payntid
rede to renne aboute in þe heuen" and adds that the gear also included "A lang small corde to gerre þe Aungels renne aboute."⁴⁰
The reconstruction of Johnston and Rogerson suggests that
these are puppets circling about the top of the pageant under the
roof, but their design seems to be speculation for which it would
be hard to find much support. It is more likely here that the
model which would provide a more sound iconography might
be the restored glass in the West Window at Fairford where the
cherubin, who are painted red in the glass, move in a circle
about the figure of Christ as Judge.⁴¹ This iconography is also
corroborated by a Doom at Gloucester Cathedral.⁴²

In the York *Doomsday*, Christ was provided with apparatus
to descend to take his place on the Judgment seat amidst the
seated apostles in a tableau that is a very similar to contemporary
illustrations in English art. A windlass seems to have been provided both in the earlier pageant and in Drawswerd's new
pageant, and the descent would surely have been designed to be
seen as similar to the ascent at the time of the Ascension in the
play on that subject. In the *Holkham Bible Picture Book*, Christ
descends on a cloud (fol. 42)—a stage property noted in the
1433 indenture and also in the 1526 inventory—while in the wall
painting at St. Thomas, Salisbury, the small figures of the
apostles are seated below him. At York, the initial scene, which
in a solemn and affecting moment of medieval stagecraft remains static while angels sing, shows Christ seated on a rainbow
made up of two pieces "of tymber."⁴³ He is clearly suspended in
the air on his seat, and from this position he will judge the
world.⁴⁴ Now the time of mercy will be past, and the actual
judging of souls will begin which will distribute the bad souls to
their proper dwelling among the "fendis blake" (XLVII.198–99).
He has come like a king to establish his court among the souls of

men in order that he might "deme [their] dedis and make ending" (XLVII.234). The 1433 indenture gives him "a Sirke Wounded a diademe with a veserne gilted."[45] Nothing is said in the dramatic records about a royal robe, which of course would be opened to show the wounds on his body (represented by the shirt, presumably of leather, with wounds painted upon it), yet the visualizing of a royal garment as in the *Bolton Hours* would seem to be obligatory here. Along with the gilt mask would also be a cross nimbus which would have been attached.

According to John Mirk's *Festial*, Christ will come on the Last Day of history with his apostles and saints in order that he might be the ultimate judge among sinners. He may be expected to "schow all his wondys all fresch, as that day that he deyet on the crosse"; everyone will see the bloody cross also, along with "all other ynstrumentys of his passyon."[46] So it will be therefore in the York *Doomsday*, when Christ appears to the souls of all men and reveals his wounds, which are surely intended to inspire "love-teeris" and sweet sorrow for his suffering among the viewers of the scene.[47] Christ's words are reminiscent of the lyric complaints of the Savior from the cross:

> Here may ȝe see my woundes wide,
>   Þe whilke I tholed for youre mysdede.
> Thurgh harte and heed, foote, hande and hide,
>   Nought for my gilte, butt for youre nede.
> Beholdis both body, bak and side,
>   How dere I bought youre brotherhede.
> Þes bittir peynes I wolde abide —
>   To bye you blisse þus wolde I bleede.
>
> Mi body was scourged withouten skill,
>   As theffe full thraly was I thrette;
> On crosse þei hanged me, on a hill,
>   Blody and bloo, as I was bette,
> With croune of thorne throsten full ill.
>   Þis spere vnto my side was sette —
> Myne harte-bloode spared noght þei for to spill;
>   Manne, for thy loue wolde I not lette.
>
> Þe Jewes spitte on me spitously,
>   Þei spared me no more þan a theffe.

Whan þei me strake I stode full stilly,
   Agaynste þam did I nothyng greue.
Behalde, mankynde, þis ilke is I,
   Þat for þe suffered swilke mischeue,
Þus was I dight for thy folye —
   Man, loke, thy liffe was to me ful leffe.

Þus was I dight þi sorowe to slake;
   Manne, þus behoued þe to borowed be.
In all my woo toke I no wrake,
   Mi will itt was for þe loue of þe.
Man, sore aught þe for to quake,
   Þis dredfull day þis sight to see.
All þis I suffered for þi sake —
   Say, man, what suffered þou for me? (XLVII.245-76)

But to the good souls, Christ's wounds and suffering will ultimately be a source of comfort; to the bad ones, however, the
same wounds and pain will serve as a source of existential terror
that is beyond comprehension.

The emphasis at the end of the York play is upon the mercy
which he has extended to his "chosen childir," whom he invites
to come with him to dwell where "joie and blisse schall euer be"
(XLVII.365-67). In contrast to Cain's kin who will be consigned
to everlasting sorrow and suffering to be endured by the side of
"Satanas þe fende" (XLVII.372), the chosen ones will forever
"belde and bide in [his] blissing" (XLVII.380). Now all God's
plan, as represented by the Book of Creation held by him in representations such as the one at the top of the tracery of the Great
East Window of York Minster, has been completed, for, as
Jesus indicates in the York play, "endid is all erthely thyng"
(XLVII.374). But most importantly, those who "mendid þame
whils þei moght" are the ones who shall forever rest in God's
"blissing" (XLVII.379-80). The way to mercy has been open,
and these men and women are the ones who have taken advantage
of the way of charity and love. As the Mass for the Dead in the
York rite reminds us, the day of wrath is also the day of joy
when his chosen people shall enter into the eternal light.[48]

The York Doomsday is, of course, a particularly valuable text
which might be studied against the iconographic evidence because

we also have available the Mercers' documents, including the 1433 indenture recently discovered. It would be very difficult to see this play as influencing in any significant way the visual arts of York in pre-Reformation times, while at the same time the play shares a great deal with examples from the visual arts both from York and elsewhere. Nevertheless, there is a great deal that can be learned from careful and systematic comparative study. Religious art and religious drama were not seen in the Middle Ages as ends themselves, but rather they were understood in terms of their function or purpose. Hence the two artistic forms come together and seem to blend, and in so doing they demand of us that we should understand more fully the cultic, social, and even economic milieu that brought both into being.

The drama and the art are first of all expressions of the civic piety that informed communities such as York and inspired the religious artistic forms in ways that we can only determine through the efforts of our scholarship. It may be refreshing for us today as scholars to reach back beyond the period dominated by the humanist and Protestant overvaluing of the *word*, and to make contact with a more visually oriented culture. This may seem particularly true in these times of instability and historical doom-saying, and more than ever we learn from the past that a viable and solidly based *supra*-rationalism of the kind provided by the religious myths of the late medieval period may be a salve for the modern malaise and our modern alienation. It cannot be forgotten that the age of the cycle plays was also an age of pestilence, war, and even at times near anarchy, and yet this was a period that more than any other supported the production of the religious arts and of religious popular theater. The rise of the Creation to Doom cycle, which flourished so strongly at York and certain other civic centers, occurred in the centuries following the arrival of the bubonic plague in 1348–49 — centuries we can hardly characterize as quiet, happy, or bucolic. England was indeed in ferment, with its population decimated by epidemic and its base of wealth sharply shifted away from what it had been in the past. By the end of the period, there was the additional upheaval of the Reformation with its strong antagonism to the old ways of seeing religious scenes and its consequent iconoclasm—an iconoclasm that extended to the scenes on the religious stage.

When communities during the fourteenth through sixteenth centuries united in a common effort to produce a religious play cycle, therefore, they deliberately were looking beyond the immediate toward the existential realities which they saw as distinct from what could be perceived through immediate sense perception. Their vision was the biblical one reaching from Alpha to Omega, from the beginning to the end of the history of the race. Through the plays they therefore participated in that vision imaginatively and directly.

NOTES

Chapter I

1. The theory that the medieval drama influenced medieval art in substantial ways was argued forcefully by Émile Mâle; see the English translation of his *Religious Art in France: The Twelfth Century,* Bollingen Ser., 90, 1 (Princeton: Princeton Univ. Press, 1978), and also Otto Pächt, *The Rise of Pictorial Narrative in Twelfth-Century England* (Oxford: Clarendon Press, 1962). The later medieval drama, including the English Creation to Doom cycles, has also been dealt with extensively. See especially M. D. Anderson, *Drama and Imagery in English Medieval Churches* (Cambridge: Cambridge Univ. Press, 1963), and W. L. Hildburgh, "English Alabaster Carvings as Records of the Medieval Religious Drama," *Archaeologia,* 93 (1949), 51-101. Widespread influence of the drama on the visual arts, however, has recently been questioned; see F. P. Pickering, *Literature and Art in the Middle Ages* (Coral Gables, Fla.: Univ. of Miami Press, 1970), *passim,* and A. M. Nagler, *The Medieval Religious Stage* (New Haven: Yale Univ. Press, 1976), pp. 74-105. See also Rosemary Woolf, *The English Mystery Plays* (Berkeley and Los Angeles: Univ. of California Press, 1972), *passim.* Pamela Sheingorn, arguing against the investigation of the primacy of either art or drama, sensibly suggests that both "are expressions of medieval Christian culture, itself based on sacred texts and changing interpretations of those texts. Religious thought generated the entire cultural complex, and it is primarily to changes in religious thought that we should look for motivating changes in art and in literature" ("On Using Medieval Art in the Study of Medieval Drama: An Introduction to Methodology," *Research Opportunities in Renaissance Drama,* 22 [1979], 106). But drama is spectacle as well as literature (if indeed it aspires to the latter may often be open to question), and there is much to be said for the *visual* element in tradition. This visual tradition was less dependent upon plays than upon less ephemeral and more universal kinds of images. Earlier in her paper (p. 103), Professor Sheingorn quotes the remarkable observation made by Meyer Schapiro in his *Words and Pictures* (The Hague: Mouton, 1973) that "the correspondence of word and picture is often problematic

and . . . surprisingly vague." It is as dangerous to underrate the strength of visual tradition as to make assumptions concerning the alleged influence of drama on art. The "motivating changes" are sometimes there in the intellectual and popular texts, but sometimes they are not. Instead, we would need to look to the model books the artists used and to ways in which the visual tradition was adapted from decade to decade. Professor Sheingorn is absolutely correct in insisting that drama and art should both be approached systematically and with the greatest scholarly tact in terms of the "entire cultural context" and of its religious basis.

2. Anderson, *Drama and Imagery,* p. 5.

3. Hildburgh, "English Alabaster Carvings," p. 53.

4. Pickering, *Literature and Art,* pp. 165–66.

5. H. T. Musper, *Die Urausgaben der holländischen Apokalypse und Biblia Pauperum* (Munich: Prestel, 1961), II, 26.

6. Jacobus de Voragine, *The Golden Legend,* trans. Granger Ryan and Helmut Ripperger (New York: Longmans, Green, 1941), p. 191.

7. Hildburgh, "English Alabaster Carvings," p. 86.

8. Pächt, *Pictorial Narrative, passim.*

9. Karl Young, *Drama in the Medieval Church* (Oxford: Clarendon Press, 1933), I, 249; trans. Joseph Quincy Adams, *Chief Pre-Shakespearean Dramas* (Boston: Houghton Mifflin, 1924), p. 9.

10. While William L. Smoldon saw the plainchant melodies as consistent with the Easter Introit ("The Melodies of the Medieval Church-Dramas and Their Significance," *Comparative Drama,* 2 [1968], 185–209), more recent scholarship has suggested that the origin of the *Quem queritis* is more complex; see especially David Bjork, "On the Dissemination of *Quem quaeritis* and the *Visitatio sepulchri* and the Chronology of Their Early Sources," *Comparative Drama,* 14 (1980), 46–69; rpt. in *Drama in the Middle Ages,* ed. Clifford Davidson, C. J. Gianakaris, and John H. Stroupe (New York: AMS Press, 1982), pp. 1–4.

11. See Thomas Bilson, *A Sermon Preached at Westminster, before the King and Queenes Majesties, at Their Coronations* (London, 1603), sig. C2.

12. See Pickering, *passim,* and Erwin Panofsky, *Early Netherlandish Painting* (Cambridge: Harvard Univ. Press, 1953), I, 2. These matters are treated below in Chapter VII.

13. James Torre, *The Antiquities of York Minster,* MS. in York Minster Library, p. 7.

14. David E. O'Connor and Jeremy Haselock, "The Stained and Painted Glass," in *A History of York Minster*, ed. G. E. Aylmer and Reginald Cant (Oxford: Clarendon Press, 1977), p. 367.

15. See Chapters VI and VII, below.

16. Panofsky, *Early Netherlandish Painting*, I, 2ff.

17. *Cur Deus Homo*, trans. Eugene R. Fairweather, in *A Scholastic Miscellany* (New York: Macmillan, 1970), pp. 104-05.

18. Young, *Drama of the Medieval Church*, II, 539, as cited by Richard Axton, *European Drama of the Early Middle Ages* (London: Hutchinson, 1974), p. 162.

19. *York*, ed. Alexandra Johnston and Margaret (Dorrell) Rogerson, Records of Early English Drama (Toronto: Univ. of Toronto Press, 1979), I, 37; II, 722.

20. *A Middle English Treatise on the Playing of Miracles*, ed. Clifford Davidson (Washington, D.C.: University Press of America, 1981), pp. 39-40.

21. Ibid., p. 35.

22. Ibid., p. 36.

23. Ibid., p. 40; italics mine.

24. Angelo Raine, *Mediaeval York* (London: John Murray, 1955), p. 251; E. A. Gee, "The Painted Glass of All Saints' Church, North Street," *Archaeologia,* 102 (1969), 151-202.

25. *York Memorandum Book A/Y*, ed. Maud Sellers, Surtees Soc., 125 (Durham, 1915), II, xliii.

26. *York*, ed. Johnston and Rogerson, I, 62.

27. On the decline of the wool trade at York, see Herbert Heaton, *The Yorkshire Woolen and Worsted Industries from the Earliest Times up to the Industrial Revolution*, 2nd ed. (Oxford: Clarendon Press, 1965), pp. 47-68.

28. *York*, ed. Johnston and Rogerson, I, 337-38.

29. Ibid., I, 37; as translated by Margaret Dorrell (Rogerson), "Two Studies of the York Corpus Christi Play," *Leeds Studies in English*, n.s. 6 (1972), 85.

30. See Dorrell, "Two Studies," p. 81; *York*, ed. Johnston and Rogerson, I, 122. In *The Medieval English Stage* (Chicago: Univ. of Chicago Press, 1974), Alan H. Nelson argues that references to the room where the mayor and aldermen saw and heard the play would tend to prove indoor production (pp. 72-79). Nelson's view has not found acceptance.

31. Thomas Gent, *The Antient and Modern History of the Famous City of York* (York, 1730), p. 188.

32. Anderson, *Drama and Imagery,* Pl. 14b.

33. Peter Gibson, "The Stained and Painted Glass of York," in *The Noble City of York*, ed. Alberic Stacpoole (York: Cerialis Press, 1972), pp. 117-18.

34. See O. F. Emerson, "Legends of Cain, Especially in Old and Middle English," *PMLA*, 21 (1906), 853-55; Anderson, *Drama and Imagery*, pp. 144-45; Meyer Schapiro, "Cain's Jaw-Bone That Did the First Murder," in *Late Antique, Early Christian, and Mediaeval Art* (New York: Braziller, 1979), pp. 249-65.

35. Lines 1073-74; quoted by Emerson, p. 854.

36. Schapiro, p. 256.

37. Clifford Davidson and David E. O'Connor, *York Art: A Subject List of Extant and Lost Art including Items Relevant to Early Drama*, Early Drama, Art, and Music, Reference ser., 1 (Kalamazoo: Medieval Institute Publications, 1978), p. 22; see also Eric Milner-White, [*York Minster*] *Friends' Annual Report*, 19 (1947), 28-29.

38. The adder's coat in this instance has wings "like a bryde" and a face of a maid. *The Chester Mystery Cycle*, ed. R. M. Lumiansky and David Mills, EETS, s.s. 3 (1974), p. 21.

39. *Non-Cycle Plays and Fragments*, ed. Norman Davis, EETS, s.s. 1 (1970), p. xxxv.

40. J. K. Bonnell, "The Serpent with a Human Head in Art and in Mystery Play," *American Journal of Archaeology*, 2nd ser., 21 (1917), 257-58.

41. Gertrud Schiller, *Iconography of Christian Art*, trans. Janet Seligman (Greenwich, Conn.: New York Graphic Soc., 1971), I, 76.

42. Hildburgh, "English Alabaster Carvings," p. 62, Pl. XIc. See also the examples cited in Philip Nelson, "Some Fifteenth-Century English Alabaster Panels," *Archaeological Journal*, 76 (1919), 135-36, Pls. IV, V; and the same author's "Some Additional Specimens of English Alabaster Carvings," *Archaeological Journal*, 84 (1927), Pls. V, VII; C. J. P. Cave, in his *Roof Bosses in Medieval Churches* (Cambridge: Cambridge Univ. Press, 1948), p. 27, points out that a fifteenth-century boss in the nave at Norwich Cathedral likewise shows the Child on the ground before the Blessed Virgin.

43. Oscar G. Farmer, *Fairford Church and Its Stained Glass Windows*, 8th ed. (1968), pp. 9-10; Gordon McN. Rushforth, *Medieval Christian Imagery* (Oxford: Clarendon Press, 1936), p. 280.

44. J. W. Robinson, "A Commentary on the York Play of the Birth of Jesus," *Journal of English and Germanic Philology*, 70 (1971),

241–54; Henrik Cornell, *The Iconography of the Nativity of Christ*, Uppsala Universitets Årsskrift (Uppsala, 1924), p. 1–15; Clifford Davidson, "Northern Spirituality and the Late Medieval Drama of York," in *The Spirituality of Western Christendom*, ed. E. Rozanne Elder (Kalamazoo: Cistercian Publications, 1976), pp. 148–50.

45. Translation quoted with alterations from Cornell, *Iconography of the Nativity*, pp. 12–13.

46. Farmer, *Fairford Church and Its Stained Glass Windows*, p. 9.

47. *The Mirrour of the Blessed Lyf of Jesu Christ*, trans. Nicholas Love (London, 1486), sig. C7^V.

48. *Habakkuk* 3.2, Septuagint; see Schiller, *Iconography of Christian Art*, I, 61.

49. See *The Apocryphal New Testament*, trans. M. R. James (Oxford: Clarendon Press, 1924), p. 74.

50. Cornell, *Iconography of the Nativity*, pp. 40–42.

Chapter II

1. See below, Chapters VI and VII. Richard Beadle notes that the alliterative stanza of this play is also found in Plays XL and XLIV (*The York Plays* [London: Edward Arnold, 1982], p. 416).

2. *York*, ed. Johnston and Rogerson, I, 17.

3. On the date of the work of the York Realist, see below, Chapters VI and VII. Burtons's *Ordo* of 1415 apparently functioned as a kind of official list which was brought up to date from time to time. A second list, perhaps compiled later but before 1422, merely listed the order of the pageants by title; see *York*, ed. Johnston and Rogerson, I, 25–26.

4. Woolf, *English Mystery Plays*, pp. 107–08; Clifford Davidson, "Thomas Aquinas, the Feast of Corpus Christi, and the English Cycle Plays," *Michigan Academician*, 7 (1974), 103–04. Cf. R. W. Hanning, "'You Have Begun a Parlous Pleye': The Nature and Limits of Dramatic Mimesis as a Theme in Four Middle English 'Fall of Lucifer' Plays," *Comparative Drama*, 7 (1973), 22–50; rpt. in *Drama in the Middle Ages*, ed. Davidson *et al.*, pp. 140–68.

5. See the evidence from alabasters for a kind of "balcony" representing heaven where angel musicians also would appear, in Hildburgh, "English Alabaster Carvings," p. 61. Some practical suggestions concerning staging are presented in the original version of this chapter, written in collaboration with Nona Mason and appearing as an article in *Theatre Survey*, 17 (1976), 162–78.

6. Davidson and O'Connor, *York Art*, p. 18.

7. For an example of a *closed* book, see the marginal illumination in Bodleian MS. e. Mus. 36, p. 1 (Otto Pächt and J. J. G. Alexander, *Illuminated Manuscripts in the Bodleian Library, Oxford*, III [Oxford: Clarendon Press, 1973], No. 137, Pl. XV).

8. Davidson and O'Connor, *York Art*, pp. 188-92; *An Inventory of the Historical Monuments in the City of York*, III (Royal Commission on Historical Monuments, 1972), 6, Pl. 43; Cave, *Roof Bosses in Medieval Churches*, p. 222.

9. On music in the cycle plays, see especially the work of JoAnna Dutka: "Music and the English Mystery Plays," *Comparative Drama*, 7 (1973), 135-49; "Mysteries, Minstrels, and Music," *Comparative Drama*, 8 (1974), 112-24 (*Studies in Medieval Drama in Honor of William L. Smoldon*); and *Music in the English Mystery Plays*, Early Drama, Art, and Music, Reference ser., 2 (Kalamazoo: Medieval Institute Publications, 1980). See also John Robert Moore, "The Tradition of Angelic Singing in English Drama," *Journal of English and Germanic Philology*, 22 (1923), 89-99, and the Appendix by John Stevens in *The York Plays*, ed. Beadle, pp. 465-74.

10. *The Towneley Plays*, ed. George England and A. W. Pollard, EETS, e.s. 71 (London, 1897), p. 4 (I.100-07, 130-31).

11. Milner-White, [*York Minster*] *Friends' Annual Report*, 19 (1947), 26.

12. Davidson and O'Connor, *York Art*, p. 19.

13. *York,* ed. Johnston and Rogerson, I, 97.

14. Ibid., p. 56.

15. Ibid., p. 55.

16. Ibid., p. 55.

17. Ibid., p. 242.

18. Thomas Sharp, *A Dissertation on the Pageants or Dramatic Mysteries Anciently Performed at Coventry* (Coventry, 1825), p. 73.

19. The effect of the scene would be much diminished if indoor production had been used in the manner suggested by Nelson in his *Medieval English Stage*.

20. Glynne Wickham, *Early English Stages 1300-1660*, I (London: Routledge and Kegan Paul, 1959), 103.

21. Ibid., I, 103.

22. As Cave notes, this is a point of some ambiguity in medieval art. "It is not always possible," he writes, "to distinguish between the Father and the Son. An aged figure with a cross-nimbus may quite well represent the Son. But there are a few cases where it is possible to say that the Father is intended" (*Roof Bosses in Medieval Churches*, p. 25).

23. M. R. James, *Illustrations of the Book of Genesis* (Oxford: Roxburghe Club, 1921), p. 6.

24. Ibid., p. 23.

25. Davidson and O'Connor, *York Art*, p. 17.

26. Rushforth, *Medieval Christian Imagery*, pp. 149–51; *The Sherbourne Missal,* introd. J. A. Herbert (Oxford: Roxburghe Club, 1920), Pl. XXIXb. See also Anthony Blunt, "Blake's 'Ancient of Days': The Symbolism of the Compasses," *Journal of the Warburg Institute,* 2 (1938–39), 53–63; M. D. Anderson, *Looking for History in British Churches* (London: John Murray, 1951), pp. 181–82.

27. *Non-Cycle Plays*, ed. Davis, p. xxxv.

28. *York,* ed. Johnston and Rogerson, I, 55. See also Sharp, p. 35.

29. *Chester Mystery Cycle*, Play I.42ff.

30. See Chapter XI, below.

31. Gee, "The Painted Glass of All Saints' Church," Pl. XXXII, pp. 170–74.

32. *Golden Legend*, trans. Ryan and Ripperger, p. 581.

33. Ibid., p. 581.

34. Ibid., p. 581. On the nine orders of angels, see also Rushforth, *Medieval Christian Imagery*, pp. 204–16.

35. Gee, "The Painted Glass of All Saints' Church," pp. 170–74, Pls. XXXIII–XXXV.

36. John A. Knowles, "The West Window, St. Martin-le-Grand, Coney Street, York," *Yorkshire Archaeological Journal,* 38 (1955), 170–72.

37. Gee, "The Painted Glass of All Saints' Church," p. 171, Pls. XXXII–XXXIII.

38. Sharp, *Dissertation on the Pageants*, p. 71. But see the accounts from London printed by Wickham, *Early English Stages*, I, 326; here angels' wings were apparently constructed of peacock feathers. Painted gilt figures of angels would seem to have been utilized in the York Mercers' play; see *York*, ed. Johnston and Rogerson, I, 55–56.

39. Sharp, *Dissertation on the Pageants*, p. 71; *Non-Cycle Plays*, ed. Davis, p. xxxv.

40. Anderson, *Drama and Imagery*, p. 167, Pl. 18. See also the thorough study of the carved angels at Warwick by Philip B. Chatwin, "The Decoration of the Beauchamp Chapel, Warwick, with Special Reference to the Sculptures," *Archaeologia,* 77 (1927), 313–34. The collars which represent rays of light are only utilized at Warwick for the very highest orders, the Cherubin and Seraphin. See Chatwin, Pls. LVIII–LX. On costumes for angels, see also Rushforth, *Medieval Christian Imagery*, p. 25.

41. Cave notes that the most common garments worn by angels on roof bosses are the alb and amice; however, the higher orders of angels, which would be presented in resplendent feathers and without a covering garment, are not very often shown on bosses (*Roof Bosses in Medieval Churches*, pp. 50–51).

42. Sharp, *Dissertation on the Pageants*, pp. 55–56, 71.

43. Davidson and O'Connor, *York Art*, p. 20; cf. Anderson, *Drama and Imagery*, pp. 171–72.

44. *Chester*, ed. Lawrence M. Clopper, Records of Early English Drama (Toronto: Univ. of Toronto Press, 1979), p. 244.

45. Davidson and O'Connor, *York Art,* p. 20.

46. Anderson, *Drama and Imagery*, p. 170.

47. *York,* ed. Johnston and Rogerson, I, 55.

48. Ibid., I, 241.

49. Sharp, *Dissertation on the Pageants*, p. 31.

40. Ibid., p. 31.

51. Ibid., p. 69.

52. Ibid., pp. 56–57.

53. This fifteenth-century manuscript has been linked with York since it contains illuminations which connect it with the glass in All Saints, North Street, York. See Pächt and Alexander, No. 803.

54. Milner-White, [*York Minster*] *Friends' Annual Report,* 19 (1947), 28.

55. Rushforth, *Medieval Christian Imagery*, p. 153.

56. M. D. Anderson notes: "It is an almost invariable convention of medieval imagery that Adam lies with his head to the right while Eve issues from his right side. In many cases he rests against an abrupt hummock behind which she could well have hidden until her cue came, as for instance on a Fitzroy tomb chest at Framlingham (Suffolk). . . . The stage directions of the Cornish *Creation of the World* say: 'let Adam laye downe and slepe wher Eva is, and she by the conveyour must be taken from Adam's side.' Before this rubric God has taken a rib from Adam. . . . " (*Drama and Imagery*, p. 142).

57. *York*, ed. Johnston and Rogerson, I, 330.

58. *Non-Cycle Plays*, ed. Davis p. xxxv.

59. Quoted by Martial Rose, *The Wakefield Mystery Plays* (1962; rpt. Garden City, N.Y.: Doubleday, 1963), p. 157.

60. Rushforth, *Medieval Christian Imagery*, p. 155.

61. Payments to both minstrels and actors are recorded in the Mercers' accounts. See Alexandra Johnston and Margaret Dorrell (Rogerson), "The York Mercers and Their Pageant of Doomsday, 1433–1526," *Leeds Studies in English*, n.s. 6 (1972), 26–29.

Chapter III

1. Hardin Craig, *English Religious Drama* (Oxford: Clarendon Press, 1955), pp. 127-50; V. A. Kolve, *The Play Called Corpus Christi* (Stanford, Calif.: Stanford Univ. Press, 1966), pp. 57-100. The best argument is Alan Nelson's claim that the principles of selection are "historical" (*Medieval English Stage*, pp. 6-7). The Old Testament plays present sacred history in a manner which establishes the origin of the race. It is my contention that these plays also stress the kinship relationship of Adam and his descendants to the Creator.

2. See especially *Summa Theologica*, I, Q. 83, Art. I; and II, Pt. II, Q. 13, Art 5.

3. See Rushforth, *Medieval Christian Imagery*, p. 158.

4. *Speculum humanae salvationis*, ed. J. Lutz and P. Perdrizet (Leipzig, 1909), Pl. 3.

5. Rushforth, *Medieval Christian Imagery*, p. 159.

6. MS. Auct. D. 4. 4, fol. 24^V (Pächt and Alexander, No. 665). See also the famous panel in Canterbury Cathedral, illustrated in Madeline Harrison Caviness, *The Early Stained Glass of Canterbury Cathedral* (Princeton: Princeton Univ. Press, 1977), fig. 6, and additionally T. S. R. Boase, *The York Psalter* (London: Faber and Faber, 1962), Pl. 1.

7. As Rosemary Woolf points out (*English Mystery Plays*, p. 116), the York plays introduce the Franciscan idea that even had the Fall not taken place, Christ nevertheless would have become man. Such speculation, however, does not diminish the urgency of the Incarnation and Atonement as the means whereby the effects of the Fall may be overcome.

8. Gibson, "The Stained and Painted Glass of York," Pl. 38, pp. 143-44. See also Anderson, *Drama and Imagery*, p. 211.

9. See David Lyle Jeffrey, "Stewardship in the Wakefield *Mactacio Abel* and *Noe* Plays," *The American Benedictine Review*, 22 (1971), 64-76.

10. The idea of Christ as the Good Shepherd is, of course, a commonplace, though it was not normally illustrated in late medieval art.

11. These words from St. Augustine (*Enarrationes in Psalmos* CII.8) characterize the difference between the followers of Cain and the followers of Abel. The words are quoted from the translation in *An Augustine Synthesis*, ed. Erich Przywara (New York: Harper, 1958), p. 382.

12. See Emerson, "Legends of Cain," pp. 833-37.

13. See Robert Edwards, "Techniques of Transcendence in Medieval Drama," *Comparative Drama*, 8 (1974), 167; rpt. in *Drama in the Middle Ages*, ed. Davidson *et al.*, p. 113.

14. See Clifford Davidson, "The Unity of the Wakefield 'Mactacio Abel'," *Traditio*, 23 (1967), 498–99.

15. Ernst Kitzinger, *Early Medieval Art in the British Museum*, 2nd ed. (London: British Museum, 1955), Pl. 7.

16. Saint Ambrose, *Cain and Abel*, I.1.3, trans. John J. Savage, in *Hexameron, Paradise, and Cain and Abel* (New York: Fathers of the Church, 1961), p. 360.

17. George Zarnecki, *Romanesque Sculpture at Lincoln Cathedral*, 2nd ed. (Lincoln, 1970), p. 7.

18. Attention is called to the importance of this work for the understanding of the English plays on the subject of Cain and Abel by John E. Bernbrock, "Notes on the Towneley Cycle *Slaying of Abel*," *Journal of English and Germanic Philology*, 62 (1963), 317–22.

19. Ambrose, *Cain and Abel*, pp. 361–62.

20. Davidson and O'Connor, *York Art*, p. 182. Synagogue was also illustrated on the painted ceiling of the Chapter House, but this figure was removed in 1798. See the illustration in Joseph Halfpenny, *Gothic Ornaments in the Cathedral Church of York* (York, 1795), Pl. 95.

21. Arthur Gardner, *English Medieval Sculpture*, revised ed. (Cambridge: Cambridge Univ. Press, 1951), p. 147.

22. Pächt and Alexander, No. 424.

23. Davidson and O'Connor, *York Art*, p. 182.

24. In contrast to the thirteenth-century art described by Émile Mâle (*The Gothic Image*, trans. Dora Nussey [1913; rpt. New York: Harper, 1958]), the York cycle is less "responsive" to dogma than to biblical narrative. See especially Mâle's discussion of Old Testament scenes in thirteenth-century art (ibid., pp. 131–75).

25. See Beryl Smalley, *The Study of the Bible in the Middle Ages* (Oxford: Blackwell, 1952), 264–355.

26. See Ambrose, *Cain and Abel*, p. 360.

27. See Emerson, "Legends of Cain," pp. 846–48.

28. See Anderson, *Drama and Imagery*, p. 144.

29. Susan Snyder, "The Left Hand of God: Despair in Medieval and Renaissance Tradition," *Studies in the Renaissance*, 12 (1965), 58.

30. Gregory the Great, *Moralia* IX.80, as cited in Snyder, p. 58.

31. Cave, *Roof Bosses in Medieval Churches*, fig. 148; Zarnecki, p. 7; G. McN. Rushforth, "The Windows of the Church of St. Neot,

Cornwall," *Exeter Diocesan Architectural and Archaeological Society*, 15 (1937), 157; Emerson, "Legends of Cain," pp. 874–77.

32. *Summa Theologica* I, Pt. II, Q. 40, Art. 4.

33. Rushforth, *Medieval Christian Imagery*, p. 160.

34. See Rushforth, *Medieval Christian Imagery*, p. 160.

35. Dorrell, "Two Studies of the York Corpus Christi Play," p. 102. The 1415 *Ordo* specifies that Noah will make the ark "from smoothed boards" (*York*, ed. Johnston and Rogerson, I, 18; II, 703).

36. See M. D. Anderson, *The Imagery of British Churches* (London: John Murray, 1955), pp. 91–92.

37. Pächt and Alexander, No. 883, Pl. LXXXIV.

38. Anna J. Mill, "The Hull Noah Play," *Modern Language Review*, 33 (1938), 493.

39. Ibid., p. 493.

40. Pächt and Alexander, No. 429, Pl. XXXVII.

41. Cave, *Roof Bosses in Medieval Churches*, fig. 150. See also the misericord at Ely, discussed by Francis Bond, *Wood Carvings in English Churches* (London: Oxford Univ. Press, 1910), pp. 130, fig. on p. 134.

42. *Homiliae in Hiezechihelem Prophetam* II.iv.16, Corpus Christianorum, ser. Latina 142 (1971), p. 270. The passage is cited in Rushforth, *Medieval Christian Imagery*, p. 161.

43. Rushforth, *Medieval Christian Imagery*, p. 161.

44. Cf. *Chester* III.161–92.

45. Quoted by Katherine Garvin, "A Note on Noah's Wife," *Modern Language Notes*, 49 (1934), 89.

46. Anderson, *Drama and Imagery*, p. 108, Pl. 14a.

47. The legend of Noah's wife is discussed and traced by Anna J. Mill, "Noah's Wife Again," *PMLA*, 56 (1941), 613–26. See also Woolf, *English Mystery Plays*, pp. 136–37.

48. Woolf, *English Mystery Plays*, p. 139.

49. See ibid., p. 139.

50. Curiously, Thornton's panel in the Great East Window in York Minster apparently errs in showing Noah's wife in the ark but still shrewish in mood. One of the sons is attempting to reason with her. See Anderson, *Drama and Imagery*, p. 108.

51. See Mâle, *Gothic Image*, pp. 140–41.

52. John Mirk, *Festial*, EETS, e.s. 96 (London, 1905), p. 78. The importance of Mirk's sermon is stressed by Rosemary Woolf, "The Effect of Typology on the English Mediaeval Plays of Abraham and Isaac," *Speculum*, 32 (1957), 811.

53. *The Lay Folks Mass Book*, ed. Thomas F. Simmons, EETS, o.s. 71 (London, 1879), pp. 108–09. See also Kolve, p. 72.

54. Minnie E. Wells, "The Age of Isaac at the Time of the Sacrifice," *Modern Language Notes,* 54 (1939), 579–81.

55. Anderson, *Imagery of British Churches*, p. 93, Pl. 5.

56. M. R. James, "On Paintings Formerly in the Choir at Peterborough," *Cambridge Antiquarian Society Proceedings,* No. 38 (1896), pp. 192f.

57. *Biblia Pauperum,* Pl. 24; Cologne Bible (1478–80). Rushforth, *Medieval Christian Imagery*, p. 170, discusses the scene formerly depicted at Great Malvern.

58. Woolf, *English Mystery Plays*, p. 151.

59. See William F. Munson, "Typology and the Towneley Isaac," *Research Opportunities in Renaissance Drama,* 11 (1968), 131–32.

60. See Woolf, "The Effect of Typology on the English Medieval Plays of Abraham and Isaac," pp. 823–25.

61. For examples at York, see Davidson and O'Connor, *York Art*, p. 61–65. See also J. L. André, "Saint John the Baptist in Art, Legend, and Ritual," *Archaeological Journal,* 50 (1893), 3–4.

62. Adolf Katzenellenbogen, *Allegories of the Virtues and Vices in Mediaeval Art,* trans. Alan J. P. Crick (1939; rpt. New York: Norton, 1964), p. 15, fig. 14.

63. *York Psalter,* Pls. 1–2.

64. See Anderson, *Imagery of British Churches*, p. 97. Moses' horns are derived from a mistranslation of *Exodus* 34.30 in which the Hebrew word meaning "shone" was translated as "horn" in the Vulgate.

65. Rushforth, *Medieval Christian Imagery*, pp. 182–83.

66. Woolf, *English Mystery Plays*, pp. 153–54.

67. Ibid., pp. 153–54.

68. On Moses' rod in art, see Mâle, *Gothic Image*, pp. 156f.

69. See Cynthia Haldenby Tyson, "Noah's Flood, the River Jordan, the Red Sea: Staging in the Towneley Cycle," *Comparative Drama,* 8 (1974), 105–10 . It should be noted that the texts of the Towneley and York plays on the topic of the Exodus are practically identical.

70. Cave, *Roof Bosses in Medieval Churches*, fig. 152.

71. *Biblia Pauperum,* Pl. 9.

Chapter IV

1. Anna J. Mill, "The Stations of the York Corpus Christi Play," *Yorkshire Archaeological Journal,* 37 (1951), 492–502; Meg Twycross,

"'Places to hear the play': pageant stations at York, 1398–1572," *REED Newsletter,* 1978:2, pp. 10–33.

2. *York,* ed. Johnston and Rogerson, I, 109.

3. Ibid., I, 109, 280, 317. Players not ready were fined; see ibid., I, 314.

4. Ibid., I, 283.

5. Ibid., pp. 16–24.

6. Ibid., pp. 16–26. See also Martin Stevens and Margaret Dorrell (Rogerson), "The *Ordo Paginarum* Gathering of the York *A/Y Memorandum Book,*" *Modern Philology,* 72 (1974), 45–59. According to Peter Meredith, however, the *Ordo* still requires further study; see his "The *Ordo Paginarum* and the Development of the York Tile-makers' Pageant," *Leeds Studies in English,* n.s. 11 (1980), 71.

7. *York,* ed. Johnston and Rogerson, p. 25.

8. Schiller, *Iconography of Christian Art,* I, fig. 139.

9. Davidson and O'Connor, *York Art,* pp. 49, 52.

10. *York,* ed. Johnston and Rogerson, I, 18.

11. Young, *Drama of the Medieval Church,* II, 17.

12. Anderson, *Drama and Imagery,* pp. 91–92, Pl. 10.

13. Davidson and O'Connor, *York Art,* pp. 39–44. The indication of music in the stage directions is written in the hand of John Clerke and is a sixteenth-century addition; see Beadle, ed., *York Plays,* p. 114.

14. Davidson and O'Connor, *York Art,* pp. 39–44, fig. 9.

15. *Biblia Pauperum,* Pl. 1.

16. *St. Olave's Church, York* (Gloucester: British Publishing Co, 1950), p. 15.

17. Fol. 23^v; see Margaret Rickert, "The So-Called Beaufort Hours and York Psalter," *Burlington Magazine,* 104 (1962), 238, fig. 8.

18. See Schiller, *Iconography of Christian Art,* I, 42.

19. Rushforth, *Medieval Christian Imagery,* p. 276.

20. Francis Drake, *Eboracum* (1736), p. 502.

21. *Religious Lyrics of the XVth Century,* ed. Carleton Brown (Oxford: Clarendon Press, 1939), p. 119.

22. See *The Mirrour of the Blessed Lyf of Jesu Christ,* trans. Love, sig. B8^r.

23. John Mirk, *Festial,* ed. T. Erbe, EETS, e.s. 96 (1905), p. 107.

24. Davidson and O'Connor, *York Art,* pp. 40–44.

25. Young, *Drama of the Medieval Church,* II, 249; Stanley J. Kahrl, *Traditions of Medieval English Drama* (London: Hutchinson, 1974), p. 51.

26. See Schiller, *Iconography of Christian Art*, I, 45. Sometimes the soul of Christ was not so small, as in an alabaster in the Victoria and Albert Museum (A-58-1925) which shows it in an aureole extending almost all the way from the Father to the Virgin below.

27. Christopher Woodforde, *The Norwich School of Glass-Painting in the Fifteenth Century* (London: Oxford Univ. Press, 1950), pp. 23-24; Schiller, *Iconography of Christian Art*, I, fig. 113.

28. Philip Nelson, "The Virgin Triptych at Danzig," *Archaeological Journal*, 76 (1919), 140, Pls. I, II.

29. Rickert, "The So-Called Beaufort Hours and York Psalter," p. 244.

30. Schiller, *Iconography of Christian Art*, I, fig. 99. In *Queen Mary's Psalter*, the Annunciation is illustrated above, and the Visitation below (ed. George Warner [London: British Museum, 1912], Pl. 147).

31. M. E. McIver, "Visitation of Mary," *New Catholic Encyclopedia* (New York: McGraw-Hill, 1967), XIV, 721.

32. F. Saxl, "The Ruthwell Cross," *Journal of the Warburg and Courtauld Institutes*, 6 (1943), Pl. Id.

33. Davidson and O'Connor, *York Art*, pp. 43-44.

34. *Non-Cycle Plays and Fragments*, ed. Davis, p. 2.

35. Anderson, *Imagery of British Churches*, p. 107.

36. Acquisition No. 8128-1863; *Gospel Stories in English Embroidery* (London: Her Majesty's Stationery Office, 1963), Pl. 16.

37. *Queen Mary's Psalter*, Pl. 162.

38. Rushforth, *Medieval Christian Imagery*, p. 380.

39. *Two Coventry Corpus Christi Plays*, ed. Hardin Craig, EETS, e.s. 87 (London, 1957), p. 11.

40. *Golden Legend*, trans. Ryan and Ripperger, p. 87.

41. Davidson and O'Connor, *York Art*, pp. 53-54.

42. *Historical Monuments in the City of York*, III (1972), Pl. 42f. See also Christopher Woodforde, *English Stained and Painted Glass* (Oxford: Clarendon Press, 1954), Pl. 32; John Baker, *English Stained Glass* (London: Thames and Hudson, 1960), Pl. XVII; and Emanuel Winternitz, *Musical Instruments and Their Symbolism in Western Art* (New Haven: Yale Univ. Press, 1967), pp. 80, 132ff.

43. See Schiller, *Iconography of Christian Art*, I, 87.

44. Lawrence, J. Ross, "Symbol and Structure in the *Secunda Pastorum*," *Comparative Drama*, 1 (1967), 22-23.

45. Anderson, *Drama and Imagery*, Pl. 11; Alan H. Nelson, "On Recovering the Lost Norwich Corpus Christi Cycle," *Comparative Drama*, 4 (1970-71), figs. 1-2. On the textual question with regard to the York plays, see Beadle, ed., *York Plays*, pp. 429-33.

46. See Anderson, *Drama and Imagery,* p. 165; Woolf, *English Mystery Plays,* pp. 391–92.

47. Davidson and O'Connor, *York Art,* fig. 53; *Queen Mary's Psalter,* Pl. 173.

48. Miriam Skey, "Herod's Demon Crown," *Journal of the Warburg and Courtauld Institutes,* 40 (1977), 274–76.

49. Davidson and O'Connor, *York Art,* p. 54.

50. John Browne, *The History of the Metropolitan Church of St. Peter, York* (London, 1847), I, 140–42; II, Pls. XCVI, CI, CVI. The original bosses were destroyed by fire in the nineteenth century. The present bosses are copies made from Browne's drawings.

51. *Biblia Pauperum,* Pl. 3; Rushforth, *Medieval Christian Imagery,* pp. 284–86.

52. Gee, "The Painted Glass of All Saints' Church," p. 157, Pl. XXIII.

53. *Golden Legend,* trans. Ryan and Ripperger, p. 85.

54. *Queen Mary's Psalter,* Pl. 174. See also Schiller, I, fig. 272, and Mâle, *Gothic Image,* figs. 111–12.

55. *York,* ed. Johnston and Dorrell, I, 19, 25.

56. Ibid., I, 351; Beadle, ed., *York Plays,* pp. 434–36.

57. Davidson and O'Connor, *York Art,* p. 56.

58. See Farmer, *Fairford Church and Its Stained Glass Windows,* p. 10.

59. Dorothy Shorr, "The Iconographic Development of the Presentation in the Temple," *Art Bulletin,* 28 (1946), 27.

60. Rushforth, *Medieval Christian Imagery,* pp. 106–7; *Biblia Pauperum,* Pl. 4.

61. Hildburgh, "English Alabaster Carvings," pp. 70–71, Pl. XIIIc; *Speculum Humanae Salvationis,* ed. Lutz and Perdrizet, Pl. 19.

62. Calendar, p. 4, in *Breviarum ad usum insignis ecclesie Eboracensis,* I, Surtees Soc., 71 (1880).

63. Mirk, *Festial,* p. 59.

64. See Schiller, *Iconography of Christian Art,* I, 117.

65. David Staines, "To Out-Herod Herod: The Development of a Dramatic Character," *Comparative Drama,* 10 (1976), 45; rpt. in *Drama in the Middle Ages,* ed. Davidson *et al.,* p. 223. For the Fleury play, see the edition prepared by Noah Greenberg and W. L. Smoldon (New York: Oxford Univ. Press, 1965). For evidence that the text in the Register was no longer used by John Clerke's time, see Beadle, ed., *York Plays,* p. 437.

66. Davidson and O'Connor, *York Art,* fig. 16; *Golden Legend,* trans. Ryan and Ripperger, p. 137. See also Anderson, *Drama and Imagery,* p. 137.

67. Anderson, *Drama and Imagery,* pp. 136–37.

68. *Queen Mary's Psalter,* Pl. 188.

69. Rushforth, *Medieval Christian Imagery,* p. 382.

70. The question-answer form is, of course, suggested in the apocryphal *Gospel of Thomas,* which asserts that "after the third day [his parents] found him in the temple sitting in the midst of the doctors and hearing and asking them *questions,*" and also in the biblical account in *Luke* 2.46. See *Apocryphal New Testament,* trans. James, p. 54.

Chapter V

1. *York,* ed. Johnston and Rogerson, I, 19. The second list (ibid., I, 25) gives the play to the Taverners, perhaps the earlier producers of the Marriage at Cana since the 1415 *Ordo* designates the "Vynters" in a later or different hand. See Beadle, ed., *York Plays,* pp. 192, 440. In Beadle's edition, the missing play is numbered XXIIA, while the missing Ironmongers' play on the subject of the visit of Jesus to the house of Simon is numbered XXIIIA (see Appendix, below).

2. *York,* ed. Johnston and Rogerson, I, 351.

3. *The Ancient Cornish Drama,* ed. and trans. Edwin Norris (Oxford: Oxford Univ. Press, 1859).

4. Mâle, *Gothic Image,* p. 177.

5. Ibid., p. 177.

6. Ibid., p. 181, citing Durandus, *Rationale divinorum Officiorum,* VI, xvi, and other sources.

7. W. L. Hildburgh, "An Alabaster Table of the Annunciation with the Crucifix: A Study in English Iconography," *Archaeologia,* 74 (1923–24), 203–34; Davidson and O'Connor, *York Art,* pp. 39–40.

8. Davidson and O'Connor, *York Art,* p. 184.

9. *Testamenta Eboracensia,* ed. James Raine, II, Surtees Soc., 30 (Durham, 1855), pp. 230–31.

10. *Testamenta Eboracensia,* IV, Surtees Soc., 53 (1869), p. 244.

11. John A. Knowles, "The East Window of Holy Trinity, Goodramgate," *Yorkshire Archaeological Journal,* 28 (1924–26), 1–2, 5–8.

12. See Dutka, *Music in the English Mystery Plays,* pp. 43–44. On the lacunae present in this play's text, see Beadle, ed., *York Plays,* p. 439.

13. Schiller, *Iconography of Christian Art,* I, 138–39, fig. 384.

14. Rushforth, *Medieval Christian Imagery,* p. 157; see also *Queen Mary's Psalter,* Pl. 211.

15. *York,* ed. Johnston and Dorrell, I, 19.

16. Rushforth, *Medieval Christian Imagery,* p. 289.

17. See Hardin Craig, *English Religious Drama* (Oxford: Clarendon Press, 1955), p. 200, and Beadle, ed., *York Plays,* p. 192.

18. Schiller, *Iconography of Christian Art,* I, figs. 394–96; see also Patrick J. Collins, *The N-Town Plays and Medieval Picture Cycles,* Early Drama, Art, and Music, Monograph Ser., 2 (Kalamazoo: Medieval Institute Publications, 1979), pp. 11–20.

19. Hilary Wayment, *The Windows of King's College Chapel, Cambridge* (London: Oxford Univ. Press, 1950), p. 66.

20. Woolf, *English Mystery Plays,* p. 200.

21. Davidson and O'Connor, *York Art,* p. 105 (Northeast Window, top of fifth light).

22. On the Feast of the Transfiguration, see R. W. Pfaff, *New Liturgical Feasts in Later Medieval England* (Oxford: Clarendon Press, 1970), pp. 13–39.

23. William Tydeman, *The Theatre in the Middle Ages* (Cambridge: Cambridge Univ. Press, 1978), pp. 169–70.

24. *York,* ed. Johnston and Rogerson, I, 20.

25. See the commentary of Eleanor Prosser, *Drama and Religion in the English Mystery Plays* (Stanford: Stanford Univ. Press, 1961), pp. 103–07. On textual questions, see Beadle, ed., *York Plays,* pp. 441–42.

26. Illustrated in Clifford Davidson, "The Visual Arts and Drama, with Special Emphasis on the Lazarus Plays," *Le Théâtre au Moyen Âge,* ed. Gari Muller (Montreal: Les Éditions Univers, 1981), Pl. on p. 54.

27. Pächt and Alexander, No. 665, Pl. LXVIII.

28. Gent, *Antient and Modern History,* p. 188.

29. Woolf, *English Mystery Plays,* p. 232.

30. *Holkham Bible Picture Book,* fol. 26^r.

31. Hildburgh, "English Alabaster Carvings," p. 74.

32. See *Holkham Bible Picture Book,* fol. 26^r.

33. See also Cave, *Roof Bosses,* p. 31, Pl. 192.

34. W. L. Hildburgh, "Further Miscellaneous Notes on Medieval English Alabaster Carvings," *Antiquaries Journal,* 17 (1937), 182–83.

35. Farmer, *Fairford Church and Its Stained Glass Windows,* p. 12; see also Chambers, *Mediaeval Stage,* II, 4–5.

36. *Apocryphal New Testament,* trans. James, p. 97.

37. *York,* ed. Johnston and Rogerson, I, 20; II, 706.

38. Rosemary Woolf, however, would also include the *Agony* (*English Mystery Plays,* pp. 235–37).

39. *York,* ed. Johnston and Rogerson, I, 309, 325; see also Anna J. Mill, "The York Bakers' Play of the Last Supper," *Modern Language Review,* 30 (1935), 152.

40. Rushforth, *Medieval Christian Imagery,* p. 58.

41. Davidson and O'Connor, *York Art,* p. 71; see also Schiller, *Iconography of Christian Art,* II, Pls. 89, 91.

42. *Meditations on the Life of Christ,* trans. Isa Ragusa and Rosalie B. Green (Princeton: Princeton Univ. Press, 1961), p. 314.

Chapter VI

1. The date of the work of the York Realist has not been absolutely established, but the York dramatic records indicate that some combining of shorter plays into longer and more elaborate ones would seem to have taken place c.1422-32 (*York,* ed. Johnston and Rogerson, I, 37, 48). Because the plays named are ones in the Passion series, the activity of the York Realist at this time may be conjectured. See also Peter Meredith, "The *Ordo Paginarum* and the Development of the York Tilemakers' Pageant," pp. 59, 73. Stylistic arguments for dating, though quite risky, would appear to point to a date not later than c.1435. In no case, of course, could the date be later than 1463-77, the date established for the manuscript of the Register which contains the York cycle; see Richard Beadle and Peter Meredith, "Further External Evidence for Dating the York Register (BL Additional MS 35290)," *Leeds Studies in English,* n.s. 11 (1980). Richard Beadle comments on the poor state of the text of the plays which make up the bulk of the York Realist's contribution to the Passion series; the fifteenth-century copyist apparently had great difficulty copying the play scripts which came into his hands (Beadle, ed., *York Plays,* pp. 443-51).

2. Jesse Byers Reese, "Alliterative Verse in the York Cycle," *Studies in Philology,* 48 (1951), 668, citing the opinion of Katharine Lee Bates in her book, *The English Religious Drama* (New York, 1893), p. 169. It should be noted here that Reese is not convinced that the plays in alliterative meters were all written by the same person. But see Craig, *English Religious Drama,* p. 228, and J. W. Robinson, "The Art of the York Realist," *Modern Philology,* 60 (1962-63), 241-42. The poetry of the entire cycle is considered by Richard J. Collier, *Poetry and Drama in the York Corpus Christi Play* (Hamden, Conn.: Archon Books, 1978).

3. Gee, "The Painted Glass of All Saints' Church," p. 186; *A History of Yorkshire: The City of York,* ed. P. M. Tillot (London: Oxford Univ. Press, 1961), pp. 107, 109. That Nicholas Blackburn, Sr., owned property in North Street is demonstrated by his will (*Testamenta Eboracensia,* II, 18). On Nicholas Blackburn, Jr., see

also *York,* ed. Johnston and Rogerson, I, 84, and Twycross, "'Places to hear the play': pageant stations," p. 29, for his association with a pageant station in Micklegate.

4. John A. Knowles, *Essays in the History of the York School of Glass-Painting* (London: SPCK, 1936), p. 38. The window is described in Gee, "The Painted Glass of All Saints' Church," pp. 153–57.

5. He also, for example, endowed a chantry (1424) dedicated to St. Anne in St. Anne's Chapel, Fossbridge, as we learn from his will. See *Testamenta Eboracensia,* II, 21, and Gee, "The Painted Glass of All Saints' Church," p. 186; for information about St. Anne's Chapel, see Angelo Raine, *Mediaeval York* (London: John Murray, 1955), pp. 68–70.

6. The former East Window is now in the east wall of the north aisle of the chancel. It is of fourteenth-century glass, though, unfortunately, the glass in the central Crucifixion panel is almost entirely modern—the work of the nineteenth-century glass painter Wailes of Newcastle. See Gee, "The Painted Glass of All Saints' Church," pp. 157–58, and Davidson and O'Connor, *York Art,* p. 81.

7. See below, Chapter, XI.

8. The cost of a painted glass window of the size and quality of the Blackburn window may be judged from the will of Reginald Bawtree, who left 100 shillings in 1429 to provide another window for All Saints, North Street (P. J. Shaw *et al., An Old York Church: All Hallows in North Street* [York, 1908], p. 90).

9. Gee, "The Painted Glass of All Saints' Church," p. 156. Bidding prayers of this kind "did not necessarily mean that the person mentioned has died" (ibid., p. 186). In this case, the window was surely completed before the death of Nicholas Blackburn, Sr.

10. Davidson and O'Connor, *York Art,* p. 36.

11. Gee, "The Painted Glass of All Saints' Church," p. 190.

12. See G. R. Owst, *Literature and Pulpit in Medieval England,* 2nd ed. (Oxford: Blackwell, 1961), pp. 23–47, and David L. Jeffrey, "Franciscan Spirituality and the Rise of Early English Drama," *Mosaic,* 8, No. 4 (1975), 17–46.

13. See ibid., pp. 22–23; Arnold Williams, *The Drama of Medieval England* (East Lansing: Michigan State Univ. Press, 1961), p. 120; and Prosser, *Drama and Religion,* p. 41. Of related interest is J. W. Robinson, "The Late Medieval Cult of Jesus and the Mystery Plays," *PMLA,* 80 (1965), 508–14.

14. See *York,* ed. Johnston and Rogerson, *passim,* and Alexandra F. Johnston, "The Guild of Corpus Christi and the Procession of Corpus Christi in York," *Mediaeval Studies,* 38 (1976), 372–84.

15. Johnston, "The Guild of Corpus Christi and the Procession of Corpus Christi in York," pp. 372–84.

16. Leaf R7 is lost (between fols. 136^V and 137). It contained Christ's teaching of the Lord's prayer to the disciples. On other textual problems, see Beadle, ed., *York Plays*, pp. 444–45.

17. *Meditations*, trans. Ragusa, p. 324.

18. Lines 39–41; ed. George P. Krapp in his edition of *The Vercelli Book*, Anglo-Saxon Poetic Records, 2 (New York: Columbia Univ. Press, 1932), p. 62.

19. See, for example, the Crucifixion panel at Daglingworth (Esther Jackson, *Art of the Anglo-Saxon Age* [Peterborough, N.H.: Richard R. Smith, 1964], p. 136); the illumination showing the Crucifixion in the New Minster Office, Winchester (eleventh century; Margaret Rickert, *Painting in Britain in the Middle Ages* [Baltimore: Penguin, 1954], Pl. 37B); and the ivories illustrated in John Beckwith, *Ivory Carvings in Early Medieval England* (Greenwich, Conn.: New York Graphic Soc., 1972), Pls. 67–74; cf. ibid., Pls. 46–47.

20. See the classic study by Gustaf Aulén, *Christus Victor,* trans. A. G. Herbert (New York: Macmillan, 1969), *passim,* and also Sandro Sticca, "Drama and Spirituality in the Middle Ages," *Medievalia et Humanistica,* n.s. 4 (1973), 69–87.

21. *Mirrour of the Blessed Lyf of Jesu Christ,* sig. N3^r.

22. Émile Mâle, *Religious Art from the Twelfth to the Eighteenth Century,* English trans. (1949; rpt. New York: Noonday, 1970), pp. 112–13.

23. See Rosemary Woolf, "The Theme of Christ the Lover-Knight in Medieval English Literature," *Review of English Studies,* 13 (1962), 1–16. See also the comment on the Towneley cycle in Kolve, *Play Called Corpus Christi,* pp. 192–95.

24. Schiller, *Iconography of Christian Art,* II, 184.

25. For an illustration from a photograph taken before the panel was damaged by vandals in 1970, see Knowles, *York School,* fig. 6. The glass is now in the West Window of All Saints, Pavement, York.

26. Authority usually cited for this interpretation is *Romans* 5.12–21. See Walter E. Meyers, *A Figure Given: Typology in the Wakefield Plays* (Pittsburgh: Duquesne Univ. Press, 1970), pp. 21, 59.

27. *Middle English Dictionary,* s.v. *daren* and *dideron*.

28. *St. Albans Psalter,* Hildesheim, St. Godehard, p. 34; see Pächt, *Rise of Pictorial Narrative,* fig. 41.

29. John Plummer, *The Hours of Catherine of Cleves* (New York: Braziller, n.d.), Pl. 16.

30. Courtauld Institute Collection.

31. Schiller, *Iconography of Christian Art,* II, fig. 152.

32. The Harleian MS. of the *Northern Passion* indicates that "both water and blude he sweet" (l. 457) and that the drops fell to the ground. See *The Northern Passion,* Part I, ed. Frances A. Foster, EETS, o.s. 145 (1913), p. 47. On the relationship between the *Northern Passion* and the York plays, see *Northern Passion,* Part II, ed. Foster, EETS, o.s. 147 (1916), pp. 81–86, and Frances H. Miller, "The *Northern Passion* and the Mysteries," *Modern Language Notes,* 34 (1919), 88–92.

33. In the Harleian MS. of the *Northern Passion,* Jesus prays, "Lat þis paines pas fra me" (l. 450), while the Cambridge MS. reads "late thys deth passe fro me" (l. 450).

34. See Anderson, *Drama and Imagery,* p. 147; examples include the miniature in the *Hours of Catherine of Cleves,* Gossaert's *Agony,* and an illumination in the *Albani Psalter.*

35. Davidson and O'Connor, *York Art,* p. 71.

36. *Ludus Coventriae,* p. 263.

37. Schiller, *Iconography of Christian Art,* II, fig. 166.

38. Ibid., II, 56.

39. The stage directions in the N-town play indicate that when Christ speaks, "*all þe jewys falle sodeynly to þe Erde*" (*Ludus Coventriae,* p. 265).

40. For the early appearance of the lantern in iconography, see Robert Edwards, *The Montecassino Passion and the Poetics of Medieval Drama* (Berkeley and Los Angeles: Univ. of California Press, 1977), pp. 105–08.

41. See Louis Réau, *Iconographie de l'art Chrétien* (Paris, 1956), II, 134–37.

42. Schiller, *Iconography of Christian Art,* II, 56–58, 60–66. See also Hildburgh, "English Alabaster Carvings," pp. 51ff.

43. Davidson and O'Connor, *York Art,* p. 73.

44. Plummer, *Hours of Catherine of Cleves,* Pls. 20–21.

45. *The Hours of Etienne Chevalier* (New York: Braziller, 1971), Pl. 15.

46. Bodleian Library MS. Gough liturg. 6, fol. 22^V; Pächt and Alexander, No. 812. For additional attention to the iconography of the suffering Christ, see James Marrow, *Passion Iconography in Northern European Art of the Late Middle Ages and Renaissance* (Kortrijk: Van Ghemmert, 1979), pp. 44–67.

47. Sandro Sticca, *The Latin Passion Play* (Albany: State Univ. of New York Press, 1970), pp. 69–71.

48. Cf. *Ludus Coventriae,* p. 278: *"et cantabit gallus."*

49. Robinson, "The Art of the York Realist," p. 246.

50. Sticca, *Latin Passion Play*, pp. 72–74.

51. Woolf, *English Mystery Plays*, p. 245.

52. *Hours of Etienne Chevalier*, Pl. 15. But see also the depiction of armored Roman soldiers in the painted glass at York (e.g., in the Resurrection panel in the fourteenth-century window in the East Wall, North Aisle, All Saints, North Street, and in the restored Crucifixion completed in 1339. See Davidson and O'Connor, *York Art*, pp. 79, 81.

53. See Lawrence G. Craddock, "Franciscan Influences in Early English Drama," *Franciscan Studies*, 10 (1950), 389.

54. York Minster Library MS. XVI. K. 6, fol. 1^V; printed in *The Lay Folks Mass Book*, ed. Thomas F. Simmons, EETS, o.s. 71 (1879), p. 84.

55. *History of Yorkshire: The City of York*, p. 146. For Nicholas Blackburn's membership in the Corpus Christi Guild, see *The Register of the Guild of Corpus Christi in the City of York*, ed. Robert H. Skaife, Surtees Soc., 57 (1872), p. 16.

56. Kolve, pp. 184ff.

57. Owst, p. 510; A. C. Cawley, ed., *The Wakefield Pageants in the Towneley Cycle* (Manchester: Manchester Univ. Press, 1958), p. 121.

58. Quoted by Owst, p. 510.

59. Quoted by Owst, p. 510.

60. Hildburgh, "English Alabaster Carvings," Pl. XVIIa.

61. Plummer, *Hours of Catherine of Cleves*, Pl. 19.

62. Kolve, p. 186.

63. See J. Huizinga, *Homo Ludens* (1950; rpt. Boston: Beacon Press, 1955), p. 11. "It is curious to note," writes Huizinga, "how much more lenient society is to the cheat than to the spoil-sport. This is because the spoil-sport shatters the play-world itself. By withdrawing from the game he reveals the relativity and fragility of the play-world in which he had temporarily shut himself with others. He robs play of its illusion—a pregnant word which means literally 'in-play' (from *inlusio, illudere* or *inludere*). Therefore he must be cast out, for he threatens the existence of the play-community."

64. Plummer, *Hours of Catherine of Cleves*, Pl. 19 (commentary).

65. Leyden Univ. Library Codex Burmanni Q 3, fol. 125^V; reproduction in Adolf Katzenellenbogen, *Allegories of the Virtues and Vices in Mediaeval Art*, fig. 5.

66. Ibid., p. 47.

67. Ibid., pp. 2, 57, fig. 14.

68. Migne, *PL*, XXIII, 1474, as quoted in G. von der Osten, "Job and Christ," *Journal of the Warburg and Courtauld Institutes*, 16 (1953), 156.

69. Quoted from Albert Boekler, *Die Regensburg-Prüfeniger Buch-malerei* (Munich, 1924), pp. 33ff, by von der Osten, p. 156.

70. Woolf, *English Mystery Plays,* p. 257.

71. See W. A. Craigie, "The *Gospel of Nicodemus* and the *York Mystery Plays,"* in *An English Miscellany presented to Dr. Furnivall* (Oxford: Clarendon Press, 1901), pp. 55–56.

72. For a discussion of Pilate's composite character, see Arnold Williams, *The Characterization of Pilate in the Towneley Plays* (East Lansing: Michigan State Univ. Press, 1950), pp. 1ff; but see also the study of the York Pilate by Robert A. Brawer, "The Characterization of Pilate in the York Cycle Play," *Studies in Philology,* 69 (1972), 289–303.

73. *OED,* s.v. *scathe.*

74. See also the scourge illustrated in the Arma Christi now in All Saints, Pavement; see Knowles, *York School,* fig. 6.

75. Chambers, *Mediaeval Stage,* II, 142–43. But see especially the record of expenditures by the Smiths of Coventry in 1451: "It[em] payed for vj skynnys of whitled' [white leather] to godds g[ar]ment . . . xviij^d" (Sharp, *Dissertation on the Pageants,* p. 26). See also Hildburgh, "English Alabaster Carvings," pp. 79–80.

76. See MS. Bodley 758, fol. 1; illustrated in Clifford Davidson, *Drama and Art* (Kalamazoo: Medieval Institute, 1977), Pl. VII; cf. Katzenellenbogen, fig. 14. But for another source of this iconography, see Marrow, *Passion Iconography,* pp. 52–54.

77. *Ludus Coventriae,* p. 294; *Chester Mystery Cycle,* p. 299; *Towneley Plays,* p. 247. See also the sermon quoted by Owst, p. 508. But see the *Holkham Bible Picture Book,* fol. 30^v.

78. Plummer, *Hours of Catherine of Cleves,* Pl. 22.

79. Schiller, *Iconography of Christian Art,* II, fig. 246; Sticca, *Latin Passion Play,* p. 76.

80. See Woolf, *English Mystery Plays,* p. 254.

81. National Gallery, London, Catalogue No. 4744. Cf. James Marrow, "*Circumdederunt me canes multi:* Christ's Tormentors in Northern Art of the Late Middle Ages and Early Renaissance," *Art Bulletin,* 59 (1977), 167–81.

82. *Meditations,* trans. Ragusa, p. 319.

83. *Religious Lyrics of the XIVth Century,* ed. Carleton Brown, 2nd ed. (Oxford: Clarendon Press, 1952), p. 68.

84. *York,* ed. Johnston and Rogerson, I, 353. For the effigy of Matthew Hutton, which was damaged in the fire of 1829 and restored, see G. E. Aylmer, "Funeral Monuments and Other Post-Medieval Sculpture," in *A History of York Minster,* ed. G. E. Aylmer and Reginald Cant (Oxford: Clarendon Press, 1977), fig. 138.

Chapter VII

1. Charles Mills Gayley, *Plays of Our Forefathers* (New York, 1907), p. 158.

2. Robinson, "The Art of the York Realist," pp. 241-51.

3. See, for example, Kahrl, *Traditions of Medieval English Drama,* pp. 72-98.

4. Woolf, *English Mystery Plays,* p. 400. She is referring specifically to the scenes in which Judas argues with the Porter and in which Pilate appears with Procula.

5. Panofsky, *Early Netherlandish Painting,* I, 35.

6. Robinson, "The Art of the York Realist," p. 243.

7. Meyrick H. Carré, *Phases of Thought in England* (Oxford: Oxford Univ. Press, 1949), p. 145.

8. Plummer, *Hours of Catherine of Cleves,* Pl. 20. The towel, however, is a common iconographic feature, and appears, for example, over the shoulder of the attendant in an alabaster fragment at the Louvre. See Hildburgh, "English Alabaster Carvings," p. 80. For an example at York, see Davidson and O'Connor, *York Art,* p. 73.

9. There may well be a hint that Pilate's action should be compared in some way to the washing of hands by the priest before the canon of the Mass.

10. See *John* 12.3-6.

11. *York,* ed. Johnston and Rogerson, I, 9; II, 695.

12. Extracts from Sharp, *Dissertation on the Pageants,* p. 28.

13. Sticca, *Latin Passion Play,* p. 66.

14. See Robert Edwards, *Montecassino Passion,* pp. 97-102.

15. Meyrick H. Carré, *Realists and Nominalists* (Oxford: Oxford Univ. Press, 1946), p. 110. For Ockham's rejection of universals, see his *Summa totius logicae,* 1.15, as quoted in *Philosophical Writings: A Selection,* ed. and trans. Philotheus Boehner (New York, 1957), pp. 35-37. The role of nominalism at Oxford is discussed by Gordon Leff, *Paris and Oxford Universities in the Thirteenth and Fourteenth Centuries* (1968; rpt. New York: Robert E. Krieger, 1975), *passim.*

16. See above, Chapter VI, and also Sticca, *Latin Passion Play,* pp. 72-74.

17. The quoted words are from George Boas' introduction to his translation of St. Bonaventure's *The Mind's Road to God* (New York: Library of Liberal Arts, 1953), p. xviii. The Franciscan principle of preferring "direct acquaintance with, rather than descriptions of [things]" is extremely important for an understanding of the York Realist.

18. See *Meditations*, trans. Ragusa, pp. 317ff, and also the translation by Nicholas Love, published by Caxton in 1486, beginning at sig. N3^r.

19. Prosser, in *Drama and Religion, passim,* stresses the late medieval doctrine of penance as central to the plays contained in the medieval cycles. The connection between vernacular plays and the forgiveness of sins might be very close indeed, for, as F. M. Salter notes (*Mediaeval Drama in Chester* [Toronto, 1955], p. 39), a statement on the cover of a play book containing the Chester plays (Harley MS. 2124) links the promise of indulgences by the Bishop of Chester and by the Pope with the plays.

20. Mâle, *Religious Art from the Twelfth to the Eighteenth Centuries,* pp. 112–13.

21. *Catalogue of Early Christian Antiquities,* No. 291; reproduction in Kitzinger, *Early Medieval Art in the British Museum,* Pl. 7; Beckwith, *Ivory Carvings,* figs. 47, 67–72.

22. O'Connor and Haselock, "The Stained and Painted Glass," pp. 361–63; Davidson and O'Connor, *York Art,* pp. 79–80; T. W. French, "The West Windows of York Minster," *Yorkshire Archaeological Journal,* 47 (1975), 81–85.

23. Plummer, *Hours of Catherine of Cleves,* Pl. 26. On related literary expression, see Douglas Gray, *Themes and Images in the Medieval English Religious Lyric* (London: Routledge and Kegan Paul, 1972), pp. 122–45.

24. Pickering, *Literature and Art,* pp. 273–85.

25. Davidson and O'Connor, *York Art,* pp. 75–76; Hildburgh, "English Alabaster Carvings," p. 83, Pl. XVIId. In the *Northern Passion,* which was one of the Realist's sources, we read how the executioners used rope to stretch Christ's body to fit the cross (Pt. I, p. 191). See additionally Grace Frank, "Popular Iconography of the Passion," *PMLA,* 46 (1931), 339.

26. Pickering, *Literature and Art,* pp. 285–301; Davidson, "Northern Spirituality and Late Medieval Drama in York," pp. 135–36.

27. See E. W. Tristram, *English Wall Painting in the Fourteenth Century* (London: Routledge and Kegan Paul, 1955), pp. 21–22.

28. *Religious Lyrics of the XIVth Century,* ed. Brown, p. 55.

29. *Mirrour of the Blessed Lyf of Jesu Christ,* sig. O7^r.

30. O. B. Hardison, Jr., *Christian Rite and Christian Drama in the Middle Ages* (Baltimore: Johns Hopkins Univ. Press, 1965), pp. 131–32. See also the Reproaches in the *Northern Passion,* p. 205.

31. Davidson, *Drama and Art,* Pl. VIII; Hildburgh Collection A.15-1946; Panofsky, *Early Netherlandish Painting,* fig. 39.

32. Hildburgh Collection A.49–1946. The Virgin is, of course, absent from the Deposition in the York play.

33. Schiller, *Iconography of Christian Art,* II, fig. 563.

34. *The Belles Heures of Jean, Duke of Berry, Prince of France,* introd. James J. Rorimer (New York, 1958), Pl. 9.

35. Pächt, *Rise of Pictorial Narrative,* pp. 30–31.

36. MS. XVI. K. 6; *Hours of the Cross* printed in *Lay Folks Mass Book,* p. 86.

37. Ibid., pp. 83, 86.

38. Davidson and O'Connor, *York Art,* pp. 85–87; Knowles, *Essays,* p. 170.

39. As Knowles points out, the Corpus Christi Guild was founded specifically for "the praise and honour of the most sacred body of our Lord Jesus Christ" (*Essays,* pp. 169–71).

40. See *Breviarium ad usum insignis Eboracensis,* I, Surtees Soc., 71 (1880), cols. 529–52.

41. Margaret Rickert, *The Reconstructed Carmelite Missal* (Chicago: Univ. of Chicago Press, 1952), Pl. V; British Library Additional MSS. 29704–5, 44892 (fol. 36^V in reconstructed missal).

42. *Lay Folks Mass Book,* pp. 118–19.

43. On the realism in the sermons of the Franciscans, see Owst, *Literature and Pulpit,* pp. 23–41.

44. *Religious Lyrics of the XIVth Century,* ed. Brown, p. 112.

45. Panofsky, *Early Netherlandish Painting,* I, 2.

46. Johnston, "The Guild of Corpus Christi and the Procession," p. 380.

47. *York,* ed. Johnston and Rogerson, I, 43; II, 728. Scholars were slow to see that this passage essentially approved of the plays, but see Craddock, "Franciscan Influences," pp. 389–93. J. S. Purvis, for example, is surely wrong when he suggests, in *From Minster to Market Place* (York, 1969), p. 29, that "Melton's Sermon evidently included or implied a protest of the church in opposition to the gild cycle as separated from the church and no longer interested or concerned in drama that was essentially liturgical."

48. *York,* ed. Johnston and Rogerson, I, 43.

49. E. B. Emden, *A Biographical Register of the University of Oxford to A.D. 1500* (1958), II, 1258.

50. *York,* ed. Johnston and Rogerson, I, 43; II, 728.

Chapter VIII

1. This play was the responsibility of the Saddlers, but the Glaziers also contributed to its production. See *York,* ed. Johnston and Rogerson,

I, 297-98, for documentation revealing the decline of the Glaziers in the middle of the sixteenth century.

2. See Davidson, "Northern Spirituality," pp. 125-51.

3. The Towneley play is printed by Smith, *York Plays,* pp. 372-95, for easy comparison with the York play, but citations from Towneley in this chapter are, of course, from *The Towneley Plays,* ed. England and Pollard.

4. Hardison, *Christian Rite and Christian Drama,* p. 83.

5. See Josef A. Jungmann, *The Early Liturgy,* trans. Francis A. Brunner (Notre Dame, Indiana: Univ. of Notre Dame Press, 1959), p. 263; *The Sarum Missal,* ed. J. Wickham Legg (Oxford: Clarendon Press, 1916), p. 112.

6. Ibid., p. 113; *Missale ad usum ecclesie Eboracensis* (1517), fol. h8^V.

7. Hardison, *Christian Rite and Christian Drama,* p. 97.

8. Ibid., pp. 142-43.

9. John Speirs, *Medieval English Poetry* (1957; rpt. London: Faber and Faber, 1971), p. 357.

10. Ibid., p. 357.

11. See Rushforth, *Medieval Christian Imagery,* p. 385; Réau, *Iconographie,* III, 531-37.

12. Lawrence Stone, *Sculpture in Britain: The Middle Ages* (Baltimore: Penguin, 1955), Pl. 24.

13. Trans. William Caxton (1493), fol. xxiv.

14. Ibid.; *Golden Legend,* trans. Ryan and Ripperger, p. 221. See also *The Harrowing of Hell and The Gospel of Nicodemus,* ed. W. H. Hulme, EETS, e.s. 100 (1907), and *Apocryphal New Testament,* trans. James.

15. Cf. Pickering, *Literature and Art,* pp. 223-307.

16. The role of art would have been especially great if the plays developed from the devotional *tableaux vivants.* See the speculative article by Martin Stevens, "The York Cycle: From Procession to Play," *Leeds Studies in English,* n.s. 6 (1972), 37-61.

17. Kolve, *Play Called Corpus Christi,* p. 195.

18. See especially Rosemary Woolf, "The Theme of Christ the Lover-Knight in Medieval English Literature," pp. 1-16. See also J. A. MacCulloch, *The Harrowing of Hell* (Edinburgh, 1930), p. 230.

19. See also the representation, noted in previous chapters, showing the *arma Christi* now in All Saints, Pavement.

20. Davidson and O'Connor, *York Art,* pp. 87-89.

21. See also the representation of the Harrowing in the *Holkham Bible Picture Book,* fol. 34^r.

22. Alan H. Nelson, "The Temptation of Christ; or, The Temptation of Satan," *Medieval English Drama,* ed. Jerome Taylor and Alan H.

Nelson (Chicago: Univ. of Chicago Press, 1972), p. 219. See also Peter Stuart Macaulay, "The Play of the Harrowing of Hell as a Climax in the English Mystery Cycles," *Studia Germanica Gandensia,* 8 (1966), 115-19.

23. MacCulloch, *Harrowing,* pp. 203-04.

24. Young, *Drama of the Medieval Church,* I, 103-04. See also Hardison, *Christian Rite and Christian Drama,* pp. 112-14, on the Palm Sunday procession.

25. Woolf, *English Mystery Plays,* p. 404; Tertullian, *De resurrectione mortuorum,* XLIV.7.

26. Rushforth, *Medieval Christian Imagery,* p. 385.

27. Ibid., p. 385, fig. 177. Cf. the *De Lisle Psalter,* which contains a representation of the Harrowing; reproduction in O. Elfrida Saunders, *English Illumination* (1933; rpt. New York: Hacker, 1969), I, Pl. 107. In this miniature, Christ's staff-end is in the mouth of a devil beneath his feet, while the broken gates are behind him.

28. Tristram, *English Wall Paintings of the Fourteenth Century,* p. 154; Victoria and Albert Museum, Hildburgh Collection A.1-1955.

29. Sharp, *Dissertation,* p. 73.

30. "Popular Iconography of the Passion," p. 339.

31. See Alfred W. Pollard, ed., *English Miracle Plays, Moralities, and Interludes* (Oxford: Clarendon Press, 1927), p. 169.

32. This explanation solves the problems cited by Martial Rose in his translation of *The Wakefield Mystery Plays,* p. 545. See also the description of the King's College Chapel window in E. M. W. Tillyard, *Some Mythical Elements in English Literature* (London, 1961), pp. 19-20.

33. *Chester Mystery Cycle,* p. 333.

34. See G. H. Lightfoot, "Mural Paintings in St. Peter's Church, Pickering," *Yorkshire Archaeological Journal,* 13 (1895), 367.

35. Rose, *Wakefield Mystery Plays,* pp. 545-46.

36. Harley MS., ll. 1541-48, ed. Hulme in *Harrowing of Hell and The Gospel of Nicodemus,* p. 120. See also *Apocryphal New Testament,* trans. James, p. 140.

37. Plummer, *Hours of Catherine of Cleves,* Pl. 48.

38. William Dunbar, *The Poems,* ed. W. Mackay Mackenzie (London: Faber and Faber, 1932), pp. 159-60.

39. Walter Lowrie, *Art in the Early Church,* revised ed. (1947; rpt. New York: W. W. Norton, 1969), p. 61.

40. Mâle, *Gothic Image,* p. 194; Rushforth, *Medieval Christian Imagery,* p. 77.

41. Eric George Millar, *A Thirteenth Century York Psalter* (Oxford: Roxburghe Club, 1952), Pl. VII.

42. Davidson and O'Connor, *York Art,* p. 92.

43. Pächt and Alexander, No. 1065, Pl. XCIX.

44. Hildburgh, "English Alabaster Carvings," Pl. XXI.

45. Anderson, *Imagery of British Churches,* p. 126.

46. Woolf, *English Mystery Plays,* p. 276.

47. *Apocryphal New Testament,* trans. James, p. 106.

48. Dutka, *Music in the English Mystery Plays,* Nos. 23-24; *Breviarium ad usum insignis ecclesie Eboracensis,* I, 415. See also Meg Twycross, "Playing 'The Resurrection'," *Medieval Studies for J. A. W. Bennett,* ed. P. L. Heyworth (Oxford: Clarendon Press, 1981), p. 290, and Pamela Sheingorn, "The Moment of Resurrection in the Corpus Christi Plays," *Medievalia et Humanistica,* n.s. 11 (1982), 116.

49. *York,* ed. Johnston and Rogerson, I, 22; II, 708.

50. Young, *Drama of the Medieval Church,* I, 393-97; practical music edition edited by William L. Smoldon (London: Oxford University Press, n.d.).

51. W. L. Hildburgh, "Iconographic Peculiarities in English Alabaster Carvings," *Folk-Lore,* 44 (1933), Pl. XXI.

52. Browne, *History,* Pl. CXI; Davidson and O'Connor, *York Art,* pp. 91-92.

53. Dunbar, *Poems,* p. 160.

Chapter IX

1. F. C. Gardiner, *The Pilgrimage of Desire* (Leiden: E. J. Brill, 1971), p. 147 (italics mine).

2. Ibid., p. 147.

3. Edwards, "Techniques of Transcendence," p. 164; rpt. *Drama in the Middle Ages,* ed. Davidson *et al.,* p. 110.

4. Gee, "The Painted Glass of All Saints' Church," Pl. XXVII.

5. On Mary Magdalene, see Marjorie M. Malvern, *Venus in Sackcloth* (Carbondale and Edwardsville: Southern Illinois Univ. Press, 1975), esp. pp. 100-13.

6. Cf. ibid., pp. 57-70. See also St. Bernard's devotion to the humanity of Christ and his insistence upon an affective experience that transcends ordinary life.

7. Davidson and O'Connor, *York Art,* pp. 96-97.

8. Torre, *Antiquities of York Minster,* p. 63.

9. Hildburgh, "English Alabaster Carvings," Pl. XXI.

10. M. D. Anderson, *The Choir Stalls of Lincoln Minster* (Lincoln: Friends of Lincoln Cathedral, 1967), fig. 4.

11. Of particular relevance here is Gerhart B. Ladner's article, "*Homo Viator*: Mediaeval Ideas on Alienation and Order," *Speculum,* 42 (1967), 233–59.

12. See Rosemary Woolf, *The English Religious Lyric in the Middle Ages* (Oxford: Clarendon Press, 1968), p. 163.

13. *PL*, CLXXXIV, 967, as quoted in Gardiner, *Pilgrimage,* p. 51.

14. Rushforth, *Medieval Christian Imagery*, p. 80, citing J. Wilpert, *Die Römischen Mosaiken und Malereien der kirklichen Bauten vom IV. bis XIII. Jahrhundert,* II (1916), 904.

15. See Lucy Freeman Sandler, *The Peterborough Psalter in Brussels and Other Fenland Manuscripts* (London: Harvey Miller, 1974), fig. 55; cf. *Holkham Bible Picture Book*, fol. 36, and see also Rushforth, *Medieval Christian Imagery,* pp. 79–80.

16. Davidson and O'Connor, *York Art,* p. 97.

17. See, for example, the glass of c.1440 in All Saints, North Street (Gee, "The Painted Glass of All Saints' Church," Pl. XXXVI). On the iconography, see Rushforth, *Medieval Christian Imagery,* pp. 93–96.

18. *York,* ed. Johnston and Rogerson, I, 23.

19. A. L. Laishley, *The Stained Glass of York* (York: Oldfield, n.d.), p. 32.

20. See also my review of Richard J. Collier's *Poetry and Drama in the York Corpus Christi Play*, in *Comparative Drama,* 12 (1978), 275–76.

21. Young, *Drama of the Medieval Church,* I, 481; quoted by Gardiner, *Pilgrimage,* p. 87.

22. Meyer Schapiro, "The Image of the Disappearing Christ: The Ascension in English Art Around the Year 1000," in *Late Antique, Early Christian and Mediaeval Art,* pp. 267–87.

23. Davidson and O'Connor, *York Art,* pp. 99, 101.

24. Browne, *History,* Pl. CXVI. See also Rushforth, *Medieval Christian Imagery,* p. 387; Schapiro, p. 273.

25. *York*, ed. Johnston and Rogerson, I, 23. The cloud may have been constructed of cloth, since the Tailors were responsible for the play at York.

26. Davidson and O'Connor, *York Art,* p. 101; Gibson, "Stained and Painted Glass," Pl. 39.

27. Davidson and O'Connor, *York Art,* p. 101.

28. James Torre, *Antiquities Ecclesiastical of the City of York,* MS. in York Minster Library.

Chapter X

1. *Testamenta Eboracensia*, II, 19–20.

2. The will includes provision for the endowment of a chantry chapel dedicated to St. Anne, the Virgin's mother, on Foss Bridge in York (ibid., p. 21).

3. See Davidson and O'Connor, *York Art*, pp. 36-37.

4. Millard Meiss, *Painting in Florence and Siena after the Black Death* (New York: Harper and Row, 1964), pp. 151-52; Theresa Coletti, "Devotional Iconography in the N-Town Marian Plays," *Comparative Drama*, 11 (1977), 37; rpt. in *Drama in the Middle Ages*, ed. Davidson *et al.*, p. 264.

5. Cf., however, *Speculum Humanae Salvationis*, Vol. II, Pls. 73, 75.

6. *Testamenta Eboracensia*, V (1884), 101.

7. *Meditations on the Life and Passion of Christ*, ed. Charlotte d'Evelyn, EETS, o.s. 158 (London, 1921), p. 59.

8. *York Hours* (1517), fol. cxii; see Davidson and O'Connor, *York Art*, p. 116.

9. W. L. Hildburgh, "An English Alabaster Carving of St. Michael Weighing a Soul," *Burlington Magazine*, 89 (1947), 128-31.

10. See F. L. B. Cunningham, "The Relationship between Mary and the Church in Medieval Thought," *Marian Studies*, 9 (1958), 52-78.

11. Gray, *Themes and Images in the Medieval English Religious Lyric*, pp. 81-83.

12. See M. G. A. Vale, *Piety, Charity and Literacy among the Yorkshire Gentry, 1370-1480*, Borthwick Papers, 50 (York: Borthwick Institute, 1976), p. 16.

13. *Religious Lyrics of the XVth Century*, p. 39.

14. On devotional images, see Sixten Ringbom, "Devotional Images and Imaginative Devotions," *Gazette des Beaux-Arts*, 111 (1969), 159-70, and Theresa Coletti, "Spirituality and Devotional Images," dissertation (Univ. of Rochester, 1975), *passim*.

15. M. R. James, *The Sculptures in the Lady Chapel at Ely* (1895), *passim*; for an example, see Gardner, *English Medieval Sculpture*, fig. 347.

16. *York*, ed. Johnston and Rogerson, I, 293, 331-32; Anna J. Mill, "The York Plays of the Dying, Assumption, and Coronation of Our Lady," *PMLA*, 65 (1950), 876.

17. Martin Stevens, "The Missing Parts of the Towneley Cycle," *Speculum*, 45 (1970), 254-65.

18. See the Lollard treatise against Images and Pilgrimages in *English Wycliffite Writings*, ed. Anne Hudson (Cambridge: Cambridge Univ. Press, 1978), pp. 83-88.

19. *The York Mercers and Merchant Adventurers, 1356-1917*, ed. Maud Sellers, Surtees Soc., 129 (Durham, 1918), p. iv.

20. *Apocryphal New Testament,* trans. James, pp. 209–16.

21. Davidson and O'Connor, *York Art,* pp. 103–04; Mark R. Sullivan, "The Missing York *Funeral of the Virgin,*" *EDAM Newsletter,* 1, No. 2 (April 1979), 5–7.

22. Cf. *York,* ed. Johnston and Rogerson, I, 23.

23. Ibid., I, 23.

24. *Golden Legend,* trans. Ryan and Ripperger, p. 451.

25. Ibid., p. 453.

26. Ibid., p. 453.

27. *York,* ed. Johnston and Rogerson, I, 23; the reference to the angel is written in a different and presumably later hand.

28. M. R. James and E. W. Tristram, "The Wall Paintings in Eton College Chapel and in the Lady Chapel of Winchester Cathedral," *Walpole Society Publications,* 17 (1928–29), 19–20, Pl. IV.

29. Ibid., p. 20; the source named for the inscription is the *Speculum* of Vincent of Beauvais, Book VII.75–79.

30. Tristram, *English Wall Painting in the Fourteenth Century,* pp. 154–55, Pl. 36.

31. *York,* ed. Johnston and Rogerson, I, 26.

32. Sullivan, "Missing York *Funeral of the Virgin,*" p. 5; *York,* ed. Johnston and Rogerson, I, 110.

33. Ibid., I, 47–48; II, 732.

34. Ibid., I, 110; see also Beadle, ed., *York Plays,* pp. 429–33.

35. *York,* ed. Johnston and Rogerson, I, 136, 216.

36. O'Connor and Haselock, "Stained and Painted Glass," p. 357, fig. 113.

37. *Ludus Coventriae,* pp. 367–70. An element of anti-semitism may have been present in the York play's production and audience reception. This element in general is discussed by Stephen Spector, "Anti-Semitism and the English Mystery Plays," *Comparative Drama,* 13 (1979), 3–16, rpt. in *Drama in the Middle Ages,* ed. Davidson *et al.,* pp. 328–41.

38. Sullivan, "Missing York *Funeral of the Virgin,*" p. 7.

39. Dutka, *Music in the English Mystery Plays,* p. 27.

40. Ibid., pp. 38–42, 44–50.

41. *Golden Legend,* trans. Ryan and Ripperger, p. 454.

42. Carolyn Wall, "The Apocryphal and Historical Backgrounds of 'The Appearance of Our Lady to Thomas' (Play XLVI of the York Cycle)," *Mediaeval Studies,* 32 (1970), 177–92.

43. Cave, *Roof Bosses,* fig. 181.

44. Augusta S. Tavender, "Mediaeval Alabasters in American Museums," *Speculum,* 30 (1955), 65. Legends concerning the girdle owe

much to its preservation at Prato near Florence (see Wall, "Apocryphal and Historical Backgrounds," pp. 178-80).

45. *York*, ed. Johnston and Rogerson, I, 142.

46. Ibid., I, 26.

47. Ibid., I, 134, 54. See also Margaret Dorrell (Rogerson), "The Mayor of York and the Coronation Pageant," *Leeds Studies in English,* n.s. 5 (1971), 35-45.

48. See, for example, James Raine, ed., *The Fabric Rolls of York Minster*, Surtees Soc., 35 (Durham, 1859), pp. 113-14, and E. Brunskill, "Two Hundred Years of Parish Life in York," *Annual Report and Proceedings of the Yorkshire Archaeological Society, 1950-51* (York, 1951), p. 32. See also the indispensable general work on Protestant iconoclasm by John Phillips, *The Reformation of Images: Destruction of Art in England, 1535-1660* (Berkeley and Los Angeles: Univ. of California Press, 1973).

49. Davidson and O'Connor, *York Art*, pp. 109-10.

50. *York Plays*, ed. Smith, pp. 514-15.

Chapter XI

1. *York*, ed. Johnston and Rogerson, I, 24.

2. See Mirella Levi d'Ancona, *The Iconography of the Immaculate Conception in the Middle Ages and Early Renaissance,* Monographs on Archaeology and Fine Arts, 7 (Chicago: College Art Assoc., 1957), pp. 30, 35-36.

3. Hildburgh, "Iconographic Peculiarities," pp. 48ff. See also Tristram, *English Wall Painting in the Fourteenth Century*, p. 19, and Mary Phillips Perry, "On the Psychostasis in Christian Art," *Burlington Magazine,* 22 (1912-13), 215.

4. Davidson and O'Connor, *York Art*, p. 116.

5. Peter Meredith, "The Development of the York Mercers' Pageant Waggon," *Medieval English Theatre,* 1, No. 1 (1979), 5. The 1433 indenture was reported by Alexandra Johnston and Margaret Dorrell (Rogerson) in *Leeds Studies in English,* n.s. 5 (1971), 29-34; their article also provides some explanations and conjectures concerning the Mercers' Doomsday pageant based on the indenture. See also their article, "The York Mercers and their Pageant of Doomsday," *Leeds Studies in English,* n.s. 6 (1972), 10-35, and Peter Meredith, "Item for a grone—iij d'—Records and Performance," *Proceedings of the First Colloquium,* ed. JoAnna Dutka (Toronto: Records of Early English Drama, 1979), pp. 26-60, esp. 46-50.

6. Vale, *Piety, Charity, and Literacy,* p. 26; Shaw, *Old York Church,* pp. 86, 89.

7. Davidson, "Northern Spirituality," pp. 138-39; Raine, *Mediaeval York, passim.*

8. This glass was the gift of Nicholas Blackburn, Sr., and his family; see above, Chapter VI.

9. Chester's Play XXII provides the only full dramatization of the Fifteen Signs, but the Towneley plays utilize one of the signs in a crucial way; see Clifford Davidson, "The End of the World in Medieval Art and Drama," *Michigan Academician,* 5 (1972), 257-61.

10. *York,* ed. Johnston and Rogerson, I, 188-89, 242; Meredith, "Development of the York Mercers' Pageant Waggon," pp. 6-7.

11. See Davidson and O'Connor, *York Art,* pp. 119-23. The vividness with which the wounds were portrayed in the Passion (see the 1415 *Ordo* with its emphasis on Christ's bleeding even before the Crucifixion [*York,* ed. Johnston and Rogerson, I, 21]) surely would have been carried over to this scene.

12. B. P. Johnson, "The Gilds of York," in *The Noble City of York,* ed. Alberic Stacpoole *et al.* (York: Cerialis Press, 1972), p. 476.

13. *York,* ed. Johnston and Rogerson, I, 56.

14. Davidson and O'Connor, *York Art,* pp. 115-16.

15. *York Mercers and Merchant Adventurers,* ed. Sellers, p. 98.

16. Gent, *Antient and Modern History,* p. 188.

17. E. W. Tristram, *English Medieval Wall Painting: The Thirteenth Century* (London: Oxford Univ. Press, 1950), pp. 44-45; Tristram, *English Wall Painting in the Fourteenth Century,* p. 19; A. Caiger-Smith, *English Medieval Mural Paintings* (Oxford: Clarendon Press, 1963), pp. 31-43.

18. Tristram, *English Wall Painting in the Fourteenth Century,* p. 19.

19. Durandus, *The Symbolism of Churches and Church Ornaments* [*Rationale Divinorum Officiorum,* Book I], trans. John Mason Neale and Benjamin Webb (London, 1893), pp. 24-26.

20. John Bilson, "On a Sculptured Representation of Hell Cauldron, Recently Found at York," *Yorkshire Archaeological Journal,* 19 (1906-07) 435-45.

21. Meredith, "Development of the York Mercers' Pageant Waggon," pp. 10, 14.

22. Anderson, *Imagery of British Churches,* Pl. 1.

23. Cambridge University Library MS. Gg. vi. 16, fol. 49^V, as quoted in Owst, *Literature and Pulpit,* p. 523.

24. *York,* ed. Johnston and Rogerson, I, 95.

25. Ibid., I, 95.

26. Johnston and Dorrell, "The York Mercers and Their Pageant," p. 18. See also Tydeman, *Theatre in the Middle Ages,* p. 111, and the Doom painting at Pickworth, Lincolnshire, where the souls are emerging from coffer tombs (E. Clive Rouse, "Wall Paintings in St. Andrew's Church, Pickworth, Lincolnshire," *Journal of the British Archaeological Association,* 13 [1950], Pl. XXXI). Cf. *Holkham Bible Picture Book,* fol. 42.

27. *York,* ed. Johnston and Rogerson, I, 55. The Coventry records as reported by Sharp, p. 69, indicate that the good souls are white and the bad ones are black.

28. See Clifford Davidson, "An Interpretation of the Wakefield *Judicium,*" *Annuale Mediaevale,* 10 (1969), 110-12.

29. *York,* ed. Johnston and Rogerson, I, 96.

30. Ibid., I, 55. On the question of masks on the early stage, see Meg Twycross and Sarah Carpenter, "Masks in the English Theatre: The Mystery Plays," *Medieval English Theatre,* 3 (1981), 7-44.

31. *York,* ed. Johnston and Rogerson, I, 241.

32. Ibid., I, 55-56. Tydeman notes a Mons reference to painting Raphael's face red (*Theatre in the Middle Ages,* p. 170; the citation is to Gustave Cohen's edition of *Le Livre de conduite du regisseur* [Paris, 1925], pp. 410-11).

33. See Perry, "On the Psychostasis," 94-105, 208-18; W. L. Hildburgh, "An English Alabaster Carving of *St. Michael Weighing a Soul,*" *Burlington Magazine,* 89 (1947), 129-31.

34. Davidson and O'Connor, *York Art,* p. 116.

35. Davidson, "Interpretation of the Wakefield *Judicium,*" pp. 114-15. On Michael, see also Chapter VIII, above.

36. *Missale ad usum insignis ecclesiae Eboracensis*, ed. Dr. Henderson, Surtees Soc., 60 (Durham, 1874), II, 184.

37. See, for example, Sidney W. Clarke, *The Miracle Play in England* (London: William Andrews, n.d.), p. 13.

38. See the extended examples at Winchester; described by C. J. P. Cave, "The Bosses on the Vault of the Quire of Winchester Cathedral," *Archaeologia,* 76 (1927), 165ff.

39. H. H. J. Westlake, *A History of Design in Painted Glass* (London, 1881-94), III, Pl. VI.

40. *York,* ed. Johnston and Rogerson, I, 55-56.

41. See Westlake, *History of Design,* III, 104-05, for comment on damage sustained by the window before restoration and the extent of the restoration.

42. G. Scharf, "Observations on a Picture in Gloucester Cathedral, and some other Representations, of the Last Judgment," *Archaeologia,* 36 (1855), 370ff.

43. *York,* ed. Johnston and Rogerson, I, 55.

44. Cf. *Chester Mystery Cycle,* p. 450.

45. York, ed. Johnston and Rogerson, I, 55. In 1462, God's new shirt and hose were painted (ibid., I, 95), surely making the wounds more fresh and realistic. The 1415 *Ordo* indicated that Christ in the *Road to Calvary* (Play XXXIV in the Register) was covered with blood (ibid., I, 21).

46. Mirk, *Festial,* p. 3.

47. *Religious Lyrics of the XIVth Century,* ed. Brown, p. 112.

48. *Missale ad usum insignis ecclesiae Eboracensis,* II, 183–84.

APPENDIX

The following list indicates the numbering of the plays in the Register according to the order established by Richard Beadle in his edition of *The York Plays* (1982) with the previous numbering of Lucy Toulmin Smith in parentheses when it differs. The play titles are in most cases not present in the Register, and are supplied here whenever possible from the Index of Alexandra Johnston and Margaret Rogerson's *York* (Records of Early English Drama, 1978), which adapts the form used in the second list prepared by the town clerk, Roger Burton, and entered in the *York Memorandum Book A/Y* c.1415-22 (Johnston and Rogerson, *York,* I, 25-26, II, 415-16). The guild designations are from the Register, and additionally I have included references to the appropriate folios in the manuscript for convenience.

I ff. 1-4	Barkers	Creation of Heaven and Earth
II ff. 4^V-6	Plasterers	Creation through the Fifth Day
III ff. 6^V-8	Cardmakers	Creation of Adam and Eve
IV ff. 10^V-11^V	Fullers	Prohibition of the Tree of Knowledge
V ff. 13^V-15^V	Coopers	Fall of Man
VI ff. 16^V-18	Armorers	Expulsion from the Garden
VII ff. 19-20^V	Glovers	*Sacrificium Cayme et Abell*
VIII ff. 21^V-23^V	Shipwrights	Building of Noah's Ark
IX ff. 25-29^V	Fishers, Mariners	Noah's Ark during the Flood

X ff. 31–36^V	Parchmentmakers, Bookbinders	Abraham and Isaac
XI ff. 38–43	Hosiers	Pharaoh with Moses
XII ff. 44–47^V	Spicers	Annunciation to Mary
XIII ff. 48–52	Pewterers, Founders	Joseph's Troubles about Mary
XIV ff. 54–56	Tilethatchers	Nativity
XV ff. 59–61	Chandlers	Offering of the Shepherds
XVI (XVI–XVII) ff. 62^V–73^{V*}	Masons, Goldsmiths	Herod Questioning Three Kings; Offering of the Magi
XVII (XLI) ff. 227^V–232	Hatmakers, Masons, Laborers	Purification of the Virgin
XVIII ff. 75–78^V	Marshals	Flight into Egypt
XIX ff. 80–84^V	Girdlers, Nailers	Slaughter of the Innocents
XX ff. 86–90^V	Spurriers, Lorimers	Christ and the Doctors
XXI ff. 92–94	Barbers	Baptism of Christ
XXII ff. 95–97	Smiths	Temptation in the Wilderness
XXIIA (not entered)	Vintners	Marriage in Cana
XXIII ff. 102–106	Curriers	Transfiguration
XXIIIA (not entered)	Ironmongers	Feast in Simon's House
XXIV ff. 111–114^V	Cappers	Woman Taken in Adultery; Raising of Lazarus
XXV ff. 115^V–121^V	Skinners	Entry into Jerusalem

XXVI ff. 123–130	Cutlers	Conspiracy
XXVII ff. 131^V–134^V	Bakers	Last Supper
XXVIII ff. 136–142^V	Cordwainers	Agony and Betrayal
XXIX ff. 144–151	Bowers, Fletchers	Trial before Caiaphas
XXX ff. 152^V–163	Tapiters, Couchers	First Trial before Pilate
XXXI ff. 164–171^V	Listers (Dyers)	Trial before Herod
XXXII ff. 172^V–178^V	Cooks, Waterleaders	Remorse of Judas
XXXIII ff. 180–187^V	Tilemakers	Second Trial before Pilate
XXXIV ff. 189–194	Shearmen	Road to Calvary
XXXV ff. 195–200	Pinners	*Crucifixio Christi*
XXXVI ff. 201–206^V	Butchers	*Mortificacio Christi*
XXXVII ff. 207^V–213^V	Saddlers	Harrowing of Hell
XXXVIII ff. 215–220	Carpenters	Resurrection
XXXIX ff. 221^V–223^V	Winedrawers	Appearance of Christ to Mary Magdalene
XL ff. 224–227^V	Woolpackers	Travellers to Emmaus
XLI (XLII) ff. 233–235**	Scriveners	Doubting Thomas
XLII (XLIII) ff. 236^V–240^V	Tailors	Ascension
XLIII (XLIV) ff. 241–244^V	Potters	Pentecost

XLIV (XLV) ff. 245^V–248	Drapers	Death of Mary
XLIVA (not entered)	Masons, Linenweavers	Fergus
XLV (XLVI) ff. 249–256^V	Weavers	Assumption of the Virgin
XLVI (XLVII) ff. 257–259^V	Hostelers (Inholders)	Coronation of the Virgin
XLVII (XLVIII) ff. 261–266^V	Mercers	Doomsday

*For explanation of the Herod-Magi scenes presented by the Masons and Goldsmiths, see Beadle, ed., *York Plays,* p. 430.

**Also contained in Sykes Manuscript, Yorkshire Museum, York. See ibid., p. 457.

SELECT BIBLIOGRAPHY

Adams, Joseph Quincy, ed. *Chief Pre-Shakespearean Dramas*. Boston: Houghton Mifflin, 1924.

Ambrose. *Hexameron, Paradise, and Cain and Abel*. New York: Fathers of the Church, 1961.

Anderson, M. D. *The Choir Stalls of Lincoln Minster*. Lincoln: Friends of Lincoln Cathedral, 1967.

_____. *Drama and Imagery in English Medieval Churches*. Cambridge: Cambridge Univ. Press, 1963.

_____. *The Imagery of British Churches*. London: John Murray, 1955.

_____. *Looking for History in British Churches*. London: John Murray, 1951.

André, J. L. "St. John the Baptist in Art, Legend, and Ritual," *Archaeological Journal*, 50 (1893), 1-19.

Aquinas, Thomas. *Summa Theologica*, trans. Fathers of the English Dominican Province. New York: Benziger, 1947. 3 vols.

Aulén, Gustaf. *Christus Victor*, trans. A. G. Herbert. New York: Macmillan, 1969.

Axton, Richard. *European Drama of the Early Middle Ages*. London: Hutchinson, 1974.

Aylmer, G. E. "Funeral Monuments and Other Post-Medieval Sculpture," in *A History of York Minster*, ed. G. E. Aylmer and Reginald Cant. Oxford: Clarendon Press, 1977.

Baker, John. *English Stained Glass*. London: Thames & Hudson, 1960.

Bates, Katharine Lee. *The English Religious Drama*. New York, 1893.

Beadle, Richard, ed. *The York Plays*. London: Edward Arnold, 1982.

_____ and Peter Meredith. "Further External Evidence for Dating the York Register (BL Additional MS 35290)," *Leeds Studies in English*, n.s. 11 (1980), 51-55.

Beckwith, John. *Ivory Carvings in Early Medieval England*. Greenwich, Conn.: New York Graphic Soc., 1972.

Benson, Edwin. *Life in a Mediaeval City*. London: SPCK, 1920.

Benson, George. *The Ancient Painted Glass Windows in the Minster and Churches of the City of York*. York: Yorkshire Philosophical Soc., 1915.

Bernbrock, John E. "Notes on the Towneley Cycle *Slaying of Abel,*" *Journal of English and Germanic Philology,* 62 (1963), 317–22.

Bevington, David, ed. *Medieval Drama.* Boston: Houghton Mifflin, 1975.

Bilson, John. "On a Sculptured Representation of Hell Cauldron, Recently Found at York," *Yorkshire Archaeological Journal,* 19 (1906–07), 435–45.

Bilson, Thomas. *A Sermon Preached at Westminster, before the King and Queenes Majesties, at Their Coronations.* London, 1603.

Bjork, David. "On the Dissemination of *Quem quaeritis* and the *Visitatio sepulchri* and the Chronology of Their Early Sources," *Comparative Drama,* 14 (1980), 46–69.

Block, K. S., ed. *Ludus Coventriae, or the Plaie Called Corpus Christi.* EETS, e.s. 120. 1922; rpt. 1960.

Blunt, Anthony. "Blake's 'Ancient of Days': The Symbolism of the Compasses," *Journal of the Warburg and Courtauld Institutes,* 2 (1938–39), 53–63.

Boase, T. S. R. *The York Psalter in the Library of the Hunterian Museum, Glasgow.* London: Faber and Faber, 1962.

Bonaventura. *The Mind's Road to God,* trans. George Boas. New York: Library of Liberal Arts, 1953.

Bond, Francis. *Wood Carvings in English Churches.* London: Oxford Univ. Press, 1910.

Bonnell, J. K. "The Serpent with a Human Head in Art and in Mystery Play," *American Journal of Archaeology,* 2nd ser., 21 (1917), 255–91.

Brawer, Robert A. "The Characterization of Pilate in the York Cycle Play," *Studies in Philology,* 69 (1972), 289–303.

Breviarum ad usum insignis ecclesie Eboracensis, I. Surtees Soc., 71. Durham, 1880.

Brown, Arthur. "Some Notes on Medieval Drama at York," in *Early English and Norse Studies Presented to Hugh Smith,* ed. Arthur Brown and Peter Foote. London: Methuen, 1963. Pp. 1–5.

Brown, Carleton, ed. *Religious Lyrics of the XIVth Century,* 2nd ed. Oxford: Clarendon Press, 1952.

————, ed. *Religious Lyrics of the XVth Century.* Oxford: Clarendon Press, 1939.

Browne, John. *The History of the Metropolitan Church of St. Peter, York.* London, 1847. 2 vols.

Brunskill, E. "Two Hundred Years of Parish Life in York," *Annual Report and Proceedings of the Yorkshire Archaeological Society, 1950–51* (York, 1951), 17–58.

Butterworth, Philip. "The York Mercers' Pageant Vehicle, 1433–67," *Medieval English Theatre*, 1 (1979), 72–81.

Carré, Meyrick H. *Phases of Thought in England*. Oxford: Oxford Univ. Press, 1949.
_____. *Realists and Nominalists*. Oxford: Oxford Univ. Press, 1946.
Cave, C. J. P. "The Bosses on the Vault of the Quire of Winchester Cathedral," *Archaeologia*, 76 (1927), 165–78.
_____. *Roof bosses in Medieval Churches*. Cambridge: Cambridge Univ. Press, 1948.
Caviness, Madeline Harrison. *The Early Stained Glass of Canterbury Cathedral*. Princeton: Princeton Univ. Press, 1977.
Cawley, A. C., ed. *The Wakefield Pageants in the Towneley Cycle*. Manchester: Manchester Univ. Press, 1958.
Chambers, E. K. *The Mediaeval Stage*. Oxford: Oxford Univ. Press, 1903. 2 vols.
Chatwin, Philip B. "The Decoration of the Beauchamp Chapel, Warwick, with Special Reference to the Sculptures," *Archaeologia*, 77 (1927), 313–34.
Clarke, Sidney W. *The Miracle Play in England*. London: William Andrews, n.d.
Clopper, Lawrence M., ed. *Chester*. Records of Early English Drama. Toronto: Univ. of Toronto Press, 1979.
Cohn, Norman. "The Horns of Moses," *Commentary* (1958), pp. 220–26.
Coletti, Theresa. "Devotional Iconography in the N-Town Marian Plays," *Comparative Drama*, 11 (1977), 22–44.
_____. "Spirituality and Devotional Images." Univ. of Rochester diss., 1975.
Collier, Richard J. *Poetry and Drama in the York Corpus Christi Play*. Hamden, Conn.: Archon Books, 1978.
Collins, Patrick J. "Narrative Bible Cycles in Medieval Art and Drama," *Comparative Drama*, 9 (1975), 125–46.
_____. *The N-Town Plays and Medieval Picture Cycles*. Early Drama, Art, and Music, Monograph Ser., 2. Kalamazoo, Mich.: Medieval Institute Publications, 1979.
_____. "Typology, Criticism, and Medieval Drama: Some Observations on Method," *Comparative Drama*, 10 (1976–77), 298–313.
Cornell, Henrik. *The Iconography of the Nativity of Christ*. Uppsala Universitets Årsskrift. Uppsala, 1924.

Craddock, Lawrence G. "Franciscan Influences on Early English Drama," *Franciscan Studies,* 10 (1950), 399–415.

Craig, Hardin. *English Religious Drama.* Oxford: Clarendon Press, 1955.

――――, ed. *Two Coventry Corpus Christi Plays.* EETS, e.s. 87. London, 1957.

Craigie, W. A. "The *Gospel of Nicodemus* and the *York Mystery Plays,*" in *An English Miscellany presented to Dr. Furnivall.* Oxford: Clarendon Press, 1901. Pp. 52–61.

Cunningham, F. L. B. "The Relationship between Mary and the Church in Medieval Thought," *Marian Studies,* 9 (1958), 52–78.

Davidson, Clifford. *Drama and Art.* Early Drama, Art, and Music, Monograph Ser., 1. Kalamazoo: Medieval Institute, 1977.

――――. "The End of the World in Medieval Drama and Art," *Michigan Academician,* 5 (1972), 257–63.

――――. "An Interpretation of the Wakefield *Judicium,*" *Annuale Mediaevale,* 10 (1969), 110–12.

――――. "Northern Spirituality and the Late Medieval Drama of York," in *The Spirituality of Western Christendom,* ed. E. Rozanne Elder (Kalamazoo: Cistercian Publications, 1976), pp. 125–51, 205–08.

――――. "Thomas Aquinas, the Feast of Corpus Christi, and the English Cycle Plays," *Michigan Academician,* 7 (1974), 103–10.

――――, ed. *A Middle English Treatise on the Playing of Miracles.* Washington: Univ. Press of America, 1981.

――――. "The Unity of the Wakefield 'Mactacio Abel'," *Traditio,* 23 (1967), 495–500.

――――. "The Visual Arts and Drama, with Special Emphasis on the Lazarus Plays," in *Le Théâtre au Moyen Âge,* ed. Gari Muller. Montreal: Les Éditions Univers, 1981.

――――, C. J. Gianakaris, and John H. Stroupe, eds., *Drama in the Middle Ages.* New York: AMS Press, 1982.

―――― and David E. O'Connor. *York Art: A Subject List of Extant and Lost Art including Items Relevant to Early Drama.* Early Drama, Art, and Music, Reference Ser., 1. Kalamazoo: Medieval Institute Publications, 1978.

Davies, R. *Extracts from the Municipal Records of York.* 1843.

Davis, Nicholas M. "The Playing of Miracles, c.1350 to the Reformation." Cambridge Univ. diss., 1978.

Davis, Norman, ed. *Non-Cycle Plays and Fragments.* EETS, s.s. 1. London, 1970.

d'Evelyn, Charlotte, ed. *Meditations on the Life and Passion of Christ.* EETS, o.s. 158. London, 1921.

Dorrell, Margaret. "The Butchers', Saddlers', and Carpenters' Pageants: Misreadings of the York *Ordo*," *English Language Notes*, 13 (1975), 1–4.

_____. "The Mayor of York and the Coronation Pageant," *Leeds Studies in English*, n.s. 5 (1971), 35–45.

_____. "Two Studies of the York Corpus Christi Play," *Leeds Studies in English*, n.s. 6 (1972), 63–111.

Drake, Francis. *Eboracum*. 1736.

Dunbar, William. *The Poems*, ed. W. Mackay Mackenzie. London: Faber and Faber, 1932.

Durandus. *The Symbolism of Churches and Church Ornaments*, trans. John Mason Neale and Benjamin Webb. London, 1893.

Dutka, JoAnna. "Music and the English Mystery Plays," *Comparative Drama*, 7 (1973), 135–49.

_____. *Music in the English Mystery Plays*. Early Drama, Art, and Music, Reference Ser., 2. Kalamazoo: Medieval Institute Publications, 1980.

_____. "Mysteries, Minstrels, and Music," *Comparative Drama*, 8 (1974), 112–24.

_____, ed. *Proceedings of the First Colloquium*. Toronto: Records of Early English Drama, 1979.

Edwards, Robert. *The Montecassino Passion and the Poetics of Medieval Drama*. Berkeley and Los Angeles: Univ. of California Press, 1977.

_____. "Techniques of Transcendence in Medieval Drama," *Comparative Drama*, 8 (1974), 157–72.

Emden, E. B. *A Biographical Register of the University of Oxford to A.D. 1500*. 1958. Vol. II.

Emerson, O. F. "Legends of Cain, Especially in Old and Middle English," *PMLA*, 21 (1906), 831–77.

England, George, and A. W. Pollard, eds. *The Towneley Plays*. EETS, e.s. 71. London, 1897.

Fairweather, Eugene R., trans. *A Scholastic Miscellany*. New York: Macmillan, 1970.

Farmer, Oscar G. *Fairford Church and Its Stained Glass Windows*, 8th ed. Bath, 1968.

Foster, Frances A., ed. *The Northern Passion*, Pt. I, EETS, o.s. 145. London, 1913.

Fouquet, Jean. *The Hours of Etienne Chevalier*, introd. Claude Schaefer. New York: Braziller, 1971.

Frampton, Mendal G. "The York Play of *Christ Led up to Calvary*," *Philological Quarterly*, 20 (1941), 198–204.

Frank, Grace. "Popular Iconography of the Passion," *PMLA,* 46 (1931), 333–40.

French, T. W. "The West Windows of York Minster," *Yorkshire Archaeological Journal,* 47 (1975), 81–85.

Gardiner, F. C. *The Pilgrimage of Desire.* Leiden: Brill, 1971.

Gardiner, Harold C. *Mysteries' End.* New Haven: Yale Univ. Press, 1946.

Gardner, Arthur. *English Medieval Sculpture.* Cambridge: Cambridge Univ. Press, 1951.

Garvin, Katherine. "A Note on Noah's Wife," *Modern Language Notes,* 49 (1934), 88–90.

Gee, E. A. "The Painted Glass of All Saints' Church, North Street, York," *Archaeologia,* 102 (1969), 151–202.

Gent, Thomas. *The Antient and Modern History of the Famous City of York.* York, 1730.

Gibson, Gail McMurray. "Long Melford, Suffolk: Some Suggestions for the Study of Visual Artifacts and Medieval Drama," *Research Opportunities in Renaissance Drama,* 21 (1978), 103–15.

Gibson, Peter. "The Stained and Painted Glass of York," in *The Noble City of York,* ed. Alberic Stacpoole. York: Cerialis Press, 1972.

Gospel Stories in English Embroidery. London: HSMO, 1963.

Gray, Douglas. *Themes and Images in the Medieval English Religious Lyric.* London: Routledge and Kegan Paul, 1972.

Greenberg, Noah, and W. L. Smoldon, eds. *The Play of Herod.* New York: Oxford Univ. Press, 1965.

Halfpenny, Joseph. *Gothic Ornaments in the Cathedral Church of York.* York, 1795.

Hanning, R. W. "'You Have Begun a Parlous Pleye': The Nature and Limits of Dramatic Mimesis as a Theme in Four Middle English 'Fall of Lucifer' Plays," *Comparative Drama,* 7 (1973), 22–50.

Hardison, O. B., Jr. *Christian Rite and Christian Drama in the Middle Ages.* Baltimore: John Hopkins Univ. Press, 1965.

Harrison, F. "The Bedern Chapel, York," *Yorkshire Archaeological Journal,* 27 (1923–24), 197–209.

————. *The Painted Glass of York.* London: SPCK, 1927.

Hassall, W. O. *The Holkham Bible Picture Book.* London: Dropmore Press, 1954.

Heaton, Herbert. *The Yorkshire Woolen and Worsted Industries from the Earliest Times up to the Industrial Revolution,* 2nd ed. Oxford: Clarendon Press, 1965.

Herbert, J. A., introd. *The Sherbourne Missal.* Oxford: Roxburghe Club, 1920.

Hildburgh, W. L. "An Alabaster Table of the Annunciation with the Crucifix: A Study in English Iconography," *Archaeologia*, 74 (1923-24), 203-34.
_____. "An English Alabaster Carving of St. Michael Weighing a Soul," *Burlington Magazine*, 89 (1947), 128-31.
_____. "English Alabaster Carvings as Records of the Medieval English Drama," *Archaeologia*, 93 (1955), 51-101.
_____. "Further Miscellaneous Notes on Medieval Alabaster Carvings," *Antiquaries Journal*, 17 (1937), 182ff.
_____. "Iconographic Peculiarities in English Alabaster Carvings," *Folk-Lore*, 44 (1933), 123-50.
Hollaender, Albert. "The Doom Painting of St. Thomas of Canterbury, Salisbury," *Wiltshire Archaeological and Natural History Magazine*, 50 (1942), 351-70.
Hoskins, Edgar. *Horae Beatae Mariae Virginis, or Sarum and York Primers*. London: Longmans, Green, 1901.
Hudson, Anne, ed. *English Wycliffite Writings*. Cambridge: Cambridge Univ. Press, 1978.
Huizinga, J. *Homo Ludens*. 1950; rpt. Boston: Beacon Press, 1955.
Hulme, W. H., ed. *The Harrowing of Hell and The Gospel of Nicodemus*. EETS, e.s. 100. London, 1907.
Inventory of the Historical Monuments in the City of York. Royal Commission on Historical Monuments, 1972-75. Vols. III-IV.
Jackson, Esther. *Art of the Anglo-Saxon Age*. Peterborough, N.H.: Richard R. Smith, 1964.
Jacobus de Voragine. *The Golden Legend*, trans. William Caxton. London, 1483; trans. Granger Ryan and Helmut Ripperger. New York: Longmans, Green, 1941.
M. R. James, trans. *The Aprocryphal New Testament*. Oxford: Clarendon Press, 1924
_____. *Illustrations of the Book of Genesis*. Oxford: Roxburghe Club, 1921.
_____. "On Paintings Formerly in the Choir at Peterborough," *Cambridge Antiquarian Society Proceedings*, No. 38 (1896), 178-93.
_____. *The Sculptures in the Lady Chapel at Ely*. London: D. Nutt, 1895.
_____ and E. W. Tristram. "The Wall Paintings in Eton College Chapel and in the Lady Chapel of Winchester Cathedral," *Walpole Society Publications*, 17 (1928-29), 1-44
Jameson, [Anna], and Lady Eastlake. *The History of Our Lord*. London: Longmans, Green, 1864.
Jeffrey, David L. "Franciscan Spirituality and the Rise of Early English Drama," *Mosaic*, 8, No. 4 (1975), 17-46.

————. "Stewardship in the Wakefield *Mactacio Abel* and *Noe* Plays," *American Benedictine Review,* 22 (1971), 64–76.

Johnson, B. P. "The Gilds of York," in *The Noble City of York*, ed. Alberic Stacpoole *et al.* York: Cerialis Press, 1972.

Johnston, Alexandra F. "The Guild of Corpus Christi and the Procession of Corpus Christi in York," *Mediaeval Studies,* 38 (1976), 372–84.

———— and Margaret Dorrell. "The Doomsday Pageant of the York Mercers, 1433," *Leeds Studies in English,* n.s. 5 (1971), 29–34.

———— and Margaret [Dorrell] Rogerson, *York*. Records of Early English Drama. Toronto: Univ. of Toronto Press, 1979. 2 vols.

———— and Margaret Dorrell. "The York Mercers and Their Pageant of Doomsday, 1433–1526," *Leeds Studies in English,* n.s. 6 (1972), 10–35.

Jungmann, Josef A. *The Early Liturgy,* trans. Francis A. Brunner. Notre Dame, Ind.: Univ. of Notre Dame Press, 1959.

Kahrl, Stanley J. *Traditions of Medieval English Drama.* London: Hutchinson, 1974.

Katzenellenbogen, Adolf. *Allegories of the Virtues and Vices in Mediaeval Art,* trans. Alan J. P. Crick. 1939; rpt. New York: Norton, 1964.

Kitzinger, Ernst. *Early Medieval Art in the British Museum,* 2nd ed. London: British Museum, 1955.

Knowles, David, and R. Neville Hadcock. *Medieval Religious Houses: England and Wales.* London: Longmans, Green, 1953.

Knowles, John A. "The East Window of Holy Trinity, Goodramgate," *Yorkshire Archaeological Journal,* 28 (1924–26), 1–24.

————. *Essays in the History of the York School of Glass-Painting.* London: SPCK, 1936.

————. "The West Window, St. Martin-le-Grand, Coney Street, York," *Yorkshire Archaeological Journal,* 38 (1955), 148–84.

Kolve, V. A. *The Play Called Corpus Christi.* Stanford: Stanford Univ. Press, 1966.

Krapp, George, ed. *The Vercelli Book.* Anglo-Saxon Poetic Records, 2. New York: Columbia Univ. Press, 1932.

Laishley, A. L. *The Stained Glass of York.* York: Oldfield, n.d.

Leff, Gordon. *Paris and Oxford Universities in the Thirteenth and Fourteenth Centuries.* 1968; rpt. New York: Robert E. Krieger, 1975.

Legg, J. Wickham, ed. *The Sarum Missal.* Oxford: Clarendon Press, 1916.

Levi d'Ancona, Mirella. *The Iconography of the Immaculate Conception in the Middle Ages and Early Renaissance.* Monographs on Archaeology and Fine Arts, 7. Chicago: College Art Assoc., 1957.

Lightfoot, G. H. "Mural Paintings in St. Peter's Church, Pickering," *Yorkshire Archaeological Journal,* 13 (1895), 353-70.

Love, Nicholas, trans. *The Mirrour of the Blessed Lyf of Jesu Christ.* London, 1486

Lumiansky, R. M., and David Mills, eds. *The Chester Mystery Cycle.* EETS, s.s. 3. London, 1974.

Lutz, J., and P. Perdrizet, eds. *Speculum humanae salvationis.* Leipzig, 1909.

Macaulay, Peter Stuart. "The Play of the Harrowing of Hell as a Climax in the English Mystery Cycles," *Studia Germanica Gandensia,* 8 (1966), 115-34.

MacCulloch, J. A. *The Harrowing of Hell.* Edinburgh, 1930.

Mâle, Émile. *The Gothic Image,* trans. Dora Nussey. 1913; rpt. New York: Harper, 1958.

_____. *Religious Art from the Twelfth to the Eighteenth Centuries.* English trans. 1949; rpt. New York: Noonday, 1970.

_____. *Religious Art in France: The Twelfth Century,* trans. Marthiel Mathews. Bollingen Ser., 90, 1. Princeton: Princeton Univ. Press, 1978.

Malvern, Marjorie M. *Venus in Sackcloth.* Carbondale and Edwardsville: Southern Illinois Univ. Press, 1975.

Marcousé, Renée. *Figure Sculpture in St. Mary's Abbey, York.* York: Yorkshire Philosophical Soc., 1951.

Marrow, James. "*Circumdederunt me canes multi:* Christ's Tormentors in Northern Art of the Late Middle Ages and Early Renaissance," *Art Bulletin,* 59 (1977), 167-81.

_____. *Passion Iconography in Northern European Art of the Late Middle Ages and Early Renaissance.* Kortrijk: Van Ghemmert, 1979.

McIver, M. E. "Visitation of Mary," in *New Catholic Encyclopedia.* New York: McGraw-Hill, 1967. XIV, 721.

Meiss, Millard. *Painting in Florence and Siena after the Black Death.* New York: Harper and Row, 1964.

Meredith, Peter. "The Development of the York Mercers' Pageant Waggon," *Medieval English Theatre,* 1 (1979), 5-18.

_____. "Item for a grone—iij d'—Records and Performance," *Proceedings of the First Colloquium,* ed. JoAnna Dutka. Toronto: Records of Early English Drama, 1979.

————. "John Clerke's Hand in the York Register," *Leeds Studies in English,* n.s. 12 (1981), 245–71.

————. "The *Ordo Paginarum* and the Development of the York Tile-makers' Pageant," *Leeds Studies in English,* n.s. 11 (1980), 59–73.

Meyers, Walter E. *A Figure Given: Typology in the Wakefield Plays.* Pittsburgh: Duquesne Univ. Press, 1970.

Mill, Anna J. "The Hull Noah Play," *Modern Language Review,* 33 (1938), 489–505.

————. "Noah's Wife Again," *PMLA,* 56 (1941), 613–26.

————, "The Stations of the York Corpus Christi Play," *Yorkshire Archaeological Journal,* 37 (1951), 492–502.

————. "The York Bakers' Play of the Last Supper," *Modern Language Review,* 30 (1935), 145–58.

————. "The York Plays of the Dying, Assumption, and Coronation of Our Lady," *PMLA,* 65 (1950), 866–76.

Millar, Eric George. *A Thirteenth Century York Psalter.* Oxford: Roxburghe Club, 1952.

Miller, Frances H. "The *Northern Passion* and the Mysteries," *Modern Language Notes,* 34 (1919), 88–92.

Milner-White, Eric. *Friends of York Minster: Annual Reports,* 17–35. York, 1945–63.

Mirk, John. *Festial.* EETS, e.s. 96. London, 1905.

Missale ad usum ecclesie Eboracensis. Rouen, 1517.

Missale ad usum insignis ecclesiae Eboracensis, ed. Dr. Henderson. Surtees Soc., 60. Durham, 1874.

Moore, John Robert. "The Tradition of Angelic Singing in English Drama," *Journal of English and Germanic Philology,* 22 (1923), 89–99.

Muir, Lynette. "The Fall of Man in the Drama of Medieval Europe," *Studies in Medieval Culture,* 10 (1977), 121–31.

————. "The Trinity in Medieval Drama," *Comparative Drama,* 10 (1976), 116–29.

Munson, William F. "Typology and the Towneley Isaac," *Research Opportunities in Renaissance Drama,* 11 (1968), 129–39.

Musper, H. T. *Die Urausgaben der holländischen Apokalypse und Biblia Pauperum.* Munich: Prestel Verlag, 1961.

Nagler, A. M. *The Medieval Religious Stage.* New Haven: Yale Univ. Press, 1976.

Nelson, Alan H. *The Medieval English Stage.* Chicago: Univ. of Chicago Press, 1974.

————. "On Recovering the Lost Norwich Corpus Christi Cycle," *Comparative Drama,* 4 (1970–71), 241–52.

_____. "The Temptation of Christ; or, The Temptation of Satan," in *Medieval English Drama,* ed. Jerome Taylor and Alan H. Nelson. Chicago: Univ. of Chicago Press, 1972. Pp. 218-29.

Nelson, Philip. "Some Additional Specimens of English Alabaster Carvings," *Archaeological Journal,* 84 (1927), 114-24.

_____. "Some Fifteenth-Century English Alabaster Panels," *Archaeological Journal,* 76 (1919), 133-38.

_____. "The Virgin Triptych at Danzig," *Archaeological Journal,* 76 (1919), 139-42.

Norris, Edwin, ed. and trans. *The Ancient Cornish Drama.* Oxford: Oxford Univ. Press, 1859.

O'Connor, David E., and Jeremy Haselock. "The Stained and Painted Glass," in *A History of York Minster,* ed. G. E. Aylmer and Reginald Cant. Oxford: Clarendon Press, 1977. Pp. 313-93.

Owst, G. R. *Literature and Pulpit in Medieval England,* 2nd ed. Oxford: Blackwell, 1961.

Pächt, Otto. *The Rise of Pictorial Narrative in Twelfth-Century England.* Oxford: Clarendon Press, 1962.

_____ and J. J. G. Alexander, *Illuminated Manuscripts in the Bodleian Library, Oxford.* Oxford: Clarendon Press, 1973. Vol. III.

Panofsky, Erwin. *Early Netherlandish Painting.* Cambridge: Harvard Univ. Press, 1953.

Perry, Mary Phillips. "On the Psychostasis in Christian Art," *Burlington Magazine,* 22 (1912-13), 94-105, 208-18.

Pfaff, R. W. *New Liturgical Feasts in Later Medieval England.* Oxford: Clarendon Press, 1970.

Phillips, John. *The Reformation of Images.* Berkeley and Los Angeles: Univ. of California Press, 1973.

Pickering, F. P. *Literature and Art in the Middle Ages.* Coral Gables, Fla.: Univ. of Miami Press, 1970.

Plummer, John. *The Hours of Catherine of Cleves.* New York: Braziller, n.d.

Pollard, A. W. *English Miracle Plays, Moralities, and Interludes.* Oxford: Clarendon Press, 1927.

Prosser, Eleanor. *Drama and Religion in the English Mystery Plays.* Stanford: Stanford Univ. Press, 1961.

Przywara, Erich, ed. *An Augustine Synthesis.* New York: Harper, 1958.

Purvis, J. S. *From Minster to Market Place.* York, 1969.

Ragusa, Isa, and Rosalie B. Green, trans. *Meditations on the Life of Christ.* Princeton: Princeton Univ. Press, 1961.

Raine, Angelo. *Mediaeval York.* London: John Murray, 1955.

Raine, James, ed. *The Fabric Rolls of York Minster.* Surtees Soc., 35. Durham, 1859.

Réau, Louis. *Iconographie de l'art Chrétien.* Paris: Presses Universitaires de France, 1955–59. 3 vols.

Reese, Jesse Byers. "Alliterative Verse in the York Cycle," *Studies in Philology,* 48 (1951), 639–68.

Register of the Guild of Corpus Christi in the City of York, ed. Robert H. Skaife. Surtees Soc., 57. Durham, 1872.

Remnant, G. L. *A Catalogue of Misericords in Great Britain.* Oxford: Clarendon Press, 1969.

Rickert, Margaret. *Painting in Britain in the Middle Ages.* Baltimore: Penguin, 1954.

_____. *The Reconstructed Carmelite Missal.* Chicago: Univ. of Chicago Press, 1952.

_____. "The So-Called Beaufort Hours and York Psalter," *Burlington Magazine,* 104 (1962), 238–45.

Ringbom, Sixten. "Devotional Images and Imaginative Devotions," *Gazette des Beaux-Arts,* 111 (1969), 159–70.

Robb, David M. "The Iconography of the Annunciation in the Fourteenth and Fifteenth Centuries," *Art Bulletin,* 18 (1936), 480–526.

Robinson, J. W. "The Art of the York Realist," *Modern Philology,* 60 (1962–63), 241–51.

_____. "A Commentary on the York Play of the Birth of Jesus," *Journal of English and Germanic Philology,* 70 (1971), 241–54.

_____. "The Late Medieval Cult of Jesus and the Mystery Plays," *PMLA,* 80 (1965), 508–14.

Rogerson, Margaret (*née* Dorrell). "The York Corpus Christi Play: Some Practical Details," *Leeds Studies in English,* n.s. 10 (1978), 97–106.

Rorimer, James. J., introd. *The Belles Heures of Jean, Duke of Berry, Prince of France.* New York, 1958.

Rose, Martial, ed. and trans. *The Wakefield Mystery Plays.* 1962; rpt. Garden City, N.Y.: Doubleday, 1963.

Ross, Lawrence J. "Art and the Study of Early English Drama," *Renaissance Drama,* 6 (1963), 35–46.

_____. "Symbol and Structure in the *Secunda Pastorum,*" *Comparative Drama,* 1 (1967), 122–49.

Rouse, E. Clive. "Wall Paintings in St. Andrew's Church, Pickworth, Lincolnshire," *Journal of the British Archaeological Association,* 13 (1950), 24–33.

Rushforth, Gordon McN. *Medieval Christian Imagery.* Oxford: Clarendon Press, 1936.

_____. "The Windows of the Church of St. Neot, Cornwall," *Exeter Diocesan Architectural and Archaeological Society*, 15 (1937), 150–90.

St. Olave's Church, York. Gloucester: British Publishing Co., 1950.

Salter, F. M. *Mediaeval Drama in Chester*. Toronto: Univ. of Toronto Press, 1955.

Sandler, Lucy Freeman. *The Peterborough Psalter in Brussels and Other Fenland Manuscripts*. London: Harvey Miller, 1974.

Saunders, O. Elfrida. *English Illumination*. 1933; rpt. New York: Hacker, 1969.

Saxl, F. "The Ruthwell Cross," *Journal of the Warburg and Courtauld Institutes*, 6 (1943), 1–18.

Schapiro, Meyer. "Cain's Jaw-Bone That Did the First Murder," in *Late Antique, Early Christian, and Mediaeval Art*. New York: Braziller, 1979. Pp. 249–65.

_____. "The Image of the Disappearing Christ: The Ascension in English Art Around the Year 1000," in *Late Antique, Early Christian, and Mediaeval Art*. New York: Braziller, 1979. Pp. 267–87.

_____. *Words and Pictures*. The Hague: Mouton, 1973.

Scharf, G. "Observations on a Picture in Gloucester Cathedral, and some other Representations, of the Last Judgment," *Archaeologia*, 36 (1855), 370–91.

Schiller, Gertrud. *Iconography of Christian Art*, trans. Janet Seligman. Greenwich, Conn.: New York Graphic Soc., 1971. 2 vols.

_____. *Ikonographie der christlichen Kunst*. Gütersloh: Gerd Mohn, 1971. 4 vols.

Schorr, Dorothy. "The Iconographic Development of the Presentation in the Temple," *Art Bulletin*, 28 (1946), 17–32.

Sellers, Maud. "The City of York in the Sixteenth Century," *English Historical Review*, 9 (1894), 275–304.

_____, ed. *York Memorandum Book A/Y*. Surtees Soc., 125. Durham, 1915.

_____, ed. *The York Mercers and Merchant Adventures, 1356–1917*. Surtees Soc., 129. Durham, 1918.

Sharp, Thomas. *A Dissertation on the Pageants or Dramatic Mysteries Anciently Performed at Coventry*. Coventry, 1825.

Shaw, P. J., *et al. An Old York Church: All Hallows in North Street*. York, 1908.

Sheingorn, Pamela. "On Using Medieval Art in the Study of Medieval Drama: An Introduction to Methodology," *Research Opportunities in Renaissance Drama*, 22 (1979), 101–09.

_____. "The Moment of Resurrection in the Corpus Christi Plays,"
Medievalia et Humanistica, n.s. 11 (1982), 111-29.

Simmons, Thomas F., ed. *The Lay Folks Mass Book*. EETS, o.s. 71.
London, 1879.

Skey, Miriam. "Herod's Demon Crown," *Journal of the Warburg and
Courtauld Institutes,* 40 (1977), 274-76.

_____. "The Iconography of Herod the Great in Medieval Art," *EDAM
Newsletter,* 3, No. 1 (1980), 4-10.

Smalley, Beryl. *The Study of the Bible in the Middle Ages.* Oxford:
Blackwell, 1952.

Smith, Lucy Toulmin, ed. *York Plays.* 1885; rpt. New York: Russell
and Russell, 1963.

Smoldon, W. L. "The Melodies of the Medieval Church-Dramas and
Their Significance," *Comparative Drama,* 2 (1968), 185-209.

_____. *The Music of the Medieval Church Dramas*, ed. Cynthia
Bourgeault. London: Oxford Univ. Press, 1980.

Spector, Stephen. "Anti-Semitism and the English Mystery Plays,"
Comparative Drama, 13 (1979), 3-16.

Speirs, John. *Medieval English Poetry.* 1957; rpt. London: Faber and
Faber, 1971.

Snyder, Susan. "The Left Hand of God: Despair in Medieval and Renaissance Tradition," *Studies in the Renaissance,* 12 (1965), 18-59.

Staines, David. "To Out-Herod Herod: The Development of a Dramatic Character," *Comparative Drama,* 10 (1976), 29-53.

Stevens, Martin. "The Missing Parts of the Towneley Cycle," *Speculum*,
45 (1970), 254-65.

_____. "The York Cycle: From Procession to Play," *Leeds Studies in
English*, n.s. 6 (1972), 37-61.

_____ and Margaret Dorrell. "The *Ordo Paginarum* Gathering of the
York *A/Y Memorandum Book*," *Modern Philology,* 72 (1974), 45-59.

Sticca, Sandro. "Drama and Spirituality in the Middle Ages," *Medievalia et Humanistica,* n.s. 4 (1973), 69-87.

_____. *The Latin Passion Play*. Albany: State Univ. Press of New
York, 1970.

Stone, Lawrence. *Sculpture in Britain: The Middle Ages.* Baltimore:
Penguin, 1955.

Stuart, D. C. "The Stage Setting of Hell and the Iconography of the
Middle Ages," *Romanic Review,* 4 (1913), 330-42.

Sullivan, Mark R. "The Missing York *Funeral of the Virgin*," *EDAM
Newsletter*, 1, No. 2 (April 1979), 5-7.

Tavender, Augusta S. "Mediaeval Alabasters in American Museums,"
Speculum, 30 (1955), 64-71.

Taylor, Jerome, and Alan H. Nelson, eds. *Medieval English Drama.* Chicago: Univ. of Chicago Press, 1972.

Testamenta Eboracensia, ed. James Raine and John W. Clay. Surtees Soc., 4, 30, 45, 53, 79, 106. Durham, 1836-1902. 6 vols.

Tillott, P. M., ed. *A History of Yorkshire: The City of York.* Victoria County History of the Counties of England. London: Oxford Univ. Press, 1961.

Tillyard, E. M. W. *Some Mythical Elements in English Literature.* London, 1961.

Torre, James. *The Antiquities of York Minster.* York Minster Library MS.

Travis, Peter W. *Dramatic Design in the Chester Cycle.* Chicago: Univ. of Chicago Press, 1982.

Tristram, E. W. *English Medieval Wall Painting: The Thirteenth Century.* London: Oxford Univ. Press, 1950.

_____. *English Wall Painting in the Fourteenth Century.* London: Routledge and Kegan Paul, 1955.

Twycross, Meg. "'Places to hear the play': Pageant Stations at York, 1398-1572," *REED Newsletter*, 1978:2, pp. 10-33.

_____. "Playing 'The Resurrection'," *Medieval Studies for J. A. W. Bennett*, ed. P. L. Heyworth. Oxford: Clarendon Press, 1981. Pp. 273-96.

_____ and Sarah Carpenter. "Masks in the English Theatre: The Mystery Plays," *Medieval English Theatre*, 3 (1981), 7-44.

Tydeman, William. *The Theatre in the Middle Ages.* Cambridge: Cambridge Univ. Press, 1978.

Tyson, Cynthia Haldenby. "Noah's Flood, the River Jordan, the Red Sea: Staging in the Towneley Cycle," *Comparative Drama*, 8 (1974), 101-11.

Vale, M. G. A. *Piety, Charity and Literacy among the Yorkshire Gentry, 1370-1480.* Borthwick Papers, 50. York: Borthwick Institute, 1976.

von der Osten, G. "Job and Christ," *Journal of the Warburg and Courtauld Institutes*, 16 (1953), 153-58.

Wall, Carolyn. "The Apocryphal and Historical Backgrounds of 'The Appearance of Our Lady to Thomas' (Play XLVI of the York Cycle)," *Mediaeval Studies*, 32 (1970), 172-92.

Walsh, Mary Margaret. "The Judgment Plays of the English Cycles," *American Benedictine Review*, 20 (1969), 378-94.

Warner, George, ed. *Queen Mary's Psalter.* London: British Museum, 1912.

Wayment, Hilary. *The Windows of King's College Chapel, Cambridge.* London: Oxford Univ. Press, 1950.

Wells, Minnie. "The Age of Isaac at the Time of the Sacrifice," *Modern Language Notes,* 54 (1939), 579–82.

Westlake, H. H. J. *A History of Design in Painted Glass.* London, 1881–94. Vol. III.

Wickham, Glynne. *Early English Stages, 1300 to 1660.* London: Routledge and Kegan Paul, 1959. Vol. I.

William of Ockham. *Philosophical Writings: A Selection,* ed. and trans. Philotheus Boehner. New York, 1957.

Williams, Arnold. *The Characterization of Pilate in the Towneley Plays.* East Lansing: Michigan State Univ. Press, 1950.

———. *The Drama of Medieval England.* East Lansing: Michigan State Univ. Press, 1961.

Wilpert, J. *Die Römischen Mosaiken und Malereien der kirklichen Bauten vom IV. bis XIII. Jahrhundert.* 1916. Vol. II.

Winternitz, Emanuel. *Musical Instruments and Their Symbolism in Western Art.* New Haven: Yale Univ. Press, 1967.

Woodforde, Christopher. *English Stained and Painted Glass.* Oxford: Clarendon Press, 1954.

———. *The Norwich School of Glass-Painting in the Fifteenth Century.* London: Oxford Univ. Press, 1950.

Woolf, Rosemary. "The Effect of Typology on the English Mediaeval Plays of Abraham and Isaac," *Speculum,* 32 (1957), 805–25.

———. *The English Mystery Plays.* Berkeley and Los Angeles: Univ. of California Press, 1972.

———. *The English Religious Lyric in the Middle Ages.* Oxford: Clarendon Press, 1968.

———. "The Theme of Christ the Lover-Knight in Medieval English Literature," *Review of English Studies,* n.s. 13 (1962), 1–16.

Young, M. James. "The York Pageant Wagon," *Speech Monographs,* 34 (1967), 1–20.

Young, John, and P. Henderson Aitken. *A Catalogue of the Manuscripts in the University of Glasgow.* Glasgow: James Maclehose, 1908.

Young, Karl. *The Drama of the Medieval Church.* Oxford: Clarendon Press, 1933. 2 vols.

Zarnecki, George. *Romanesque Sculpture at Lincoln Cathedral.* Lincoln Minster Pamphlets, 2nd ser., 2. Lincoln: Friends of Lincoln Cathedral, 1970.

INDEX